The World's Greatest Football Team

R.K. Sawyer & Jim Moloney

The World's Greatest Football Team

R.K. Sawyer & Jim Moloney

www.nuecespress.com

Library of Congress Control Number: 2024910265

Sawyer, R.K., Jim Moloney   THE WORLD'S GREATEST FOOTBALL TEAM

Published in the United States of America by NUECES PRESS

www.nuecespress.com

ISBN 978-1-7339524-8-4

Includes bibliographical references and index.

1. United States—National Guard—Mobilization—History. 2. Texas Football—History. 3. Southwest Conference Football—History. 4.University of Texas Football—History. Corpus Christi, Texas—History. World War 1—History.

Printed and bound in the United States of America.

10 9 8 7 6 5 4 3 2 1

Cover design by Jeff Chilcoat.

For information on all Nueces Press titles please see www.nuecespress.com.

Dedication

The World's Greatest Football Team is dedicated to the fourteen men of the Second Texas Infantry's starting lineup:

Oscar Bergstrom "Ock" Abbott

Kearie Lee Berry

William S. "Bill" Birge

Phillip Solomon "Spitz" Clarke

Warren "Rip" Collins

John Cabot Diller

Eugene Malcolm Dotson

Addison Baker Duncan

James Marcellus "Big Jim" Kendrick

George H. Lane

Charles Wesley "June" or "Charley" Ogden

Sylvan Blum Simpson

Charles E. "Charlie" Turner

Grady "Rats" Watson

Publisher's Remarks

*Y*ears ago, I uncovered some of the history of Corpus Christi's Camp Scurry and the Texas Brigade, which was one of many National Guard units sent to Texas from across America before World War I. During my early research, I acquired written material and many photographic postcards of Camp Scurry, including some of its football players from the Second Texas National Guard Infantry Regiment who participated in the National Guard's competitive football league. The more I learned about the football team, the more I became convinced that there was a great story here, and only partially told. But it was going to take some digging.

I met Rob Sawyer when he was researching his first books on the history of waterfowl hunting in Texas. I was able to provide photographs and postcards related to hunting from the Corpus Christi area of South Texas. We kept in touch as he made presentations on his books and I was able to help with more photos for his third book, *Images of the Hunt*.

As I read the *Images* book, I came across my photo of the Tarpon Club on St. Joseph's Island from the 1890s. I always felt there was a book waiting to be written on the club, as it was the most exclusive in America at the time, and its founder, E.H. R. Green, was the son of the wealthiest, and perhaps the most miserly and eccentric woman in the world. After a conversation, Rob felt the same way. We collaborated on the project, doing what each of us does best – Sawyer finding buried research gems, with me uncovering one-of-a-kind images and esoteric publications. The result was publication of our book, *The Tarpon Club of Texas and the Genius of E.H.R. Green* (2022).

We enjoyed the process of creating the *Tarpon Club*, and after its publication, I suggested we collaborate on another book. This one. I provided Rob with my prior research and files on the Second Texas team, and he commenced his investigation into the team and its players. What a story he found closeted away in college yearbooks, letters, and old newspapers of the day!

We have titled the book *The World's Greatest Football Team* mostly because that's what the press – and many of their opponents – called it. During its unparalleled 1916-17 reign, the team averaged 54 points per game and outplayed their rivals 434 to 6 in eight contests. While impressive, the record was certainly not unheard of during the era. What gained the players their reputation was who they played. The team lined up across the scrimmage line from the best-known college and regional professional franchise football players and coaches in the country, all of whom were confident they would pummel the unknown, upstart Texans. None even came close. Before the Second Texas Infantry, Texas was not a recognized football state. After the Second Texas Infantry, it could no longer be ignored.

I hope you enjoy reading *The World's Greatest Football Team*.

Jim Moloney
Nueces Press

Foreword

*U*ndefeated, and at first, unheard of. The National Guard football team of the Second Texas Infantry that came together in the months before World War I was composed largely of players from the University of Texas, Texas A&M, and a few from Baylor, Rice, and Southwestern. In their single playing season, they outscored their opponents by a margin of 432 to 6. They chafed over the one touchdown scored against them for as long as they lived. The legacy of the Second Texas Infantry team, however, is as much about the athletes who put Texas football on the national map as it is about their stunning performance. Before the Second Infantry, most believed that serious football was only played in the North and the East. The Second Texas Infantry was the team that changed that.

The World's Greatest Football Team was Jim Moloney's idea. He'd read the available material on the Texas National Guard's Second Infantry football team and even contributed to the historical record with an article that was published by the Nueces County Historical Commission (2006). But Jim thought the football games were worthy of a more detailed examination and hoped that new information might emerge. I thought the history of the football squad was probably greater than just the gridiron, reasoning that if these young men were so gifted that they could consistently swamp the most recognized football teams in America, they probably had other noteworthy achievements during their lives. We were both right.

One of my earliest concerns was that the story of the Second Texas Infantry was already told. Every decade or so after 1917, newspaper sportswriters penned praise of the team in their columns. In 1957, Associated Press sportswriter Harold Ratliff offered a well-researched chapter in his book *The Power and the Glory: The Story of Southwest Conference Football*. In 1997, University of Texas-Pan American Department Chair Joseph E. Chance provided another telling titled *Texas' Greatest Football Team: On the Border with the Texas Second Infantry, 1916-1917*. There was a third offering in Harris and Sadler's 2015 tome titled *The Great Call-up*. Wasn't the story already told? And if new details were to emerge, would anyone care? For the first question, I think the answer is no. For the second, we'll have to wait and see.

There were few play-by-play sportswriters in Texas in 1916-17, and certainly no one equivalent to today's sports analysts. As a result, there is no record of each player's offensive and defensive scorecard. Game descriptions were equally lacking. It wasn't until the last two games that big city sportswriters paid much attention to the Second Infantry. Before that, if their games were followed at all, they were mostly recorded in small-town newspapers by generalists who shared their sports writing duties with coverage of such things as farm reports, the weather, births, marriages, and deaths.

It's also safe to say that any reader of a football game from a hundred years ago would struggle to understand the precise nature of play because of the terminology that was used. Much of the lingo is obsolete and too general. On offense, backfielders weren't called running backs, tailbacks, or wingbacks, and ends weren't differentiated as tight ends or wide receivers. Kicking was integral in early football, yet it was rare for a writer to differentiate between a punt, drop kick, or place kick. They were just kicks. It was worse on defense. There were no cornerbacks or safeties, and the term secondary was never used for players behind defensive linemen. No one was called a linebacker, and certainly not a nickelback. No defensive player ever blitzed, they just made tackles. Not a single writer ever noted whether the Second Infantry, or their opponents, used the popular offensive formations of the era known as the T, single or double wing, box, or any other configuration, although their lineup was hinted at in later writings. We wanted to convert both positions and plays into more modern terminology, but there was rarely enough information to make a confident interpretation. Instead, we chose to preserve the language of the game at the time. Although it's sometimes vague, it's honest.

There were other challenges. Both local and national publications spelled the names of the Texas players in a dizzying number of ways, and sometimes even introduced players who were not on the team. It was worse for the players on the opposing team. We solved the latter and whittled away at the former. There was also no agreement on many of the final game scores. As many as three or four final Second Texas Infantry scores were sometimes printed for the same game. But they never got the opponent's tally wrong. Zero was an easy number to remember.

For most on the famous Second Texas Infantry roster, the celebrated 1916-17 football season was not the signal achievement of their lives. After their legendary season, most of them went to war, and they were as fearless on the battlefield as they were on the football field. At the end of World War I, many who were leaders on the gridiron became leaders in their professions and communities. A few of the Second Infantry players went on to play professional football or baseball. Others remained in the military, with three footballers later becoming generals in the Regular Army or Texas National Guard.

Aside from occasional interviews, none of the Second Texas Infantry players lived in the past. Not so, however, for avid sports enthusiasts. For them, the team would be forever immortalized, frozen in time for two or three months between 1916 and 1917. Decades later, a new generation of sportswriters continued to ponder the question of what made the team so much better than their rivals, and what the team might have achieved had World War I not put an end to it. They – and we – never got to find out.

A weakness of this treatise – or perhaps, in the end, a strength – is its diversion into Texas college football during the early 1900s. In part, the deep dive is justified because college ball laid the foundation for most of the players on the Second Texas Infantry football team. But another reason is because the topic, particularly the depth and intensity of the UT-A&M rivalry that dates to the early 1900s, was too good of a story to leave untold.

Sometimes unexpected links to earlier projects are discovered in history research. In researching this book, I found that the father of Second Texas Infantry team member Charles Wesley Ogden Jr. was a founding member of E.H.R. Green's Tarpon Club that was, at the time, the most exclusive sporting club in America. Jim and I wrote about Ogden Sr. in our book *The Tarpon Club of Texas*. History can be a small world.

To tell the story of the Second Texas Infantry football squad necessitates a less-than-ideal organization of the text. It would have been preferable to provide a chronological overview, moving from Texas college football to the Mexican Revolution, the Bandit Wars on the Texas-Mexico border, the National Guard call-up, then to the Second Infantry football section, and finally off to war. Ultimately, we agreed that we needed to introduce the players earlier, so that the reader knew something about them before we joined them in their sports and life triumphs. It is not an ideal organization of the text, but we hope you understand the logic.

Acknowledgements

*T*he authors are indebted to:

Ward McCampbell, grandson of Charles Ogden. for copies of Ogden's correspondence with sportswriter and historian Harold Ratliff, author of *The Power and the Glory: The Story of Southwest Conference Football.*

Jospeh E. Chance for copies of his articles and research on the Second Texas Infantry Football Team.

Denis Crawford, Historian and Exhibit Designer at the College Football Hall of Fame in Atlanta for images we used in the football history section.

Don Bryan (deceased) for a copy of the Calvary Frolics Program (see the Appendix).

Lori Poldolski of Texas A&M University-Corpus Christi, who found several helpful references and secured a copy of the Second Texas Infantry chapter in Harold Ratliff's *The Power and the Glory: The Story of Southwest Conference Football.*

Chris McDougal of the Texas Military Force Museum, for helping to fill the holes in our research on the 36th Division during and after World War I.

Michael J. Schroeder, Professor Emeritus of History at Lebanon Valley College in Annville, Pennsylvania, who filled in the gaps in Mike Bloor's military service after World War I from his research in *The Sandino Rebellion, Nicaragua, 1927-1934.*

The *Portal to Texas History* and *Handbook of Texas Online*, critical resources to this and every Texas history project the authors have done.

John Kemp of Kemp Publishing, Mark S. McDonald Sr. of Dust Devil Publishing, and retired professor Joseph E. Chance, who deserve a special thanks as our editors. The latter two were particularly helpful by challenging us to do better to explain *why* the subject of this book was better a team than any other at the time.

Table of Contents

Introduction

*T*he 74th New York Infantry football players should have kept quiet. They still would have lost the match, but it wouldn't have been so demoralizing. Instead, the Texans mostly remembered them bragging that they wouldn't "ruin the morale of our club by scoring too many points against us," or how they would run the score up to just 40 points before sending in their second-string players. With their bravado, the New Yorkers poked the bear, so to speak, and it was a mistake. The Texans set a goal to score more than a hundred points. They did. It was New Year's Day, 1917, and 3,000 fans had gathered at Camp Scurry in Corpus Christi to watch what they thought would be a close contest. Instead, the Second Texas Infantry National Guard footballers – soon to earn the name "the famous Second Infantry" – ran over New York with 15 touchdowns and 12 extra points.[1]

The game's leading scorers were a who's who of Lone Star State college football. University of Texas backfield star Phillip Clarke and Baylor fullback Eugene Dotson each made three touchdowns. Texas A&M College end Jim Kendrick and A&M quarterback Ock Abbott scored twice. UT center John Diller crossed the goal twice on defensive pass interceptions, and Southwestern's Grady Watson and A&M's George Lane each scored once. Out of 15 possible extra points, Jim Kendrick kicked eight, and A&M kicker Warren Collins went for four. When the final whistle blew, the Second Texas Infantry deflated the New Yorkers 102-0. The score might have been higher, but the game was called in the final quarter. The New Yorkers had run out of players, having exhausted their entire starting roster and every player on the bench.[2]

Between November 20 and the January 1 game against the 74th New York Infantry, the Texans played six games and won them all, scoring 329 points to their opposition's total of zero. That sixth game was supposed to be the last for the National Guard football season. It wasn't. Some of the most prominent college footballers from the North and East Coast heard it was touted as the best team in the land and wanted a chance to set the record straight. America's best-known footballers challenged the Texans to two more games. Hailing from such sterling collegiate programs as Cornell, Dartmouth, Harvard, Illinois, Indiana, Pennsylvania, Princeton, Syracuse, Virginia, Washington and Lee, West Virginia, West Point, and Wisconsin, these recognized institutions dominated the All-America All-Star selections of Yales' legendary Water Camp. They still lost. The underdog Second Texas Infantry, in their final two games, scored 103 points against their distinguished adversary's total of just six.

By the winter of 1917, the Second Texas Infantry's football performance was recognized across America. Red Wilkinson, a two-time All-American and a member of Jim Thorpe's renowned Canton Professionals offered that it was the greatest football team he'd ever seen. His sentiments were echoed by Walter Camp, who wrote it was "the greatest football team on the American gridiron." Years after their last game, commentaries continued to flow with accolades like: "The Second Texas Infantry team was a pioneer in Texas' bid for national football fame. It was one of the greatest teams in the country and perhaps the greatest," and "the North and the East did not know Texas ever saw a football until the Second Texas Infantry."[3]

To tell the story of the world's greatest football team is to also tell the story of other influencing moments in Texas and American history. First and foremost was the game they played – the American version of football – and how it evolved between the late 1800s and the 1910s. It was also a game played mostly by the country's universities and colleges. Apart from some Northern and Eastern athletic clubs organized into regional leagues, there was no professional football as we know it today.

The seeds of the Second Texas Infantry team were sown in college competitions between 1909 and 1915. In Texas, football was synonymous with UT, called Texas University during the time, and Texas A&M, known then as the Agricultural and Mechanical College of Texas. Most of the Second Infantry team members played for those two teams, with 11 of its first and second-squad players from the UT roster and five from A&M. They played during a period in which relations between UT and A&M were strained to the point of breaking. Although the UT Longhorns lost only one game to the Texas A&M Aggies between 1894 and 1908, they lost three straight to the Aggies during 1909 and 1910. Pronouncing that they weren't poor losers but objected to A&M's "unsportsmanlike and unmanly" conduct, the Longhorns terminated their relationship with the Aggies the next year. The Longhorns continued to boycott A&M on the football field until the feud was resolved, and relations restored, in 1915.[4]

A telling of the history of the Mexican Revolution and the Bandit Wars on the Texas-Mexico border is also important to this story because the American military response – the National Guard call-up of 1916 – was the event that brought the Second Texas Infantry football team together. Between 1910 and 1916, Mexico had four different presidents, with the revolving door of its leadership occurring against a backdrop of a bloody civil war. The unrest spread north into the United States across the Rio Grande as a series of often violent raids. Some of the confrontations were at the hands of the so-called legitimate government and others by guerrilla Pancho Villa and his supporters. After a particularly bold and bloody raid into Columbus, New Mexico in March 1916, US President Wilson had enough, sending Brigadier General John "Black Jack" Pershing into Mexico to put an end to the bloodshed. Called the "Punitive Expedition," they unsuccessfully scoured the countryside for Villa and his raiders for nearly a year.[5]

Raiders continued to slip around Pershing despite pouring thousands of reinforcements into Mexico, and the Regular Army was quickly running out of troops to handle border defense. US President Wilson responded by pressing the National Guards of Texas, New Mexico, and Arizona into federal service in May 1916. A month later, a second call-up encompassing the rest of the United States brought the total guardsmen stationed along the US-Mexico border to 156,414 troops. When the future Second Texas Infantry footballers volunteered for duty during the May call-up, most were either still enrolled in college or were recent graduates.[6]

Sports consumed any spare time the guardsmen had while posted along the border. Wrestling, boxing, and rifle contests were popular, as was baseball. Then, in October, the military authorized regiments to organize a football league. The Second Texas Infantry hadn't waited for any official order. Just days after they arrived at Corpus Christi's Camp Scurry, the regiment announced it was organizing a football team, and 26 players were quickly selected for the squad. They practiced every day and sometimes twice a day. Word spread that they were "a force to be reckoned with."[7]

The Second Texas Infantry wasn't really discovered by Texas sportswriters until after the team had rolled over its first six opponents during the fall and winter of 1916. After that, the media couldn't get enough of them. Articles appeared across the state, an infatuated press closely following each player and printing narratives on their colleges, hometowns, academic majors, sports records, and meticulous summaries of their weight and height. Even before they played their first game, a Texas newspaper was quick to point out that the Second's offensive line averaged 190 pounds, the backfield 185, and the ends a nimble 170 pounds. Throughout the 1916-17 season, such close attention was paid to each player's weight and height that readers were reminded more of a record saltwater gamefish than a college football player.[8]

Football fans were as mesmerized by the team as the media. Even after the guard was disbanded in February 1917, supporters desperately wanted to see them on the field again. There was a glimmer of hope when America recalled its guardsmen after declaring war on Germany in April 1917. But fans would be disappointed – the US military had restructured its National Guard, separating the famous footballers and scattering them among various Texas units. Then, in the fall of 1918, they left the gridiron for the battlefield. Fate may have brought them together for their history-making season, but World War I was the event that ended their reign. They made their gridiron mark in just a single season.

The Second Infantry players were born in the late 1800s in a Texas that was, in part, still colored by its Wild West character, and in part beginning to embrace a more industrialized, progressive future. Some players spent their formative years in a rural Texas that was not too different from a Texas that, less than a century earlier, was a fledgling republic that had only just declared its independence from Mexico. These future footballers would have traveled dirt and mud tracks by horseback or wagon, shot or trapped wild game to supplement the farm animals they raised, and worked the land with mules and oxen to grow vegetables and other crops. Others of the young men were from Texas' growing towns or cities and were inured to many of the modern technologies of the day, such as automobiles, electricity, telephones, indoor plumbing, and city markets where food could be bought rather than hunted, raised, or grown.

The evolving Texas culture was reflected not just in its athletes but was mirrored, as well, by the fans in the bleachers and boxes. Some in the stands were former war heroes, such as the graybeards who had fought in the Civil War 50 years earlier, and some who had faced Comanche warriors during the final vestiges of the Texas frontier. These old men contrasted with the next generation of veterans in the stands, the young National Guardsmen there to root for their regiments and who were called to duty as America was on the threshold of the world's first global conflict. Other onlookers represented a new breed of Texan, titans of financial circles whose wealth was no longer tied to just cattle and land but investments in railroads, oil and gas, and America's advancing technologies. There were women spectators as well, most of whom, in those days, remained relegated to homemaker and society roles.

During their formative years, the Second Texas Infantry players lived more comfortably than their parents had before them. Although rural residents still relied on kerosene-fueled lanterns for light, and wood and coal for heat, Texas' larger cities were lit by electrical plants, with steam radiators all the rage for winter warmth. Just seven years after the Wright brothers *Flyer* made its historic 12-second flight over the dunes of North Carolina's Outer Banks, aviator C.P. Rodgers flew across the continental United States, paving the way for the coming reality of commercial air passenger service. Automobiles were increasingly superseding travel by horse and buggy, and by the time the Second played its last game, there were nearly 200,000 of the new-fangled mechanical contraptions in the state – so many that the only way to keep track of them was, in 1917, to introduce mandatory license plates.[9]

The technological advancements of the early 20th century also afforded Texans more time for leisure activities. Football games, with all the social and celebratory customs that went with it, grew as a pastime for college athletes and fans alike. The Second Texas Infantry came to glory during this wave of leisure. But there were clouds on the horizon, and world events were to culminate in a war with a fury like none before it. America would have embraced the Second Texas' return to the field if they had stayed together after the Great War. Instead, their sports achievements were relegated to history. But during the player's lifetime, articles and interviews would return them back, briefly, to their former National Guard gridiron glory days. They seemed to savor the attention, the opportunity to reminisce, and to relive some of the memories. This is their story.

CHAPTER 1

The American Football Game
1880s to 1915

*A*merican football first emerged during the late 1800s and originated from English rugby. The architect of its early structure and governing rules was Walter Camp, an 1882 graduate of Yale and an athlete with varsity honors in baseball, rugby, track and field, tennis, and rowing. As the sport of rugby evolved into American football, it was Camp who, for nearly half a century, was at its center as the organizer and an influential member of the American Football Rules Committee.

Camp is credited with abolishing rugby's 15-man rule and instituting a field of 11 players. He defined the scrimmage and invented the quarterback position. In 1882, he added a possession rule requiring the offense to gain five yards in three downs, and since it required a form of measurement, he contributed to the design of a playing field that was marked in five-yard increments and gained the name "gridiron."

Early football was a kicking game, in which the rounded, rugby ball of the day could be punted, dropkicked, or placekicked at any time, on any down, to gain field position. Camp's 1883 scoring structure reflected kicking's importance – a touchdown was worth four points to a field goal valued at five points. Camp's scoring system remained unchanged until 1897, the only revision the addition of two points to "the offended side" for an off-sides penalty or for slugging a player or referee.

Camp initiated and supported other changes during the late 1800s, such as reducing the size of the playing field, standardizing goal post widths, modifying the length of the game, defining offensive line positions, dispensing with the rugby rule forbidding tackles below the waist, and hiring salaried referees and umpires who began using whistles and stopwatches. With the game's foundation built by the turn of the 20th century, college football was one of the most-watched sports in America. The only cloud on the horizon was that America's favorite sport was killing its participants.[1]

Mass Play. Initially, American football scoring rewarded kicking. To move the ball towards their goal line, players gained field position through a ground game and its main feature, the "mass play." Mass plays comprised the entire offense, its object to "all strike the line at as nearly as possible the same time to form a tightly massed wedge" and, with the ball carrier near the center of the throng, "all push forward with the greatest possible force in a solid and tightly formed mass." When the mass formation moved from the line of scrimmage or was applied to the kick-off, it was termed the "flying wedge." The momentum of the linked bodies as they ran at the defense in a flying wedge was nearly impossible to penetrate, and the only way an opponent could reach the ball was to hurdle themselves – the "flying tackle" – into the mass. Players were dying to do it.[2]

The nature of football's injuries was reminiscent more of Roman gladiator contests than an American collegiate past-time. Players with cracked and fractured skulls, others with broken necks and spinal columns, and some with internal injuries. No high school or college program was immune. An unnamed sportswriter for the *Houston Post* was one of the few in Texas who compiled and regularly reported on the casualties, and they shocked him. He counted 13 who died in 1903, 16 in 1904, and 21 in 1905. Most of his estimates were, it turned out, low.[3]

Although Houston was a long way from Walter Camp and the northern football decision-makers, the *Post* writer who so closely monitored the carnage believed the solution was to eliminate "the constant heavy mass plays." That style of play, he wrote, was "dull and stupid" and he suggested replacing it with "more open football." The *Post* journalist was far from alone in his recommendations. The themes of an open game and abolishing mass play were emerging rapidly in a growing number of football circles.[4]

Persistent reformist howls grew loud after the 1904 season, but Walter Camp and the collegiate football advisory board made few modifications to game rules during their annual 1905 summer meeting in New York. Regulations that could have produced a more open game, like the highly anticipated liberalization of the forward pass, went unchanged, and elimination of the game's "roughness" was not even seriously considered.[5]

The President and Football. In early October 1905, Harvard freshman Theodore Roosevelt Jr. donned his yellow and crimson football uniform for the first time. The son of the US president was said to have "looked slight in appearance" and, at 145 pounds, was lighter than the average 165-pound weight of the team. Three days later, he earned the distinction as "the first freshman of the year to be laid out" on the Harvard football field, his injury a cut above the right eye.[6]

A week later, the President of the United States invited the college athletic faculty elite from Harvard, Princeton, and Yale to the White House to discuss ways to eliminate football's "mortality and brutality." Among the attendees was intercollegiate football rules committee chairman Walter Camp, who afterward pledged to address the game's "roughness, holding, and foul play." Harvard President Charles William Eliot, already a vocal opponent of "brutality and unnecessary roughness" in college football, did not need much in the way of presidential persuasion. After the meeting, he told the press that, if his school did not initiate playing changes, he would eliminate the game at Harvard.[7]

Roosevelt's presidential interest in the game was the subject of some debate, but it wasn't his first foray into the subject. In a 1903 address to University of Minnesota students, he proclaimed his support for the virtues of "manly sports" and "rough games for schools," adding that "I don't feel any particular sympathy for the person who gets battered about a good deal, so long as it is not fatal." He ended his speech with the motto "Don't flush, don't foul, and hit the line hard."[8]

Just two years after the bravado of his University of Minnesota speech, the president seemed to have reversed his opinion. Now, he was espousing that "brutality in playing a game should awaken the heartiest contempt for the player guilty of it." Some believed the president's change of heart was due to his slightly injured son, but that was not consistent with his character. The *St. Louis Post-Dispatch* preferred that Roosevelt's new-found sentimentality was because he was "yielding to the seductions of calmness, peace and quiet" of middle age.[9]

In November, Roosevelt Jr. was injured again, the culprits a few players who "take great pleasure in stamping the lights out of the presidential progeny." Harvard football coach W.T. Reid was again summoned to the White House. The president wanted to "talk over the football season," he was told. During the second White House council, the president had a good deal more to discuss than just his son's latest mishap.[10]

Dying to Play Ball. November 1905 may not have been the deadliest in football, but increasingly, the fatalities were striking established high-profile collegiate programs. One of the prevailing beliefs had been that football deaths were mostly confined to small schools with their rosters of inexperienced, even weak players. But that fall, the Harvard football team captain suffered a blood clot on the brain, and Union College halfback Harold Moore died from a cerebral hemorrhage during a game with New York University.[11]

Harold Moore's demise was something of a catalyst for football reform. In his last play, Moore received a downfield lateral, his teammates forming a flying wedge around him. The defense stopped the charge, but when the writhing bodies clambered from the pile, Moore was at the bottom and wasn't breathing. He never regained consciousness. Newspapers that day also reported on an Indiana high school ballplayer killed during a tackle, a broken rib piercing his heart. In Missouri, another footballer was paralyzed during a game, the injury "probably fatal." He died three days later.[12]

The President of the United States was not the only person alarmed by the Harold Moore tragedy, but an appropriate course of action – if any – was hotly debated. As quickly as football reform supporters advanced their agendas, so did the opposition. Responding to what he thought was biased press coverage, C.C. Cragin, captain of the rival NYU team, told newsmen that Moore must have had a weak heart. Any other man "in good physical condition," he said, "would have finished the game, even if he had met with the same accident." Even Cragin's father weighed in. Forgetting that Moore was carrying the ball, he opined that "Moore tackled his opponent too high." Then he added that "Moore had been injured in a football three games three weeks ago" and already "had a blood clot on his brain." It was apparent that football rulebook revisions were as feared in one camp as it was considered imperative in the other.[13]

The sides grew more polarized when Harvard President Eliot called for a one-year ban on the game at all US colleges. Opponents circled the wagons. One Yankee writer remarked that Harvard's position was not humanitarian, but instead evidence that the Ivy League college was a sore loser, still smarting from its 1904 loss to underdog Pennsylvania whose team had resorted to rough play. The writer insisted that Harvard take the blame for all the agitator nonsense now jeopardizing the "fabled contest for American manhood."[14]

Reforms. Before the New Year, representatives of 68 colleges and universities were invited to New York for a referendum on intercollegiate football reform. The University of Texas was the single attendee from the Lone Star State. Even with Roosevelt's presidential posturing, however, a compromise was far from assured as the conferees quickly divided into two camps – one for football's "old guard" and another representing the progressives. When reformists made little headway during their winter meeting, it looked as if the status quo would prevail. Harvard president Eliot bitterly concluded that "it is impossible to believe that the committees, coaches, and umpires, who have ruined the game, are to be trusted with its reform or replacement." Then the Harvard faculty announced it was canceling its football program for the 1906 season.[15]

Despite the delays and cross-currents of opinion, the intercollegiate governing body surprised proponents and detractors alike in April with their announcement of an ambitious and innovative slate of football amendments. Most were true to the mission of abolishing brutal, rough play. The least controversial of the new mandates were those governing player conduct. There would be heavy penalties for "unnecessary roughness" and "foul play" that would cost the offensive yardage and possible player suspension. Unsportsmanlike conduct carried a one-game suspension. The committee also agreed on guidelines for kicking and punt return fair catch calls, tripping, interference, and they adopted a six-man rule on the line of scrimmage. A neutral zone was established that prevented "the two lines of scrimmage men from bucking up against each other at the snap" and was also extended to a punt and the still common drop kick.[16]

Two of the most controversial mass plays were abolished by the reform committee. First on the chopping block was "all the bad features of flying tackles." So was "hurdling the line," in which a backfield receiver jumped onto the back of one of the guards, then leaped into the air and over his opponent's head. Perfectly executed, "the man carrying the ball can leap entirely over the line without stepping on another man's back." More debatable, however, were the rules to "invite an open game," particularly the introduction of a ten-yard, first-down rule and sanctioning of the forward pass. Of these, everybody seemed to have an opinion.[17]

The ten-yard rule provided the offense with three attempts to gain that yardage and maintain possession of the ball. Supporters thought it would contribute to "a more open style of play" because the offense would attempt more end runs or short passes, and the defense would invariably play the ends back from the ball. Challengers, however, were convinced the ten-yard rule would paralyze the game, fretting that the offense "will almost never gain its distance" for a first down, the result an "uninteresting kicking contest" with scores "determined [only] by flukes and fumbles."[18]

The Forward Pass. Despite the critics, a pass over the line of scrimmage was permitted for the first time, although an incomplete pass still carried yardage penalties. Advocates argued that passing would open the field of play because the defensive ends would be forced to move from the scrimmage line to cover it. Detractors, such as Harvard coach W.T. Reid, maintained that the ability of a player to throw and complete long passes was "so uncertain as to make the results almost a gamble." Yale coaches agreed, predicting "little use of the forward pass" because the play was so risky it would be used only when "desperation demands it." The forward pass was by far the most contentious new feature of college football, and Walter Camp, who personally opposed it, deserves credit for bowing to the majority at the 1906 Interscholastic Athletic Association winter meeting.[19]

In September, as practice for the controversial 1906 season was underway, Walter Camp consented to an interview and gave his thoughts on the games ahead. Uncharacteristically, he admitted he didn't know what to think. The revisions were "experimental," he divulged, and of the recommendations, the forward pass was the boldest move. "It might turn the game upside down," he said, or "may not have any effect." In a far-sighted statement, he said he was sure of one thing – that the game would now call for coaches and players to understand the use of strategy, particularly on the offense.[20]

Importantly, the instituted reforms appeared to achieve the goal of improving player safety. At the end of the "experimental" 1906 season, a writer espoused that unnecessary roughness "seems bound to be cured for good." The body count supported the optimism. The grim reaper at the *Houston Post*, who counted the football dead again in 1906, put the total at 12, about half of what it was in 1905. In 1907 there were 14 casualties and 13 in 1908. The *Austin American-Statesman* concluded that it "goes to show the modified game is less brutal than the old one." For a few years, the writer was correct.[21]

Old football was to die-hard among its veterans. Their baying, however, was hard to hear over the animated crowd who relished the restructured game that now offered "agility, speed, and nimbleness of evasion" as compared to the old sport of "ponderous aggression," where ground was contested foot by foot. The "much denounced" forward pass was a big part of the success.[22]

Passing plays were part of nearly every 1906 game. One devotee, citing the games of Princeton and the Carlisle Indian Industrial School, gushed that passing was "one of the most spectacular plays ever introduced into football" and described his satisfaction in watching a Princeton quarterback "pass the ball exactly 17 yards forward to an end, who continued down the field for a touchdown." That year there were fans across the county who counted every pass thrown in each game. The same was true in Texas, where game coverage of the 1906 season was replete with the outcome of every toss. Sometimes they miscounted, such as a UT game against TCU in which the Longhorns attempted "one forward pass but failed twice."[23]

The forward pass's honeymoon was short. By 1909, both the unfamiliarity of pass execution and a reversal in the number of injuries made its future uncertain. Of the former, one foe called the forward pass "a hobby of certain college men, but it is not football play. It belongs to basketball." Even the early passing heroes were subject to criticism. For all their deserved passing credit, the Carlisle Indians during the 1907 season earned a reputation for throwing long downfield passes "with no particular aim or direction" and "trusting to luck" that its offense would recover it. The tactic was not only unsportsmanlike, it was charged, but their opponents began to push, shove, and hold the offense with impunity because, according to existing rules, the penalty for an incomplete forward pass had precedence over any defensive penalty.[24]

Still Dying to Play Ball. In 1909, the number of footballers who died during play exploded, reaching 33 by the end of the season. Many thought that open-field collisions between pass receivers and defenders were the cause of the most serious injuries. The statistics, however, told a different story – a gradual return to rough play. As in 1905, there was a public outcry over the death of players from notable teams that were still thought to be immune from the carnage. This time it was Eugene Byrne and Earl Wilson, both from nationally regarded programs.[25]

During the October 1909 Harvard-West Point game, left tackle Eugene Byrne was buried beneath a mass of humanity, the weight of the crushing pile above him twisting his neck and breaking his spine. After he was buried on November 2, West Point canceled the remainder of its season games. As sports fans mourned Byrne, they were also watching the condition of Naval Academy midshipman Earl Wilson who, a week earlier, was paralyzed from the neck down from a supposedly outlawed "flying tackle." In December, an optimistic father reported that his son had gained some use of his arms. By April, he was dead.[26]

9

Saving the Game. When the Interscholastic Athletic Association (IAAUS) met that December, their most important agenda item was, once again, addressing football safety. US colleges were anxious, this time less about the details and more about whether the game would even survive. Few doubted that "the fate of football rests in the hands of the committee."[27]

Guidelines for more open play were a central theme of the IAAUS 1910 amendments. Short onside kicks were banned. The rule that a forward pass had to clear the scrimmage line by more than five yards was scrapped, although in a nod to receiver protection, throws greater than 20 yards were prohibited. Other important player safeguards came from banning the diving tackle, as well as "piling on a prostrate player." One of the last relics of the mass play – the grabbing of the player with the ball, then pulling and pushing him through the line – was prohibited. On the scoring side, the four-point field goal was reduced to three, but the five-point touchdown remained unchanged.[28]

Just as in the football reforms of 1906, there was pushback to the 1910 game changes. Yale players were particularly vocal, their spokesman predicting "that within a week after the college squads report for practice, such a howl will go up that the rules committee will issue a hurried call for a meeting." He anticipated the revisions wouldn't survive until the end of the season. There were complaints, too, that the regulations were unnecessarily "perplexing, contradictory, or impractical," with Yale coach Tad Jones adding that referees and umpires would never be able to keep up with all the changes. Portending the future, he thought their job would be easier if players wore a number on their jerseys.[29]

Where some saw only doom and gloom, others saw opportunity. One was Glenn Scobey "Pop" Warner, the shrewd Carlisle Indians coach who commented that he was "pleased with the new rules," because "it will result in a more spectacular game and much more interesting to the public as well as less dangerous for the players." Then he said essentially the same thing that Walter Camp did in 1906 – that football was now a contest of brains over brawn. Every football strategist, according to the influential Carlisle coach, "will have to depend on his originality in working up an offensive system."[30]

Refining the Game. After 1910, the game of football more closely resembled the modern game. The IAAUS, renamed the National Collegiate Athletic Association by 1911, enacted plenty of rule changes between 1911 and 1915, but the new regulations were mostly refinements to the existing structure. Highlights included a change from three to four downs to gain ten yards for a first down, and the value of a touchdown was increased from five to six points. The playing field size was reduced from 110 yards to 100 yards to provide sufficient room for a new ten-yard addition beyond each goal line – it would be called the end zone – that would "provide ample space for execution of the forward pass." And that forward pass was no longer confined to 20 yards.[31]

The body count in 1910, reported by the New York Medical Society, was still high at 19 deaths and 400 injuries. In 1911, according to the *Houston Post*, there were 12 deaths, 509 injuries, and 64 players carried from the field unconscious. From 1912 to 1915, the number of players killed in the game remained steady, if not comparatively respectable, at between 11 and 16.[32]

The Rise of Texas. The year 1915 was the last season that most of the future Second Texas Infantry footballers would play for their respective colleges before their service in the National Guard. The game they played had evolved from the late 1800s rugby union code into a sport that was truly American. It was also a game dominated by schools in the North and East. During football's early years, Lone Star State colleges were not members of the Eastern Seaboard club of celebrated school programs. Their participation and contributions to the intercollegiate football rules committee were minor, and the opinions of their collegiate advisors were not considered essential to the process or its outcome. The state's young athletes were indifferent. They just played football, and if anyone from the more renowned, established football programs was watching, they saw the Texans were getting good at it. But they weren't watching. Not until 1916 and 1917, when the Second Texas Infantry showed America that they could play the game better than anyone else. And put Texas on the national football map.

Walter Camp, the architect of modern football. Camp was an 1882 graduate of Yale and an athlete with varsity honors in baseball, rugby, track and field, tennis, and rowing. As the sport of rugby evolved into American football, it was Camp who, for nearly half a century, was at its center as the organizer and an influential member of the American Football Rules Committee. Courtesy *College Football Hall of Fame*, Atlanta, Georgia.

Leather helmets were not mandatory in the early years of football. One curious, early safety feature of the early 1900s was the nose guard, and players are wearing them in both images. The top image is Coach Amos Stagg of the University of Chicago Maroons, in 1901, and shows the players in a wedge formation on the left side. The bottom image is an unnamed team in 1902. *Library of Congress Prints and Photographs Division*, Washington, D.C., No.LC-USZ62-35725 (top) and LC-USZ62-122899 (bottom).

Top: Ethel Roosevelt, whose father weighed in on American football reform as US president, at a football game in the 1910s (front row, center). *Library of Congress Prints and Photographs Division*, Washington, D.C., No. LC-DIG-ggbain-03024.

Bottom: The Harvard football team during practice. Harvard President C.W. Eliot canceled its football program in 1906 in protest to the lack of safety reforms. *Library of Congress Prints and Photographs Division*, Washington, D.C., No. LC-DIG-ggbain-09729.

Left: A University of Michigan player in 1909 sporting the latest in protective gear – leather shoulder pads and leather vest, but no helmet. The image was taken by New York photographer George G. Bain. *Library of Congress Prints and Photographs Division*, Washington, D.C., No. LC-DIG-ggbain-08792.

Below: The Yale football team warming up before its game with West Point in 1908. A leather helmet with ear flaps is in the foreground. *Library of Congress Prints and Photographs Division*, Washington, D.C., No. LC-DIG-ggbain-02335.

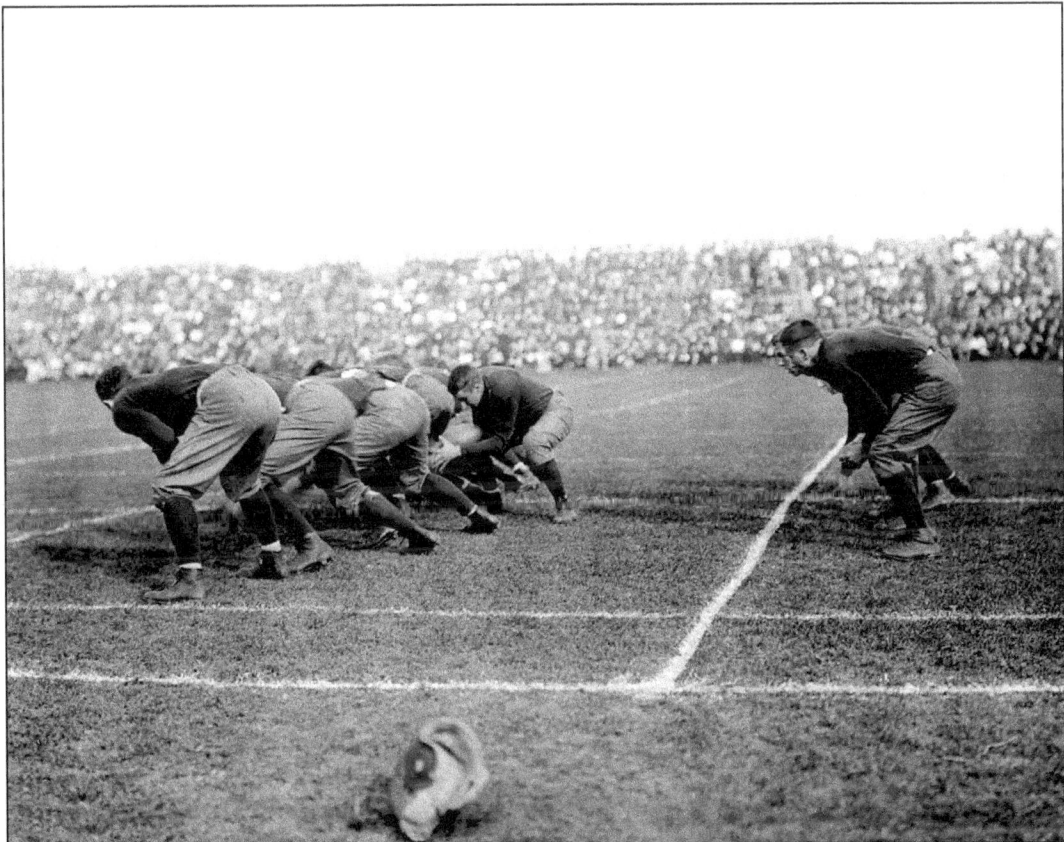

Top: Yale, Harvard, and Princeton dominated the American version of football in the late 1800s to early 1900s. Shown is Ted Coy, Yale football spokesman and All-American fullback in 1909. Coy was to later declare that the Second Texas Infantry was "the biggest, best disciplined, and most perfectly working piece of football machinery I've ever seen." *Library of Congress Prints and Photographs Division*, Washington, D.C., No. LC-DIG-ggbain-04340.

Left: In the 1910s, numbered jerseys were uncommon. Here, a 1913 Naval Academy player sports a chalked number "73" for identification. *Library of Congress Prints and Photographs Division*, Washington, D.C., No. LC-DIG-hec-03191.

Top: The Army-Navy game of 1916 shows the future of football equipment, notably the introduction of shoulder pads and thigh guards, but helmets were still optional. *Library of Congress Prints and Photographs Division*, Washington, D.C., No. LC-DIG-ppmsca-19488.

Bottom: The American football in play before 1924 was a rugby ball (below left). It was about the same length but an inch or so wider, and one to two ounces lighter, than the ball we know today. Its aerodynamics made it difficult to throw or kick accurately. Courtesy *College Football Hall of Fame*, Atlanta, Georgia.

The modern American football (below right) was developed in 1924 by Wilson Sporting Goods Company and Knute Rockne, and the result was a ball that could be thrown with greater precision than the rugby ball. Although the Wilson-Rockne design was immediately adopted in collegiate football, it was not embraced by the National Football League until 1941. Collection R.K. Sawyer.

CHAPTER 2

The Players

*T*he National Guard call-up of 1916 brought the Second Texas Infantry together for two history-making months, the team playing in eight games between November 20, 1916, and January 20, 1917. It was then, and is now, human nature to try to determine if the team members might have possessed some distinctive qualities that made them better than everyone else. Certainly, they were greater as a team than the sum of the individuals, but was there a uniqueness in their characters that set them apart from others of their gridiron era?

There were some common threads winding through their backgrounds, with athletic ability being the most recognizable. Most of the men also had a deep appreciation of country and felt an obligation to serve. They had leadership skills, and yet a willingness to share the limelight and function as a team. As only a few came from prominent families, most had to work hard to achieve success after high school, whether they chose to go to work, college, or the military, and they brought that work ethic to the playing field. Yet, in the end, there is little in their individual upbringings or collective substance that could have foretold the height of their marvelous moment.

Players. The first squad of the 1916-17 Second Infantry roster of soldier-footballers was dubbed the "Texas Eleven" and was comprised of 14 players: Oscar "Ock" Abbott, Kearie L. Berry, W.S. "Bill" Birge, Phillip "Spitz" Clarke, Warren "Rip" Collins, John Diller, Eugene Dotson, Baker Duncan, James "Big Jim" Kendrick, George H. Lane, Charley "June" Ogden, Sylvan Simpson, Charlie E. Turner, and Grady "Rats" Watson.

Seven other guardsmen composed the core of the second squad: Bart Coan, Tom Gambrell, Dick "Sugar" Lane, Bertrand "Mullie" Lenoir, T.D. "Tom" Mitchell, David R. Nelson, and Pleasant "Pleas" Rogers. These second-squad men appeared in two to five games during the 1916-17 season. Second squad men Charles T. Schaedel and John Erwin "Harry" Stullken played in one game. A disproportionate number of the first and second squads – 15 in total –were from Austin National Guard Companies E and F.[1]

Five other names showed up on the team towards the end of the 1916-1917 football season. They were Victor Bintliff, Charlie Brown, H.H. "Whitey" Davis, Louis "Tige" Halphen, and Schuyler William "Bud" Smith. These players were undoubtedly part of the Second Infantry's practice squad, but only S.W. "Bud" Smith is referenced as a substitute in any games. The five footballers were either trying out, or were already selected, for the Second Infantry's 1917-1918 season and who, if the National Guard was still in federal service for another year, were chosen to carry forward the Second's football legacy.

The roster of the Second Infantry was replete with nicknames, and by the time they were the famous Second Infantry football team, their given names always gave way to nicknames in the press. Oscar Abbott was known as "Ock," and Phillip Clarke was "Spitz," the name derived from his thick mane of blonde hair reminiscent of the wolf-like spitz dog. Howard Davis was "Whitey," Louis Halphen's moniker was "Tige," Jim Marcellus Kendrick was always "Big Jim," George Lane was referred to as "Sugar," Charles Wesley Ogden was usually "Charley" or sometimes "June," and Bertram Lenoir was "Mullie." Pleasant Roger's first name was shortened to "Pleas," and Schuyler W. Smith was "Bud." Two players were given nicknames for their athletic prowess. The unstoppable Warren Collins was "Rip," and Grady Watson was dubbed "Rats" for his scrambling ability on the field. Their coach for the last two games, D.V. Graves, arrived in camp with his nickname "Tubby."

The Unknown Soldiers. Although the names of the first and second teams of the Second Texas Infantry were listed often in the press, a casual review could be confusing. One challenge was the common use of just a surname, but no first name. Another was bad spelling. Spitz Clarke's name, for example, was nearly always spelled Clark, Tige Halphen was usually Halpin or Halpen, and an "s" was often added to Kendrick. Eugene Dotson was sometimes Dodson, and Mullie Lenoir was often Mully, his surname both LeNoire and Lenore. Bart Coan's surname was usually Cohen, and there were at least half a dozen different spellings of Stullken, including Stuken, Stulker, Stulken, Stuhlken, Stulkin, and Stulfgen. C.T. Schaedel's last name was equally challenging and included Sehaedel, Schaendel, Schraedel, and Schadle variations. The misspelled name Woodull appeared as a player in the *San Antonio Express* and was probably a reference to Walter F. Woodul, who had a business management role with the team.[2]

Beyond the first and second squads, the player names got trickier. A few names that were credited to the Second Infantry appeared in print only once. In October 1916, for example, the *San Antonio Express* listed players with the surnames Holland, Jackson, and Taylor, but with no given names. As these players appeared several weeks before the Second Infantry's first game but never emerged again, they were likely transferred to different guard companies or cut from the squad. The *Laredo Weekly News*, in November, mentioned a player called Miller, also with no given name. Miller reappeared once in January 1917 in the *San Antonio Express*, but there was never mention of his play.[3]

There were another five players mentioned as part-timers on the roster, but whose identity remains elusive – Bates, Dietel, McConnell, T. Rogers, and D. Stein or Steen. No given name was available for either Bates, Dietel, or McConnell. Bates remains unknown, and Dietel may have been Herbert A. Dietel of Austin's Company F. Of the three, only McConnell was mentioned in any games, in one account taking to the field in the Wisconsin Infantry game as a second-string end before his name vanished. T. Rogers showed up once in January 1917 in a team photograph, but it was probably an error. Another second-string player who appeared as a substitute in the last two games was D. Stein. Stein was also spelled Steen, and this player might have been Austin's Company E's Lamar "Bute" Steen. There is a single reference to Bute Steen at a 1917 Second Infantry banquet, although there is no mention of him on the field. For now, Bates, Dietel, Holland, Jackson, McConnell, Miller, Rogers, Stein or Steen, and Taylor are the unknown soldiers of the Second Infantry.[4]

Forty years after the Second Infantry played its first game, Charley "June" Ogden named the Texas Eleven, some of the second squad, and some of the team management in a 1956 letter to Associated Press sports editor Harold Ratliff. Ogden's memory was crystal clear in some areas but clouded in others. He called the team assistant manager Ed Cook instead of Dan Cook, Bud Smith was referred to as Buhl Smith, and he mistakenly confused player Dick Lane with David Lane, who was not on the roster. But he stated that Victor Bintliff, Whitey Davis, and his Buhl Smith were "out for the team," which is consistent with their appearance at the end of the 1916-1917 season and that they were among the candidates for the following year's football team. The Second Infantry, it seems was planning for its future.[5]

Coaches. Unique to the Second was that they had no formally named coach for their first six games, instead sharing the duties. Kearie Lee Berry remembered that "having the players' coach themselves wasn't very satisfactory," so "we finally pushed Jim Kendrick to the front, along with Charlie Turner," and they "finally subdued the rest sufficiently to serve as playing coaches." By the time they played their first game, the team had selected four player coaches. Lineman and team captain Bill Birge was the defensive line coach, and tackle and end Baker Duncan was offensive line coach. Jim Kendrick coached the backfield, and left end Charlie Turner was the strategist behind the team's offensive plays.[6]

It wasn't until January 6, with just two remaining games, that the Texas Eleven relented to bring in D.V. "Tubby" Graves as coach. With two tough games ahead, or so they thought, they wanted to be prepared. Graves was called one of the best football coaches in the South, his tenure including Missouri and the University of Alabama before two years with the Aggies as assistant coach.[7]

Before the First Team was the Second Texas Infantry. Most, but not all, of the team members of the Second Texas Infantry were born in Texas. Many had established reputations as high school and college athletes, and several were playing semi-professional sports in various local city leagues. Nearly all the players were either still enrolled in college or were recent graduates when the May 1916 call came to muster the Texas National Guard for active duty on the Rio Grande and Texas-Mexico border.

Oscar Abbott. Oscar Bergstrom "Ock" Abbott was born in 1890 in San Antonio to an English-born father who started a saddle-making business after settling in Texas. Abbott was a high school football star and enrolled at A&M in 1909. College gridiron circles remember him best as a Texas Aggie substitute quarterback during the historic 1909 season when the Farmers beat UT twice, by scores of 23-0 and 5-0. Abbott was on A&M's first team during most of the 1910 season and had memorable performances in a pair of October games. One was a TCU match, in which Abbott was the game's most celebrated player, gaining notoriety for huge yardage through runs and downfield catches, punt returns, and throwing a pair of forward passes for two touchdowns. The Farmers won the match 35-0. His play was equally brilliant in their 27-6 defeat against Austin College.[8]

Although an ankle injury kept him out of several November games, including UT's memorable third straight loss to the Aggies, Abbott was nominated as an All-State player that year. Abbott, in addition to football, was on the A&M track team. He took a hiatus from college in 1912 to work and raise money to finish his education. Although military records show his National Guard service began in May 1916, Abbott must have joined the Second Infantry earlier as he attained the rank of second lieutenant before the May 1916 guard call-up. The future brigadier general played in all eight games of the Second Infantry as quarterback, alternating with Grady "Rats" Watson.[9]

K.L. Berry. Born in 1893, Kearie Lee Berry was reared on a ranch near Denton, north of Dallas. He covered miles of its landscape as a boy delivering the *Denton Record-*

Chronicle newspaper from the saddle of a Shetland pony. Berry was a high school star athlete and enrolled at UT in 1911, starting his first UT season as a freshman "scrub" but moved quickly to the regular lineup, playing both the backfield on offense and defensive lineman. He gained the honor of being included among "the Immortals," the heralded UT lineup that ended the Aggie's two-year, three-game winning streak with UT's 6-0 triumph over A&M in the 1911 annual match. When the Longhorns won the state championship that year, the freshman was nominated by Dave Allerdice for the All-State nod, and he was also awarded his UT varsity football letter.[10]

Berry was a starting guard during the 1912 season. In UT's game against Arkansas, a 48-0 landslide, he was a key player in a defensive line that blocked nearly every Razorback pass or punt and broke through the line for yardage-losing backfield tackles. Berry did not attend college in 1913 but returned in 1914. That year he was nominated for the honorary All-State squad again, and the Southwestern Conference "all-star" honors. In 1915, he was elected captain of the UT football squad. Injuries kept Berry out of the lineup for most of September and played his last college game of 1915 against Notre Dame, a game UT lost 36-7.[11]

At 6-foot-1-inch and 200 pounds, Berry earned a second collegiate letter as a Southwest Conference heavyweight wrestling champion, and his third for track and field. When Berry hurled a 16-pound iron shot put 42 feet and 4 inches, he broke UT's distance record by two feet, besting the record that was made by his brother, Gene. Berry broke his own record the next year. Then he broke it again. He was also captain of the "weights" team, which included shot put, hammer throw, and discus. In UT's track team event in April, he took first place in two weight events and second in another. As late as 1919, UT had only a dozen athletes who had earned three sports letters, and Berry was on the list.[12]

The future brigadier general joined the Second Infantry, Company F, as a private during the first call-up. Berry appeared in all eight of the Second's games, starting as a fullback in six, but only played a part of the Fourth Nebraska Infantry game because of an injury.

Bill Birge. William Samuel Birge Jr. was born in 1892 in Gorman Texas, a crossroads town that was a long horse and buggy ride from Abilene to the west or Dallas to the east. He was a Longhorn freshman tackle in 1911 but in 1912 transferred to Georgia for a year. He was able to waive the player ineligibility ruling when he returned to UT in 1913 but was injured early and missed much of the season, recovering to substitute in a game with Sewanee and to start in a post-season Notre Dame game. 1915 was the last year that defensive and offensive guard Birge was on the UT team. During his tenure, he earned both All-State and All-Southwestern recognitions and his varsity football letter.[13]

Birge finished the requirements for his law degree in the spring of 1916. A natural leader, his fellow students had elected him president of the UT Law School junior class, and when the seasoned athlete and Company F lieutenant joined the Second Infantry, his teammates nominated him as team captain and defensive line coach. Birge started in all eight of the Second's games at right guard, right end, or left tackle.[14]

Phillip Clarke. Phillip Solomon "Spitz" Clarke III was born in Bryan, Texas, in 1896 and moved to Austin after his railroad conductor father accepted a job transfer. Clarke was a star Austin High School athlete, playing on the high school baseball, basketball, and football teams with Warren Collins. Both athletes received their senior year sports letters at a memorable ceremony at the Driskill Hotel. In a nod to his leadership skills, Clarke was named the school's basketball team business manager during his junior year.[15]

Clarke's Austin high school football performance was the stuff of newspaper headlines. In a tied 1913 high school game, halfback Clarke caught a pass and ran 45 yards, crossing the goal line and winning the match just as the clock ran out. The next year he made another memorable play with a 50-yard run on an interception. That year Austin played the North Fort Worth Warriors for the State High School Football Championship, clinching the title 23 to 0. The game provided another dramatic performance of Clarke's broken field running and kicking. When he missed a conversion, it was the first extra point he flubbed during the entire season. His was an amazing performance in that final game, particularly because he played with an injured shoulder, a bad ankle, and for several days before the contest had been "confined to his bed with the grippe."[16]

By 1915, Clarke was playing amateur baseball in the Austin Commercial League for the Bankers and was a standout hitter. That fall, "the plucky halfback and mainstay of the Austin High School team of last season" enrolled at UT and was named captain of the freshman scrub team. At 5'9" tall and 172 pounds, Spitz Clarke was a standout athlete. Like Bill Birge, he started in every game. He played the halfback position in six games, was starting quarterback in game two against the First Wisconsin, and in game three, the First Missouri Artillery rematch, he was at right end.[17]

Warren Collins. Henry Warren "Rip" Collins was born in 1896 in Weatherford, Texas, located west of Dallas. His mother moved the six-year-old boy to Austin after his father died, but he was raised by his aunt and uncle. Collins, like Clarke, was a star athlete at Austin High School for four years. In 1914, the graduating high schooler was named manager of the Austin High School baseball team. It was an unparalleled achievement for the teenager. Sports fans expected him to enroll at UT after graduation, but instead, he headed to Texas A&M. There are differing versions of why Collins chose A&M over UT, but the most plausible is a response to UT coach Dave Allerdice. Allegedly, the UT coach watched him hobble off the field during a high school game with a sprained ankle and was overheard remarking that Collins' lack of resolve would prevent him from ever playing on his Longhorn team.[18]

Collins made the 1915 Aggie starting lineup as a freshman. It was the "wonderful toe work" of rookie Rip Collins, the "phenomenal kicker and backfield man," that contributed to the Aggie's win over the Longhorns in their 1915 matchup. He made All-State that year. Collins' freshman season statistics would have been more impressive if he played more. He was disqualified from at least two games, however, because he failed to pass the obligatory number of courses required to participate in collegiate sports. Collins left college at the end of his first semester.[19]

During the spring and summer of 1916, Collins pitched for the Kelly Smiths in the Austin Commercial League. He never finished the season, signing up for Company F in May. Rip Collins started every game for the Second Infantry, as a halfback in seven and a fullback in the fourth game against the First Virginia Artillery.

John Diller. John Cabot Diller, born in Illinois in 1895, moved to San Antonio during the 1910s and was a high school and city YMCA basketball star. As a UT freshman in 1915, he was a standout as a forward on the undefeated Longhorn basketball team, receiving his college varsity letter. But he was relegated to the bench on its football team because, as a center, he followed in the footsteps of the legendary Gus Dittmar, considered "the best center in the whole South." Had he not left UT to join the guard, Diller would have been captain of the Longhorn football team for the 1916 season. John Diller finally ducked out from under Dittmar's long shadow in the Second Infantry, playing in every game as the starting center in six and second-string in two.[20]

Eugene Dotson. Eugene Malcolm Dotson was born in 1894 in the East Texas town of Garrison, situated between Nacogdoches on the Texas side of the Sabine River and Shreveport on the Louisiana side. The family moved to Waco in the early 1900s. Dotson enrolled at Baylor in 1913 and played halfback for their football squad, the Bears. At 210 pounds, the "big man from Baylor" was portrayed by an admiring sportswriter as "very fast for his weight" and "one of the most powerful athletes Texas has ever produced." In addition to the backfield, he was sometimes at the quarterback position. Capable of passing a pigskin some 80 yards, he "could throw a football further than anyone in the game, but his problem was accuracy."[21]

An all-around athlete, Dotson played amateur city league baseball in Waco and was on the Baylor track and field team. During his college years, he also officiated at Waco High School football games. Dotson played in seven of the eight games in halfback and fullback positions as either first- or second-string and was at left guard in game seven against the 12th Division All-Stars.[22]

Baker Duncan. Addison Baker Duncan was born in 1891 in the town of Calvert, located midway between College Station and Waco. His father, A.P. Duncan, was a founder of the Duncan-Hobson Electric Company and relocated the family to Waco so he could run the business. After graduating from Waco High School, Duncan attended UT in 1911 then transferred to the University of Virginia where he played basketball as a center. Duncan was 21 when his father was shot by an aggrieved employee in 1912, and he left Virginia to return home the next year.[23]

Duncan reenrolled at UT in 1914 but was not eligible for football because of the 12-month transfer rule. At 6-foot-6-inches and 185 pounds, he was a natural athlete. In 1914, he competed on the Waco City tennis circuit and was singles champion. He had played football at UT as a scrub in 1911, and in 1915 and was on the Longhorn basketball team. In his senior year, Duncan was back on the UT football team as a tackle and was nominated to the All-State and All-Southwestern "all-star" teams.[24]

Company F's Baker Duncan was the team's unofficial offensive line coach and started at either tackle or guard positions in all eight of the Second Infantry's games.

Jim Kendrick. James Marcellus "Big Jim" Kendrick was born in 1893 in Hillside, outside of San Angelo, and was the youngest of nine children. The family moved to a farm near Waco in 1904. After graduating from Douglas Select High School in 1910, Kendrick enrolled at Texas A&M where he played basketball and outfield on its baseball team. He was a nationally ranked sharpshooter on the collegiate rifle team and was an end on the football squad in 1911, and again from 1913 to 1915. Kendrick was nominated twice to the Texas All-State roster.[25]

1915 was Kendrick's best season on the gridiron. That year he was A&M's leading scorer, loading the scoreboard with touchdown runs and kicking extra points. His kicking and punting were second only to teammate Warren "Rip" Collins, and between the two of them, whenever the Aggies were scheduled for a game, sportswriters of the rival town predicted a kicking sensation. Before a November game against Rice, for example, the *Houston Post* carried the headline "Pigskin Booters Here on Monday," a reference to Collins and Kendrick's ability to "drop the ball over the goal from the middle of the field" and whose kicks "brought fans to their feet." Collins' and Kendrick's performance in the Aggie's 13-0 upset over the Longhorns that season was talked about in collegiate circles for years.[26]

Lt. Jim Kendrick was the Second Infantry backfield coach and was a starter at right and left end in six games, and halfback in one match. He missed only one game, the Fourth Nebraska Infantry match, because of an injury.

George Lane. George Henry Lane was born in 1894 to a frontier family that was among the first to settle in the Waco area, his grandfather deeded the first lot in the town in 1849. Lane attended Waco High School and was captain of both the football and baseball teams in 1914. In the latter sport, Lane was considered "one of the fastest fielders and best sluggers" who had played the game. He was a freshman at A&M in 1915 and a second-squad lineman.[27]

George Lane played in six Second Infantry games. He was on the first squad as an end in three games and a substitute in three others. Lane missed the first contest with the First Missouri Artillery in Corpus Christi because he was selected as one of 16 expert marksmen to compete in the National Guard's all-state rifle match held in Jacksonville, Florida in early November.[28]

Charley Ogden. Charles Wesley "June" Ogden Jr. was born in 1895 in San Antonio. His father, Charles Wesley Ogden Sr., was a judge, general legal counsel to the Texas Midland Railroad (TMR), and prominent in state and national Republican politics. Ogden Sr. was also a founding member of TMR President E.H.R. Green's sporting club, the Tarpon Club, at the time the most exclusive club in America. Son Ogden Jr. spent his teen years on the San Antonio High School football team, then enrolled at UT in 1914. That year he was a scrub, and in 1915, was a tackle on UT's second team. Ogden appeared in seven Second Infantry games, starting as a guard in five, a replacement in game 6 against the 74th New York Infantry, and a third-string fullback in the 12th Division All-Stars match.[29]

Sylvan Simpson. Sylvan Blum Simpson was born in 1893 in Llano County and attended Llano High School from 1909 to 1913. One of just ten students in his junior class, he was the class president. Simpson spent part of his first college year at Baylor, then transferred to UT for the 1915 spring semester. The following fall, he was eligible to play on the Longhorn scrub team, then moved to its first team as a versatile substitute, playing as an offensive and defensive lineman and, at the close of the 1915 season, as an end.[30]

Simpson in the first UT game of the 1915 season replaced starter Baker Duncan at left tackle in the 92-0 Longhorn waltz across Daniel Baker. He was a regular substitute for K.L. Berry, who fought injuries throughout most of the season. He replaced the injured Berry at right tackle in the Longhorn's 40-0 defeat of Southwestern on October 30 and was called in for Berry again in the memorable 1915 UT-AM game. He was also a regular replacement for his future Second Texas teammate Bill Birge, with notable substitute performances in the 1915 TCU and Sewanee games. Near the season's end, Coach Allerdice "sprung a surprise" when he moved Simpson from the line to left end. Simpson, the coach observed, was a talented pass receiver and able to "smash interference." That year he earned his varsity 'T' letter.[31]

Simpson was one of eight Second Infantry footballers who played in all eight games. He was a starting right or left tackle in seven, and a right end in the first match between the Second Infantry and First Missouri Artillery.

Charlie Turner. Charles Edgar Turner was born in Hemphill County, Texas, in 1893. The family later moved to Roswell, New Mexico, where he attended high school. Turner enrolled in UT in 1913 to study engineering. Although a diminutive 5'8" and 153 pounds in his first football season, Turner made the first squad as an end and was nominated for All-State. He was a starter during UT's 1913 win over the Baylor Baptists in what was then their highest-scoring game in UT history at 77-0.[32]

Turner showed his potential during the 1914 Longhorn season. Among his most memorable performances was in UT's 66-7 victory over Ole Miss. In one possession, Turner caught a pass for 61 yards, another for a 20-yard gain, then crossed the goal line for six points. When quarterback Clyde Littlefield passed 55 yards to Turner, who added another seven yards for the TD, the play was considered "one of the longest [forward passes] that has been executed on Clark Field." In UT's 32 to 7 defeat of Oklahoma, Turner scored three of the victor's touchdowns. Early in the game, with the Longhorns up by just six points, receiver Turner harangued coach Allerdice to let him run the ball. Allerdice conceded and let him run the next three plays. He gained five yards, then ten yards, and on his third attempt crossed the goal line. His performance prompted the editors of the 1915 *Cactus* yearbook to write that he was a player with "unlimited self-confidence" as well as "great physical strength, intuitive football acumen, and dogged determination."[33]

During his final collegiate season in 1915, Turner missed several games due to a strained ligament resulting from "bronco-busting during summer vacation." He still managed to rank as the state's third-best college scorer, racking up eight touchdowns for UT. Three of his touchdowns came in UT's 40-0 defeat of Southwestern. In the Longhorn's 27-6 march over Sewanee, Turner started in the backfield and scored the first TD of the game. Then he was swapped back to his regular end position, where he made huge receiving yardage and caught a long pass for the Longhorn's second touchdown. Turner had one bad game that year against Oklahoma and was largely blamed for UTs hard-fought 13-14 loss, the press disparaging his "poor football" and dropped passes "which should have been easily handled." Turner over his three-year career earned both All-State and All-Southwestern nominations.[34]

Charlie Turner was also a champion middleweight wrestler and was on the undefeated 1913 Longhorn wrestling team. The next year he was captain of the wrestling team, and in 1915 was the collegiate middle-weight state champion.[35]

UT engineer Charlie Turner was the mind behind organizing the Second Infantry's offensive plays. He started as an end in five of the Second's eight games, missing games four through six to visit his ill father in New Mexico.

Grady Watson. Born in Hemphill in 1894, Alfred Grady "Rats" Watson graduated from Orange High School in 1912. Orange timber baron and football benefactor H.J. Lutcher Stark, who watched the teenager play high school ball, offered Watson the money to attend college and in 1914 he enrolled at Southwestern University in Georgetown.

Weighing in at 141 pounds, he got the nickname "Rats" because no one could catch him on the field as "he scurried around like a rodent."[36]

Watson was a scrub during his first Southwestern season, one of three in line for the quarterback slot. The next year, Watson was relegated to the second team, subbing at both quarterback and backfield positions, and showing up as right end starter against TCU in November. Watson's bench-warming college football resume seems surprising given his contribution to the Second Infantry's remarkable 1916-17 playing record and his later years in the National Football League. Either coach Rix did not recognize his player's potential, which seems unlikely, or Grady Watson was a late bloomer. "Rats" Watson started as quarterback in four Second Infantry games and was a replacement quarterback in three.[37]

The Second Infantry's Second Squad. Seven players appeared during the 1916 regular season in two to five games: Bart Coan, David R. Nelson, Tom Gambrell, Dick "Sugar" Lane, Bertrand "Mullie" Lenoir, Tom Mitchell, and Pleasant "Pleas" Rogers. Three other players appeared in a single game. They were Charles T. Schaedel, "Bud" Smith, and John Erwin "Harry" Stullken. These ten players were integral members of the practice squad, and it's also likely that they were on the field more than the Texas press reported.

Bart Coan. Bartlett Elias Coan was born in Alabama in 1890, and his family relocated in the early 1900s to the outskirts of Cisco, between Dallas and Abilene, where his father bought a farm. He was one of ten children, all of whom listed their occupation as farm laborers by the time they were old enough to walk. Coan played high school football and won honors as a track star.[38]

The "big man" who was "exceptionally fast for his size" started his collegiate career at Houston's Rice University in 1914. Coan was versatile, playing tackle, sometimes guard, and fielding the team's punt returns. He earned two varsity letters in his freshman year, one in football and another in baseball. Coan left Rice to join the Houston Lights in Company A, Third Infantry at the first guard call-up. As a Second Infantry player, Bart Coan was a replacement left end against the First Virginia Artillery and started at left end in the game with the Fourth Nebraska Infantry.[39]

Tom Gambrell. Born in 1892, Thomas DeWitt Gambrell lived in Lockhart, between San Antonio and Austin, and played football at Lockhart High School as an end. His family moved to Waco before his senior year where his father was a district court judge. Gambrell enrolled at UT in 1912 and played baseball as a second baseman and shortstop for four seasons. He was captain of the baseball team in 1915, the year that UT won its first Southwest Conference championship. Gambrell led the team in hitting with a .298 batting average, 30 runs, and 16 stolen bases. Tom Gambrell was later named to the UT Sports Hall of Fame.[40]

When he enlisted in Company F in May 1916, Gambrell was enrolled in UT's Law School. He played as a substitute in at least three Second Infantry games.[41]

Dick Lane. Richard Givens "Sugar" Lane was born in 1895 in Childress, Texas, located midway between Lubbock and Oklahoma City. His father, a cattleman and ranch manager, moved the family to Oklahoma and then relocated to Austin before 1910. Lane did not attend college, and in the winter of 1915, was an amateur wrestler in the National Guard's Company E sports program that provided Austin with "a series of clean athletic exhibitions." One of his matches was against future Second footballer Victor Bintliff.[42]

Dick Lane appeared in five games. He was a starting right guard in the match against the 74th New York Infantry, a replacement fullback in the Second Infantry's 12th Division All-Star contest, and a second-string tackle in another three games.

Mullie Lenoir. Bertram Earl "Mullie" Lenoir was born in 1897 in Marlin, southeast of Waco. He played baseball and football as left end on the Marlin High School team. Lenoir tried to join the Navy in 1913, even signing up for an entrance exam, but when the recruiters learned he had just turned 16 years old, they sent him home. By 1915 he was playing baseball for the Waco City League and had applied to the University of Alabama before joining the National Guard. Mullie appeared as a substitute in the Second Infantry's last three games.[43]

Tom Mitchell. Born in 1896, Thomas Douglas Mitchell lived in Gainesville, south of Indian Territory before it was Oklahoma, on the Texas side of the Red River. He was one of five children born to a traveling salesman father. After high school, he attended Baylor and played two years on the football team during the 1913 and 1914 seasons. Freshman Mitchell started as a backup to quarterback Guy Crosslin and rapidly moved to starter, with Crosslin redeployed to the backfield. His most memorable game was against Texas A&M in a contest that ended with a 14-14 tie. Mitchell scored both Baptist touchdowns and kicked both extra points. He earned his varsity letter at the end of his first season.[44]

In the October 1914 Baylor-UT game, the Longhorns routed the Baptists 57-0. Quarterback Mitchell lined up in that game against future teammates Birge, Berry, and Turner. It was ugly. Mitchell scrambled the entire game as his line "was torn to pieces" by the Longhorns, the Baptist offense never threatening to score. Crosslin made the gain of the day at 18 yards but was hit so hard by UT's Charlie Turner that "he was thrown on his head" and dislocated his neck. Knocked unconscious, "for a time it was thought that possibly his injury might be fatal."[45]

Mitchell was expected to return for Baylor's 1915 season but instead enrolled at UT for the academic year to begin his law degree. The transfer rule made him ineligible to play UT ball. After his first UT semester, Mitchell enlisted in Company F in May 1916. He was the Second Infantry's third-string quarterback but played three games as a replacement halfback.[46]

Dave Nelson. Born in San Antonio in 1889, David Rogers Nelson was one of the oldest players on the Second Texas roster. He graduated from San Antonio's Peacock Military Academy and married Theresa Cullen in 1913. The couple settled in Lytle, southwest of San Antonio, where he took up farming and raising livestock. Nelson left his cattle and hogs long enough to run for Representative of the 18th District but lost to Judge Frank Earnest. First Lieutenant Nelson played in five games, starting as a center in two games and as a substitute in three.[47]

Pleas Rogers. Pleasant Blair Rogers was born in Austin in 1899 to a larger-than-life father, John Harris Rogers. John Rogers enlisted in the Texas Rangers in 1882, making captain in 1892. Wounded twice in the line of duty, his exploits and occasional shootouts with frontier outlaws were followed in every major Lone Star State newspaper. Lawman Rogers was appointed United States Marshal for the Western District of Texas by President Woodrow Wilson in 1913.[48]

Son Pleas was 15 when his father enrolled him in a two-year program at the Wentworth Military Academy in Lexington, Missouri. Rogers was on the track and football teams, including the Wentworth gridiron squad that went undefeated in 1914. Rogers graduated the next year, that fall enrolling at UT where he made the football squad as a scrub.[49] Rogers, who was another of the Second Infantry's future brigadier generals, enlisted in Company E in May 1916. Just six weeks later he was promoted to first sergeant. He played in at least four games as a substitute.[50]

C.T. Schaedel. Charles Theodore Schaedel was born in Alexandria, Louisiana, in 1884 and lived in Vermillion Parrish before his family relocated in 1902 to Bay City, in Matagorda County, Texas. When he first showed up as a sophomore transfer to Aggie football training camp in 1909, it was joked that "many of the boys wondered where he came from and what country could be guilty of raising such a man." Partly the bantering was because he didn't drink or swear, and partly because, in his freshman year, he joined every sports team on campus and most of its social and military organizations. By the time he graduated with a degree in civil engineering in 1912, Schaedel was a captain in the Artillery Corps, track team captain and record-holder in the hammer throw, captain of the rifle club, captain and first baseman of the 'H' Company baseball team, vice president of the Artillery Tennis Club, was on the Athletic Council, and was athletic editor for the A&M annual yearbook, ironically titled *The Long Horn*. He was a recipient of both football and track letters for 1910 and 1911.[51]

On the football field, Schaedel played mostly at center and guard but was equally adept at any position on the line. He played on the 1909 and 1910 A&M teams that won two back-to-back state championships. A&M's coach Moran nominated Schaedel for All-State in 1910 and he was awarded his second varsity letter that year. Schaedel was at left guard in the historic 1911 game against UT when the Longhorns broke their three-game losing streak with a 6-0 victory over the Farmers. During that game, he played against UT's Birge, who started opposite him at right guard, and Berry, who came in at tackle.[52]

During his senior year, Schaedel's A&M's cadet field artillery battery was chosen for advanced readiness instruction by the US Army's Coast Artillery Corps. In June, he was one of a small group of graduates recognized by the National Guard adjutant general "as having shown special military aptitude" and was commissioned as a second lieutenant. C.T. Schaedel was a substitute in at least one Second Infantry game.[53]

Bud Smith. Schuyler William "Bud" Smith was born to a Nebraska farming family in 1891. By the time he was a teenager, the family had moved to Missouri and then New Mexico. He enrolled in the UT Law School in 1913, and with Charlie Turner, was on the Longhorn wrestling team that won every state match that year. The law student was both a trainer and captain of the UT wrestling team in 1916.

Bud Smith is referenced as having been a substitute in the final Second Texas Infantry game against the First New York Cavalry, although his position is unknown.[54]

J.E. Stullken Jr. John Erwin "Harry" Stullken was born in Iowa in 1895, the family relocating to Texas while he was in grade school. Stullken attended Brenham High School before transferring to Austin where his father worked at UT as a chemist. He completed his high school education in Austin and enrolled at UT as a freshman in 1915, playing on its scrub team. Part of Company E, Stullken started in the Second's fifth game, against the Fourth Nebraska, as a left tackle.[55]

Other Players. There were four other named team members who are not known to have played in any Second Infantry games. This could have been a press omission, but the best explanation is that these were the players selected for the Second Infantry's 1917-1918 season team. Likely they scrimmaged against the first and second squads, and they may have substituted in some games. They were Victor Bintliff, Charlie Brown, H.H. "Whitey" Davis, and Louis "Tige" Halphen.

Victor Bintliff. Victor James Bintliff was born in Austin in 1894 to a tinsmith father who emigrated from England. His family owned a ranch east of the city where Bintliff took a keen interest in animal husbandry. It was here that he shot himself through the foot while rabbit hunting, but the 16-year-old's bullet hole healed with no lasting damage. Bintliff did not attend college, joining the National Guard shortly after high school. Like Dick Lane, he was an amateur boxer and wrestler who was active in Austin's National Guard's Company E athletic program exhibitions during the winter and summer of 1915. Bintliff is not referenced in any of the Second Infantry games. His name, however, surfaced during the winter of 1917 and he was almost certainly recruited for the 1917-1918 season team.[56]

Charlie Brown. Charles Wiley Brown was born in 1893 in Groesbeck, 30 miles east of Waco, and moved to Waco as a youngster. He was elected as the student manager of the Waco High School baseball team in 1914 and was the high school football team manager for two years. He enrolled at Texas A&M in the fall of 1914 and played right tackle and end during his first year. He was one of the first freshmen at the college to win a varsity letter. Like Victor Bintliff, Brown is not referenced in any of the Second Infantry games but was practicing with the team for its 1917 season.[57]

Whitey Davis. Born Howard Herndon Davis in 1894 in Spring, Texas, the family moved to San Marcos where he attended high school and was a track and field star. As a freshman in the fall of 1915 at UT, he was on the university's track and field team and captain of the broad jump squad. Davis was not mentioned as a player in any of the Second Infantry's eight games.[58]

Louis Halphen. Louis Alcide "Tige" Halphen was born in 1895 in Austin. He did not attend college and joined the guard in 1913 after high school. Halphen signed up for the Austin baseball league in 1913 and was also one of the league's umpires. In his three baseball seasons before the first call-up, he played nearly every infield and outfield position, including catcher. Halphen continually moved up in the leagues and was a star on teams such as the Moose Club, Lemon Kola, and the league-leading Oliver team. His play was followed regularly by local sportswriters, and one editor wrote that "his never-say-die spirit makes him a very valuable player." Halphen was also well-liked by city league ballplayers, and he had a sizable Austin fan base. In an unusual show of support, they started a collection and raised $5 that they sent to him while he was on the border with the National Guard. Halphen was not cited as a player in any of the Second Infantry's eight games.[59]

Management. Lieutenant Colonel A.W. "Mike" Bloor, who held degrees from both the University of Texas and Texas A&M, was the Second Texas Infantry's team organizer and carried the honorary title of athletic director throughout the Second Infantry's eight-game reign of terror. Team captain Bill Birge's fellow UT Law School mates Charlie Stewart and Dan Cook were managers of the football squad, and handled duties such as scheduling, finance, negotiations, and travel logistics. Laredo's Walter F. Woodul was never provided a formal title, but he was a force behind the scenes who negotiated many of the Second's games and venues with top army brass and various host city decision-makers. Texas University graduate Dr. Jim Seay was the team physician. D.V. "Tubby" Graves was team coach for the team's final two games.[60]

Mike Bloor. Born in Pennsylvania in 1876, Alfred Wainwright Bloor's rancher and farmer father relocated his family to Manor, 12 miles northeast of Austin, in 1880. Bloor was one of just 32 graduates in the class of 1895 at A&M College, and he played on the Farmer's first football team. He was promoted quickly in the college's Battalion Organization, making first lieutenant in his senior year. After graduation, Bloor was part of the Governor's Guard, an elite body of volunteer soldiers, before joining the First Texas Volunteer Infantry. He went overseas in 1898 to serve in the Spanish-American War, where he took part in the Army of Occupation in Cuba. At war's end, Major Bloor married and entered the University of Texas Law School, passing the bar in 1904.[61]

Attorney Bloor remained active in the guard. A first lieutenant of Company I in 1901, he was promoted to major a year later when the volunteer soldiers of the First Texas Infantry elected him to lead their unit. As one of the best rifle shots in the Texas National Guard, Bloor organized marksmanship training and competitions, and his 1910 team placed in the top 15 teams in the United States. Bloor was transferred to the Second Infantry in 1908, and in 1914 was a lieutenant colonel and second in command of the regiment under Colonel B.F. Dalameter.[62]

Former A&M footballer Mike Bloor was the Brownsville District football program's strongest advocate, and the reason is probably because of his long-term commitment to the guard organization. In 1905 he was a founder and the first chairman and president of the National Guard Association. Among its purposes was to expand military training and promote the significance of the guard to the Texas community by arranging entertainment, such as athletics, drills, and marches. Most notably, at least to the football question, was the association's goal to improve the morale of the men who were serving.[63]

Dan Cook. Dan M. Cook was born in 1889 and grew up on a farm between Mt. Pleasant and Cookville in the northeast corner of Texas. Cook played baseball in high school, then attended University of Texas. He was in his final year of UT Law School when he enlisted as a private in Company F during the first call-up. Cook was not active in collegiate sports but was a charter member of the UT Triangles and Acacia fraternities whose members were Scottish Rite Masons. Both Bill Birge and Charlie Stewart were also active in the organization.[64]

D.V. "Tubby" Graves. One of ten children born in 1886 to an Alabama doctor father, Graves always went by his nickname or his initials so that he didn't have to explain how he got his real name, Dorsett Vandeventer Graves. Graves played college football at Missouri from 1906 to 1908, then played minor league baseball before joining the University of Alabama sports program in 1912 as a baseball, football, and basketball coach. He left Alabama in 1915 to become the assistant football coach under Dana X. Bible at A&M in 1916.

Dr. Jim Seay. James Browder Seay was born in 1891 near Madisonville and graduated in 1913 from UT with a degree in dentistry. His medical specialty was an unusual choice for a team general physician position, but his lifetime passion for sports probably helped him overcome any reluctance on the part of team management.[65]

Charlie Stewart. Charles Brooks Stewart was born in 1892 in Shiloh, Louisiana, before moving to Shreveport. He was 14 when he started working as an office boy for the local Shreveport Western Union Telegraph Company. In 1911 he enrolled in UT Law School. Stewart demonstrated his business acumen as manager for the 1915 UT Varsity *Cactus* yearbook, "raising the greatest amount of money ever sought for the publication." Like Dan Cook, Stewart was not a UT athlete but was acquainted with Second Infantry team captain Bill Birge as a degreed Mason.[66]

Walter Woodul. Walter Frank Woodul was born in 1892, in Laredo, Texas. Woodul attended public schools in Corpus Christi and Alice, graduating from high school in 1909 as class valedictorian. He earned money for college by washing dishes and teaching school for two years in Oklahoma and Kansas. In 1913 he enrolled at UT and finished his law degree in just three years. In May 1916, Woodul volunteered as a private on the Austin Company F roster then in the summer of 1916 transferred to his hometown Laredo Company I. During his first months in the guard, he was elected to represent Laredo and Webb County in the Texas House of Representatives. The day after taking his seat in the legislature, January 10, 1917, he was licensed to practice law.[67]

The Achievers. The Second Texas Infantry football players carried many of the same traits through life that they either brought to the football field or developed when they got there. They were achievers, and perhaps that's a clue to why the Second Texas Infantry was better than many of their gridiron era. The most common callings that the former footballers later followed were in sports, the military, and law. Not surprisingly, they were very good at them.

Back to the Field. Sports brought them together as the Second Texas Infantry, and sports remained vital to many of the team members after their 1916-17 season. Six players who went back to college to finish their degrees played football again, and three of them repeated their stellar Second Texas performances during their college years. K.L. Berry returned to finish a graduate degree at UT and in 1924 was nominated for the All-Southwestern "all-star" laurels again. Mullie Lenoir, who enrolled at the University of Alabama and played college baseball and football, was an All-Southern running back. As late as 1951, his 1920 season score of 144 points on 24 touchdowns was still the Crimson Tide's highest individual scoring record. Rats Watson, who donned the burnt orange and white as a University of Texas Longhorn, was named the All-Southwestern quarterback of 1920.[68]

Three former National Guard footballers played professional sports. Rip Collins chose professional baseball, pitching for the New York Yankees, Boston Red Sox, Detroit Tigers, and St. Louis Browns. Jim Kendrick played professional football from 1922 to 1927, his gridiron career taking him to Jim Thorpe's Canton Bulldogs, the Chicago Bears, and the 1927 NFL champion New York Giants. He was also player-manager of the Cleveland Indians minor league baseball team. Rats Watson played 20 NFL games for four different teams between 1922-1927. At least six former footballers coached sports at the high school and college levels, and as many traveled across Texas as umpires and referees for various sports events.

Military. Duty to country, another strong common thread between most of the team's players, was evident even after they parted ways as a football squad. In 1918, most went to war, and many were the same heroes on the battlefield that they were on the gridiron. Seven former footballers were wounded during World War I. Many of the players, in their later civilian roles, remained active in the Texas National Guard after the Great War and served in some capacity during America's next global conflict, World War II.

Ten of the team players and management joined the Regular Army. Three achieved the rank of brigadier general, a remarkably high number for the small sample size of a football team. The generals were Oscar Abbott, Kearie Lee Berry, and Pleas Rogers. Berry received his star in 1946 after surviving the infamous Bataan Death March and forty months as a Japanese prisoner of war.

The Lawyers. Eleven men on the team or its management received law degrees. Of the players, Ock Abbott, K.L. Berry, Bill Birge, Baker Duncan, Tom Gambrell, Tom Mitchell, and Schuyler Smith were licensed to practice law. Duncan later became a Waco mayor and Tom Gambrell, like his father before him, was a judge who, in 1930, ran for the senate. All four team managers – Mike Bloor, Dan Cook, Charles Stewart, and Walter Woodul also earned law degrees. Woodul had a remarkable career in politics, with elected positions in the Texas House of Representatives, the Senate, and was a Texas lieutenant governor.

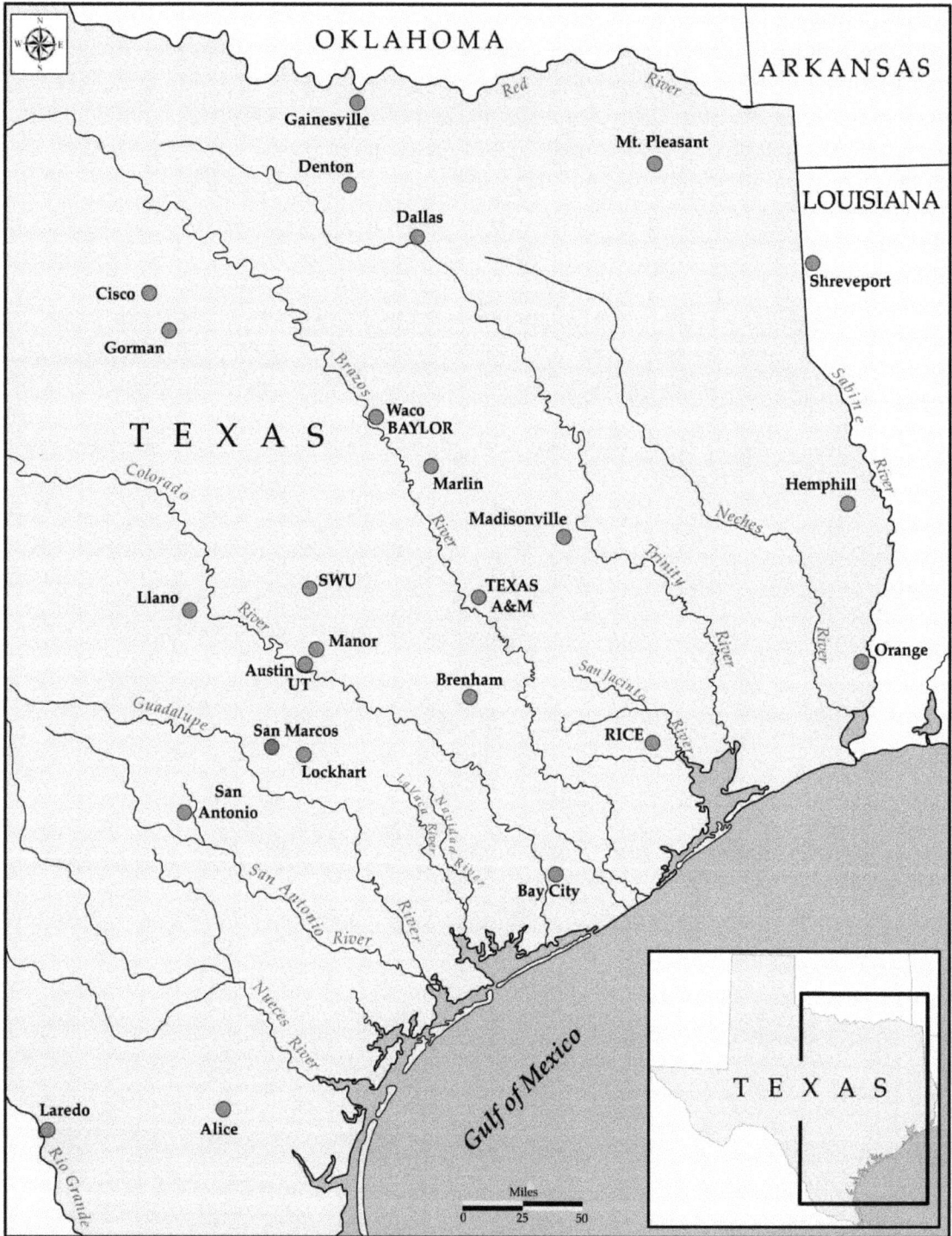

Overview map of the towns and cities where the Second Texas Infantry football squad and its management spent their formative years. The upper-case names refer to the Texas colleges mentioned in the text – University of Texas, Texas A&M College, Baylor, Rice, and Southwestern University. Drawing by R.K. Sawyer.

Left: Oscar "Ock" Abbott in a 1910 Texas A&M track team photo. Although better known for his football prowess, it is interesting his track coach said that he "possessed considerable natural ability, but needed coaching." "1911 A&M Longhorn Yearbook," *Texas A&M University Libraries*, library.tamu.edu.

Right: Bill Birge during his first year of college football, 1911. That year he was honored with inclusion in "the Immortals" for the team that beat Texas A&M in the annual Thanksgiving Day game after two years of losses. He was also Junior Class Law President in 1914. "School Yearbooks, 1900-2016," https://www.ancestry.com/discoveryui-content/view/22969988:1265.

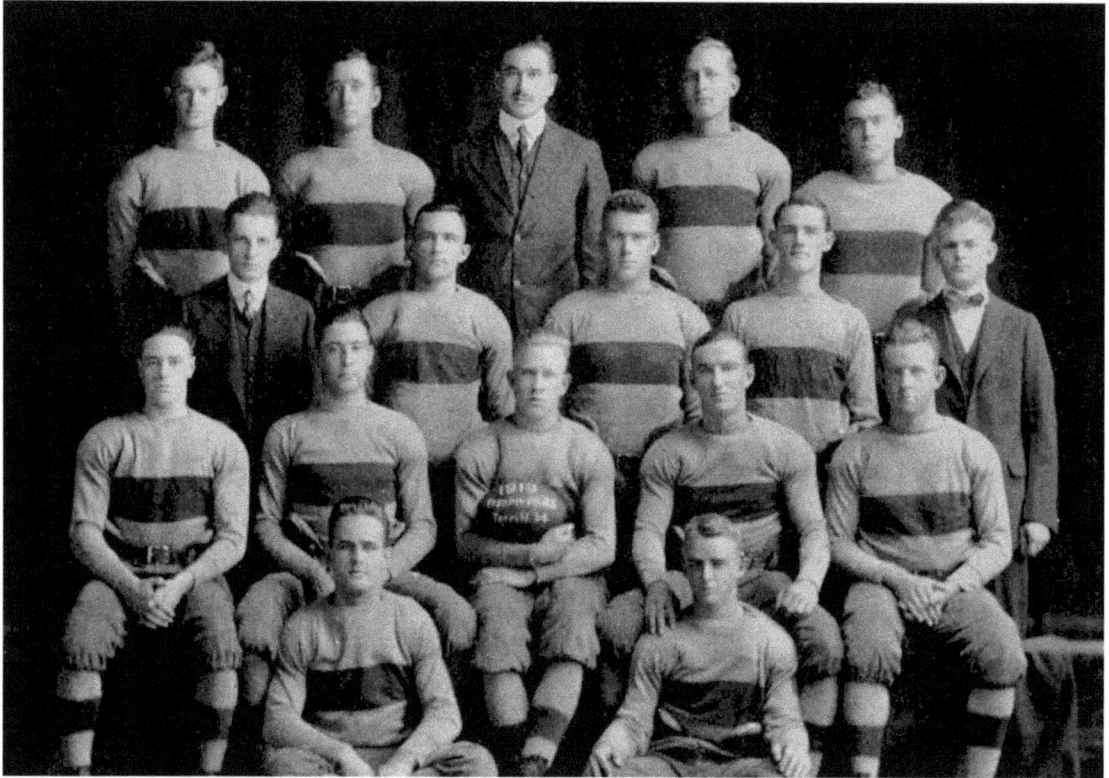

Top: The 1915 University of Texas freshmen football squad. Texas Eleven starter Phillip S. Clarke (second row, center) was captain of the freshman team. Second team player John E. "Harry" Stullken was also on the team, and is in top row, second from left. "1915 Cactus Yearbook," *Texas Scholar Works*, University of Texas Libraries, http://hdl.hande.net/2152/23763.

Left: Second Texas Infantry starting center John Diller. As a UT freshman in 1915, he was a standout as a forward on the undefeated 1916 Longhorn basketball team. "1916 Cactus Yearbook," *Texas Scholar Works*, University of Texas Libraries, http://hdl.hande .net/2152/23763.

Top: 1916 Longhorn basketball team. John Diller is on bottom row, far left, and starting Second Texas Infantry lineman Baker Duncan is in the top row, center. "1916 Cactus Yearbook," *Texas Scholar Works*, University of Texas Libraries, http://hdl.hande.net/2152/23763.

Left: Texas Eleven end and backfielder Jim Kendrick in 1915 as National Guard Regimental Ordnance Sargent Kendrick at Texas A&M. "1916 A&M Longhorn Yearbook," *Texas A&M University Libraries*, library.tamu.edu.

Left: Texas Eleven starting end Charlie Turner, from UT. Turner enrolled at UT in 1913 to study engineering, and in addition to his football performance was also a champion middleweight wrestler. "1915 Cactus Yearbook," *Texas Scholar Works*, University of Texas Libraries, http://hdl.hande.net/2152 /24283.

Right: Before Tom Gambrell was part of the Second Texas Infantry's second squad, he played baseball at UT as a second baseman and shortstop for four seasons. He was captain of the baseball team in 1915, the year UT won its first SWC championship. "1915 Cactus Yearbook," *Texas Works*, University of Texas Libraries, http://hdl.hande.net/2152 /24283.

Left: Thomas D. Mitchell was the third-string Second Texas Infantry quarterback. Known as "Tommy" during his Baylor footfall days, he was at first overlooked for its 1913 squad because "his very minuteness discouraged those in charge, and at once the opinion was formed that no good could come from a man of his build." "1915 Round-Up Yearbook," *Baylor University Archives*, digitalcollect-ions-baylor.quartexcollections.com.

Below: Pleasant B. Rogers in Wentworth Military Academy football team photo, 1914. Rogers is seated front row second from right. "Wentworth Military Academy Museum Yearbook Collection," *Annual Catalog 1914-1915*, https:// exportal.blob.core.windows.net/exportalresources/wma/Yea rbookWMA-1915.pdf.

Substitute Second Texas Infantry footballer Charles T. Schaedel was awarded Texas A&M football and track letters and graduated in 1912. "1912 A&M Longhorn Yearbook," *Texas A&M University Libraries*, library.tamu.edu.

Schuyler William "Bud" Smith enrolled at UT Law School in 1913, and with Charlie Turner, was on the Longhorn wrestling team that won every match in the state that year. The law middle-classman was both trainer and captain of the UT wrestling team in 1916. "1916 Cactus Yearbook," *Texas Scholar Works*, University of Texas Libraries, http://hdl.hande.net/2152/23763.

WRESTLING MATCH
Kopescky vs. Bintliff
At ARMORY CO. "E" 10th and CONGRESS
(Over Crescent Confectionery)
TONIGHT, 8 P. M.--ADMISSION 50c   Five Extra Good Preliminaries

Austin native Victor James Bintliff did not attend college, joining the National Guard shortly after high school. Like Dick Lane, he was an amateur boxer and wrestler who was active in the Austin's National Guard's Company E athletic program exhibitions during the winter and summer of 1915. Shown is a promotion for a 1915 wrestling match at the Austin armory. Modified from *Austin American*, Aug. 28, 1915.

Alfred Wainwright "Mike" Bloor, the Second Texas Infantry athletic director, was one of just 32 graduates in the class of 1895 at A&M College, and he played on the Farmer's first football team. After graduation, Bloor was part of the Governor's Guard, an elite body of volunteer soldiers, before joining the First Texas Volunteer Infantry. He went overseas in 1898 to serve in the Spanish-American War, where he took part in the Army of Occupation in Cuba. At war's end, Major Bloor married and entered the University of Texas Law School, passing the bar in 1904. "Texas A&M Olio 1895 Annual," *Corps of Cadets*, (Columbus: Berlin & Co, 1895).

Above: Team managers Dan Cook and Charles B. Stewart, along with Bill Birge, were active in the Acacia Masonic fraternity. Cook is in the second row from bottom, fourth from left. Stewart is in the third row from bottom, second from right. Bill Birge is on the top row, far left. "1916 Cactus Yearbook," *Texas Scholar Works*, University of Texas Libraries, http://hdl.hande.net/2152/23763.

Below: Team physician James B. Seay was in the UT Longhorn rifle club. Seay is in second row from bottom, second from right. Texas Eleven starter Sylvan B, Simpson was also on the team, and is in top row, second from left. "1916 Cactus Yearbook," *Texas Scholar Works*, University of Texas Libraries, http://hdl.hande.net/2152/23763.

CHAPTER 3

Texas College Football
1896 to 1915

*F*or a few on the National Guard gridiron roster, the Second Texas Infantry football season was their first moment in the sports limelight. Most of the Second Texas Infantry team members, however, had played college ball and their playing prowess was already well-known, if not legendary. At least in Texas. Before World War I, college football in America was regional and not yet national in its reach. That would change, and one of the catalysts was certainly the Second Texas Infantry. But until it did, athletic programs in the South and West were organized into, and governed by, three sometimes overlapping associations and conferences: the Southern Intercollegiate Athletic Association (SIAA), Southwestern Intercollegiate Athletic Association (SWIAA), and the Texas Intercollegiate Athletic Association (TIAA). In 1914 a fourth was added, the Southwest Conference (SWC), that would oversee competition among Texas, Arkansas, and Oklahoma schools for more than 80 years.

Colleges and universities were often concurrent members of more than one governing body and jockeyed between them with regularity, positioning their athletic programs for the most favorable player eligibility rules, recruiting, and season schedules. Some college programs even opted out of the oversight organizations, competing as independents and following their own rulebooks. Disagreements over player admissibility and the dominance of large collegiate programs over smaller ones precipitated no small amount of debate and sometimes bitterness between competing colleges, and it caused all but the SWC to fade away by the late 1910s.

Southern Intercollegiate Athletic Association. Formed in 1892, the Southern Intercollegiate Athletic Association (SIAA) was instrumental in bringing Walter Camp's evolving football rules and regulations to college sports programs in the South and West, including a focus on eliminating the sport's "rough features." University of Texas was the first Texas school to apply for SIAA membership, in 1895, and remained part of that body until 1906. A&M College was admitted in 1903, left in 1908, applied to rejoin in 1911, and exited again at the end of the 1914 season.[1]

SIAA began to unravel in 1914 when a Southern Conference was formed by former SIAA institutions outside of Texas that opposed its strict player eligibility mandate. In this instance, it was the one-year ruling in which a player transferring from one school was prohibited from playing for another until completing an enrollment period of 12 months. Although no Texas teams moved to the Southern Conference, the new organization had the unintended consequence of eliminating several of their large state school opponents. This, plus growing opposition to other of its by-laws, helped to precipitate the 1914 founding of the Southwest Conference.[2]

Southwestern Intercollegiate Athletic Association. The Southwestern Intercollegiate Athletic Association (SWIAA) was a regional association that encompassed Texas, Arkansas, Missouri, Kansas, Colorado, the territories of Oklahoma and New Mexico, and what remained of "Indian Territory." SWIAA paralleled SIAA from its founding in 1904 until 1914, and its first president was UT athletic program director F. Homer Curtis. It was structured like SIAA and covered the full range of intercollegiate sports. In its gridiron role, SWIAA's board assisted in arranging playing schedules and attempted to provide football with consistent regulations and standards. Inevitably, player eligibility requirements, notably the rule barring post-graduate students from athletics, led to a rebellion that hastened its demise. The organization disappeared entirely by 1916.[3]

Texas Intercollegiate Athletic Association. Texas Christian University Professor O.W. Long, then president of SWIAA, founded the Texas Intercollegiate Athletic Association (TIAA) in 1909 as a protest to the by-laws of the Southwestern Intercollegiate Athletic Association. TIAA was initially composed of most of Texas' smaller football programs, including Austin College, Baylor, Southwestern University, Texas Christian, and Trinity University. Fort Worth University was an intermittent member. University of Texas, Texas A&M, Daniel Baker College, and Fort Worth Polytechnic joined TIAA in 1910, and Rice played its first year with TIAA in 1912.[4]

Like SIAA and SWIAA before it, TIAA's support was quickly eroded by issues of player admissibility among participating schools. In 1912, for example, Baylor coach Ralph Glaze was accused of playing two ineligible men against UT, and according to TIAA guidelines, faced disbarment as a coach. A furious Glaze protested that his infraction wasn't listed in the rulebooks. It was, but TIAA had neglected to mail the new rulebook to participating TIAA schools.[5]

The 1913 TIAA president, Dr. C.C. Gumm of Polytech College, was in an equally awkward position when four of his own team players were charged with various eligibility infractions, including the unpopular rule precluding football players from participating in organized summer baseball leagues, whether they were paid athletes or not. Gumm set an example by barring the four questionable team members from play in the 1913 Polytech football season, a move that made him instantly unpopular with students and alumni alike.[6]

The same year, the embattled TIAA lost favor with the two largest Texas programs, particularly UT, that wanted access to larger schools and better opponents. The 1913 football season was a good example. Every Texas team apart from UT was defeated by teams that were not part of the TIAA, an outcome that "proved the inferiority of TIAA football." TIAA began to lose its prominence the next year and was replaced by the Southwest Conference.[7]

Southwest Conference. University of Texas athletic director L. Theo Bellmont was the driving force behind the 1914 founding of the Southwest Intercollegiate Athletic Conference, its name soon shortened to the Southwest Conference (SWC). His timing was ideal, and his initiative was well-received. No one was satisfied with the existing governing structures, and Bellmont correctly predicted that the new conference would entice larger SIAA schools, who were beginning to boycott games "in the West," to participate with a structure that promoted regional competition between schools of similar strength. The Southwest Conference was initially composed of the University of Texas, Texas A&M College, Baylor, Southwestern University, and Rice. Participating programs outside of

Texas were the University of Arkansas, University of Oklahoma, and Oklahoma A&M. The Southwest Conference survived until 1996.[8]

All-Southwestern and All-State Awards. Walter Camp, who initiated his famous All-American All-Star selection in 1889 after "years of close study and a complete grasp of the situation," never included Texas players on his coveted "first team" roster. Each year, sports enthusiasts anxiously awaited Camp's publication of his first, second, and third All-Star football teams. But it wasn't until 1914 that a Texas player finally made Camp's list. The honors went to UT's Louis Jordan, although he only got as far as the second team. Camp didn't ignore only Texas, but also most of America's South and West. The nation's preeminent football players, it seemed, were ensconced only in the North or the East, with many from Ivy League schools and a few from West Point and Annapolis.

As a result, Texas and the other college programs developed their own nominating system. With Camp's "All-Star" player moniker already taken, Texas and Southwest football player recognition came in the form of "All-Southwestern" and "All-State" designations. Likely the first use of the All-Southwestern conference label was in 1902, the year the University of Texas, A&M College, Sewanee, and Vanderbilt were called the "Big Four" of the "Southwestern Section of SIAA." That year sportswriter H.W. Lanigan of the *St. Louis Star* compiled his "All-Southwestern Team" listing, published in 1903. Texas dominated the roster with five UT players and two from A&M.[9]

F. Homer Curtis picked the All-Southwestern conference team for 1904 at the same time he rolled out his new Southwestern Intercollegiate Athletic Association. The next season, it was determined that the regional championship team coach would choose the All-Southwestern roster. This was less than effective, and in some years the rankings either weren't made or weren't published. Texas championship coaches were an exception, with A&M coach Charles B. Moran publishing the honors in 1909 and 1910, and in 1913 when UT's Dave W. Allerdice picked the All-Southwestern slate.[10]

The term "All-State" entered Texas football lexicon in 1910. By agreement, the honors were to be a consensus between five or more Texas coaches. It almost never happened. Coaches were rarely able to agree on an All-State roster, in part because many couldn't resist selecting players entirely from their own teams. In some years, sportswriters surrendered to the chaos and published individual coach lists or resorted to opinions from referees and other writers. Often, they simply published their own compilations. It got to the point where, if a Texas player was given an All-State distinction, it was usually qualified by the source of the nomination. A Galveston writer pointed out the futility of a system in which "no two [picks] coincide," so that "practically every college man in the state has been picked on some All-State Eleven." Walter Camp's coveted endorsements might have been exclusionary, but for over 35 years they were, at least, consistent.[11]

Despite the nomination maze, a remarkable number of future Second Infantry footballers were recognized as All-State players. A&M's coach Moran, in a first-team heavy with A&M players, nominated C.T. Schaedel in 1910. The next year, UT's Dave Allerdice selected K.L. Berry for the All-State nod. Bill Birge and Charlie Turner were on coach Allerdice's All-State first team in 1913, although his credibility was questioned because nine of his 11 players were from UT. Birge and Turner were on the sanctioned first-team list again in 1914.[12]

UT and A&M: The Grand Rivalry. Many players on the Second Texas Infantry football team had played for either UT or A&M between 1909 and 1915, the years that the rivalry between the two schools reached a fever pitch. Between 1894 and 1907, UT and A&M faced off 15 times. During those 11 seasons, the Texas Agricultural and Mechanical College scored a total of 30 points to the Texas University Longhorn's 282. A&M managed just two ties and only one win – in 1902 – to UT's dozen. UT's dominance persisted into 1908, but its fortunes reversed in 1909, losing both matches that year to the Aggies by a combined 28-0 score. The Aggies also won the single contest in 1910. Then all hell broke loose.[13]

The Longhorns. The football team of the Texas University, or University of Texas, played its first game in 1893. Initially, the team was called the Varsity, but after the turn of the century, the Longhorn name made its appearance. UT was the Lone Star State's football goliath, and it was the standard by which Texas football was measured. Under coach Dave W. Allerdice from 1911 to 1915, UT was 7-1 in 1912 and 1913, then went undefeated in 1914. UT won the state championship title three out of four years during Allerdice's reign.[14]

Great things were expected of the Longhorns in 1915. Instead, it produced a season record of 6-3. Four of its nine games were against other Texas teams, and that year it rolled over TCU by a score of 72-0, Brownwood's Daniel Baker 92-0, Rice 59-0, and Southwestern 45-0. But not A&M. The Aggies surprised Texas football with a 13-0 win. Citing personal reasons, the 1915 season was Allerdice's last year coaching football.[15]

The Aggies. The Agricultural & Mechanical College of Texas gridiron team was formed in 1894, its team initially called the Cadets and the Farmers before the term Aggies first showed up in 1908 sports columns. The Aggies under coach Charles B. Moran had a brilliant winning record, with two state champion spots in 1909 and 1910. But coach Moran was under nearly constant fire, initially from UT supporters over what they perceived as a win-at-any-cost mentality, and then a contentious A&M student strike over fraternity hazing in the spring of 1913 that left the beleaguered Moran without a veteran team for the following season. That year his team went 2-4-2. Despite a 6-1-1 winning record in 1914, Moran left A&M after the season. He was replaced by E.H. Harland of Princeton with Missouri's D.V. Graves as assistant coach.[16]

A&M's two winning years in 1909 and 1910 announced to Texas sports that the Farmer's had arrived. Its ascendency, however, came at a price – the termination of play between UT and A&M for three years. Although the rivals played one more game in 1911, the relationship had soured. UT made a 1911 declaration that it would sever relations with A&M, its spokesman explaining that the Longhorns didn't begrudge losing to A&M, but they did resent the way A&M played the game behind the scenes and on the field.

The Great Divide. The rift between the universities got its footing in 1908 and reached its furious peak in 1911. In the beginning, most of the contention was over player eligibility. As schools formed their squads each season, they found it advantageous to drift between the SIAA, SWIAA, and TIAA, choosing the by-laws of whatever entity was most advantageous to their programs and rosters. The lack of consistency, at its best, created confusion over the prevailing regulations for each collegiate football match. At its worst, it demonstrated that program supporters knew no bounds when digging deeply into rival player backgrounds to discredit their lineup. No Texas school was immune.[17]

In most instances, the faculty athletic councils of competing schools overcame the lack of a consistent association governing structure simply by agreeing, in advance, to the rules that would prevail for a particular match. But the compromise hardly solved the problem. Before their 1908 season, for example, UT and A&M agreed to disregard SIAA and SWIAA regulations in favor of a contract clause in which each school would be governed by their own faculty athletic council rules of professionalism. It left a gray area that would soon turn black. Before the UT-A&M Thanksgiving Day match that year, UT supporters were clamoring that A&M was violating the terms of their agreement. Outside of the faculty councils on either side, however, few even knew what the agreement was.[18]

The conflict got its formal footing in a letter of grievances penned by UT's Faculty Athletic Committee Chairman E.C.H. Bantel to A&M's Athletic Council President, E.J. Kyle, on October 30, 1908. First of Bantel's issues was a player named Kelly who, it was rumored, was enticed to A&M after the 1907 season from the Carlisle Indians football program by a salary. In doing so, A&M had violated both the one-year transfer and professional player rules. Worse, he allegedly changed his name to hide his background. Kelly wasn't the only one with alleged infractions, the list also including player Mike Balenti, and two others, referred to only as Smith and Hamilton.

E.J. Kyle probably could have swiftly closed the matter had he responded that A&M was, in fact, abiding by the agreement that each school would follow its own faculty athletic committee code. But, if he had, he risked exposing A&M's apparent disregard for the by-laws outlined in its own published "Blue Book" governing intercollegiate football conduct. Kyle, who was in an exceedingly unwinnable spot, instead attempted to refute the allegations. His position was weak.[19]

In A&M's statement to UT, Kyle wrote that former Carlisle players Kelly and Balenti were not bound by the one-year transfer rule because Carlisle's football was a "secondary program," an odd admission given Carlisle's college football dominance during the era. Equally anemic was his retort to charges that veteran player Kelly used an assumed name, in which he advised it was not to conceal his eligibility, but "to keep the knowledge of his playing from his parents." With no wiggle room on the question of former LSU player Smith's eligibility, Kyle resorted to playing the UT independent faculty rules clause card which, under "A&M's faculty regulations," deemed him a legitimate player.

As for the Hamilton charges, Kyle responded that his investigation could neither refute nor substantiate the rumor. Rather than address another concern, he demanded instead to know the source of UT's information. To yet another he penned that, since it was not a specific charge, it could not be specifically answered. As he concluded his correspondence, he was unable to resist citing similar "rumors of unprofessionalism" against two of UT's players. In the end, despite his best efforts, all that Kyle managed to accomplish was add fuel to the fire.[20]

The correspondence between UT's Bantel and Kyle was courteous. Bantel made no official indictments and Kyle, for his part, gave the appearance of answering honorably. Later, Bantel and UT even advised that they were satisfied with Kyle's responses. Not so the student body or the program supporters. The following season, at the first 1909 game, Longhorn students "hissed" and shouted charges of "ringers" towards their opponents. It was the start of a contentious two years.

47

During the 1910 season, the contested players were removed from the Aggie lineup. But A&M's altruism was short-lived. At the beginning of the season, unnamed A&M sources leaked that four Longhorn players were salaried men, and one player changed his name to conceal his identity. UT published a defense hardly stronger than A&M's the year before. In it, they provided references to various signed affidavits and sworn statements, but offered nothing irrefutable and, borrowing a page from their rivals' playbook, asserted that the player who changed his name did so "because his parents objected to his playing."[21]

The next move on the sports chessboard was A&M's. In January 1911, A&M announced it was signing a contract with Baylor for the 1911 and 1912 Thanksgiving Day games, rescheduling its matches with UT to other dates. Then the college went a step further, terminating the entirety of its spring UT baseball schedule. Relations were strained between the Lone Star State's leading schools, but they were about to get much worse.[22]

The game played between UT and A&M in early November 1911 would be their last for three seasons. Immediately after the game, which UT won 6-0, the *Austin American-Statesman* carried the headline "Texas University Severs Athletic Relations with the A&M College for Year 1912." In a "secret session," the UT athletic council was evidently unanimous in its decision to ban future matches with A&M, citing the school's "unsportsmanlike and unmanly" conduct. The statement, communicated to A&M and the press in a terse telegram by UT's Athletic Council Chairman W.T. Mather, was followed by an announcement to the student body.

UT's Mather was less measured in his second proclamation to a gathering crowd of students on the university grounds. He began his diatribe while "mounted [on] a wheelbarrow conveying some dead Farmer cadet" and adorned with flowers and dummy mourners, his oration whipping the horde into a frenzy. Mather and the crowd then marched in front of the capitol to celebrate while UT football manager Stephen F. Pinckney clung to "one of the highest posts" reading dozens of telegrams of support from "other colleges, coaches of other teams," and allegedly even A&M alumni. The festivities that afternoon were accompanied by music and cheers raised to "the whole damn world except [for] A&M."[23]

The *Austin American-Statesman* followed the boycott announcement with pages of indictments against A&M. Written skillfully, the newsmen might have crafted a worthy exposé. Instead, their credibility was eroded by emotionally charged and unsubstantiated reporting. In one of their first pronouncements, the paper's writers charged that LSU shared their disgust of A&M, not only canceling its next game with the Aggies but threatening "to sever all athletic relations with that institution in the future." At best, this was an exaggeration. So was the statement that "Mississippi, Auburn, and Sewanee have already taken such steps."

The reporting also featured a litany of interviews with seemingly noteworthy persons who were supposed to provide irrefutable evidence of misconduct. They failed, offering instead only opinions and a flow of bombast aimed at the university and its coach, Charles Moran. Moran, according to one interviewee, was the man responsible for the college's "squad of trained thugs" whose winning methods were based mostly on slugging and maiming "the star players of the opposing team and get them out of the game." One article offered the unlikely opinion that A&M's alumni even sided with UT, and they "expressed their disgust and loathing" for coach Moran and his "reputation for rotten athletics that has shamed the Agricultural and Mechanical alumni."

Most egregious were the writer's conflicting versions of the three UT players who were injured at the hands of the Aggie "thugs" in the 1911 game. Copious press surrounded lineman Marion Harold's broken leg, a mishap that was allegedly shrouded in "much mystery." Unnamed spectators swore they saw an unnamed A&M player "grab hold of it" and "twist it until it snapped." That version, while sensational, was not consistent with Harold's own account. Harold, instead, had told reporters that his leg was accidentally broken during a tackle. Then there was UT end Woodhull who was reportedly "badly injured," although the writer overlooked the UT team physician's report of a strained leg ligament. Painful, but not so serious to prevent him from being back in the UT lineup by the end of November.[24]

UT manager Stephen F. Pinckney, in his enthusiasm, inadvertently let slip that the attack on A&M was about more than just rough football. Instead, it was the same issue that had been dividing them for the past several years – player eligibility. UT would not play ball again with A&M, he declared, "until a certain ring of professional players [was] booted out of the institution." Others offered that normal relations could only be restored after coach Moran was fired.[25]

Texas newspapers relished the collegiate clash and were as eager to carry A&M's retort as they were the original UT charges. A&M's response came not from the usual athletic faculty council but from representatives selected from the faculty, team management, and student body. One of the latter was Charles T. Schaedel, a player in the notorious 1911 game and a future Second Texas Infantry team member. A&M and Schaedel attempted to answer each charge under the weighty headline "Slanderous Charges of Texas University Athletic Authorities Refuted by Positive and Incontestable Evidence." But as in the previous exchanges, they neglected to provide their "incontestable evidence."[26] The words of a *Houston Post* writer perhaps best sum up the three years of back-and-forth tirades between the colleges. The charges by both sides, he wrote, were "so cleverly worded as to give the average reader a maximum of false impressions and a minimum of facts."[27]

UT anticipated that its arguments would cause A&M to be "barred from any athletic relations with any reputable school in the South." In that, they would be disappointed. Barely a month later the Aggies were readmitted to membership in SIAA. Then A&M announced a 1912 season schedule that was its most ambitious to that date. Before later game changes were made, its original regional opponents were to be Arkansas, Oklahoma, Kansas, Mississippi, Oklahoma, and Tulane. The intra-state competition included Baylor, Daniel Baker, and TCU.[28]

Several future Second Infantry players were part of either the UT or A&M teams during the contentious 1908 through 1911 seasons. On the UT side, the roster included fullback K.L. Berry, and linemen Bill Birge and Baker Duncan. For A&M, it was quarterback Oscar Abbott, right end Jim Kendrick, and C.T. Schaedel, the student author of A&M's last salvo fired between the two football foes in 1911. Many of these players made up the leadership of the Second Infantry lineup, and while none of them ever discussed it, the hostility between the schools may have been one reason they worked so hard to develop a sense of teamwork when it was their turn to lead. Quite possibly their college years taught them what failure looked like, and they learned its lesson.[29]

By 1914 the feud had run its course. A&M Athletic Director Charles Moran retired just before Christmas that year, replaced by E.H. Harlan. Both A&M and UT were now members of the new Southwest Conference and talks between the two adversaries suggested the possibility of renewing their games.[30]

The first UT-A&M contest since 1911 was played at Kyle Field on November 19, 1915, and players and fans from both schools made every demonstration to show that the fight was over. The entirety of the A&M College section stood to croon Auld Lang Syne in tribute to UT. Longhorn yell leader Casey Jones crossed to the opposing team's rooters to lead a cheer, and A&M's Runt Hanson did the same on the UT side. During halftime, a thousand UT fans paraded over to the Farmer seats and cheered them. Next, the A&M cadet corps and band marched by the opposition, forming the letter 'T' to return the compliment. The overt show of respect was the first such public gesture in the history of the two schools.[31]

Their Last College Football Season. Most of the Second Texas Infantry team members who attended college played their last college games in the 1915 season. Sixteen of the future Second Infantry were on the roster of the two Texas collegiate football giants, the University of Texas and Texas A&M College. A total of 11 players on the Second Infantry's first and second squads came from UT and five from A&M. Just two were from Baylor, and there was one player from Rice and one from Southwestern.

1915 was the second year of play in the Southwestern Conference, and that year neither UT nor A&M dominated the field. Instead, Oklahoma's 10-0 record earned it the SWC champion laurels, with underdog Baylor winning the number two spot. Baylor technically clinched the Texas state champion spot with a 7-1 season, but the title was hotly contested because its schedule did not include contests with UT or A&M. Admittedly, the statistics weren't in Baylor's favor. UT was the highest-scoring team in 1915, with a daunting 335 points to Baylor's 154. The three highest scorers in the state were from UT, although Baylor took the next two spots. The Longhorns also set a new state scoring record, walking over Daniel Baker College 92-0.[32]

The Baylor controversy impacted the 1915 All-State designation process, throwing it into "a three-cornered endless tale of the Texas championship." It became a free-for-all after A&M coach Edwin H. Harlan, Southwestern's J. Burton Rix, and UT's Dave Allerdice announced they would boycott the proceedings. A glib Phillip Arbuckle, of Rice, also didn't make any official All-State nominations, and instead invented his own process, offering a list of players that he considered "potential All-State material." The *Houston Post* cobbled together something close to a consensus, and on this list were future Second Infantry players Berry, Birge, Duncan, and Turner from UT, Aggie right end Jim Kendrick and freshman Warren Collins, and Rice's Bart Coan.[33]

Many of the Second Infantry players were teammates or opponents during the 1915 collegiate football season, and it allowed them an opportunity to assess the strengths and weaknesses of some of its roster before their first practice on the sandy scrub on the outskirts of Corpus Christi. The game that featured the most players in 1915 was the November 19 UT-A&M contest at Kyle Field, the first year the two teams had met since 1911.

The 1915 UT-A&M Game. During the UT-A&M Thanksgiving game, future Second Infantry players on the Longhorn roster included team captain and right tackle Berry, Birge at right guard, left tackle Duncan, end Charlie Turner, and lineman Sylvan B. Simpson. Substitutes were Charley Ogden, Pleas Rogers, and Harry Stullken. In the Aggie's lineup were freshman Warren Collins at right halfback, Jim Kendrick at right end, and Charlie Brown as a sub. The University of Texas was heavily favored, but the experts hadn't counted on the one-man wrecking machine that was Warren Collins. Austin, however, was only too aware of its 1914 high school state championship team star, and to the more fanatical, his enrollment in rival A&M was an act of treachery.[34]

Some said that Collins was "carrying a grudge into the game" because UT coach Dave Allerdice, who watched him hobble off the field in a high school game with a sprained ankle, remarked that he lacked courage and would never play on a Longhorn team. Others say it was because UT supporters booed and jeered him as he came on the field. Regardless of the version, Collins played as he had never played "before or after on that day." Facing the "terrific charging of the greatest line in Texas," the "yellow" Collins, as he was taunted, kicked two field goals that put the Aggies ahead 6-0 at the half. In the third quarter, with A&M on the 17-yard line, Collins ran the ball twice downfield and within threatening distance of the Longhorn goal. No one expected Collins to get the ball a third time, but when he did, he "tore eight yards through the supposedly invincible" defense for the game's only touchdown. In that game, he punted 23 times and averaged 55 yards on his "spiraling boots." The Longhorns found the spin he put on the ball impossible to handle and fumbled 13 times.[35]

Although Collins was the game's standout player, "Big Jim" Kendrick's playing performance was called "a thing of beauty." Kendrick kicked the only extra point of the game, and on defense was a force to be reckoned with. He was credited with numerous tackles behind the offensive line, causing the loss of "10 to 30 yards on every exchange of punts" during the upset.[36]

After the "Farmers" 13-0 triumph over "Varsity," the headlines of the *Bryan Daily Eagle* crowed that it was the "greatest football game ever witnessed in Texas." Its sports editor then added that the win, witnessed by 7,000 to 10,000 fans, "proved beyond all question A&M's superiority."[37]

Austin newspapers, usually full of sports bluster and bombast, were entirely silent on the outcome. One of the few articles written on the loss was coverage of a post-game student rally, and it was almost ominous in its tone. The gathered students were reminded that, despite the "recent fiasco at College Station" and the "seriousness of the football situation," the sports program still needed the student's support. Four future Second Texas Infantry starting players – Bill Birge, team captain K.L. Berry, Baker Duncan, and Charlie Turner – each took to the podium, and each pronounced the importance of a winning outcome in their next game, against Notre Dame. The exception was Bill Birge. Birge reminded the assembly that the world might not end after all, as it was just football. He said simply of the upcoming Notre Dame contest that "we're going to put on our football togs, go down to Clark Field, and engage in a little scrimmage." The Longhorns lost the Notre Dame match, the last game of their 1915 season, by a score of 36 to 7.[38]

1915 Baylor Season. The Baylor College football team, located in Waco, began play in 1898 on an off-campus field scraped from sand and scrub. Just eight years after their first game, Baylor trustees canceled the college's football program, joining in the protest to the sport's brutality. The backlash was so great that the well-intentioned boycott lasted just a single season. They were called the Baylor Baptists until the 1915 college season when they were renamed the Bears. Few in college football took the Baptists seriously, particularly UT, which dropped Baylor from their schedule before the 1915 season because of three straight years of "poor or indifferent football." When Charles "Bubs" Mosely took the helm in 1914, he was Baylor's eleventh coach in 15 years.[39]

Mosely turned the newly minted Bears team around in 1915, his success heralded by the *Waco Times-Herald* with: "Four years of football tragedy at Baylor are recorded now as ancient history." That year Baylor, a member of the SWC, had a 7-1 record and nabbed the number two conference spot behind Oklahoma. Baylor also won the Texas state championship laurels, but most in the sports world objected to the title. At issue was that, while the Bears played against Rice and Southwestern in the 1915 season, neither A&M nor UT were on their schedule. To gridiron fans, those two teams were Texas football.[40]

Houston Post sportswriter William B. Ruggles, under the headline "Baylor Looms Up as an Unsatisfactory State Champion in Muddled Outcome," opined that, while "the Texas title of the season is clouded and carries little honor with it," Baylor was the only logical conclusion. He based his case on the fact that Baylor beat Rice, Rice had bettered A&M, and A&M defeated UT. No one at Baylor, however, had any doubts about who won the title – the team's lettermen received a gold football at the end of the season with the engraving "Baylor State Champions – 1915."[41]

Tom Mitchell had left Baylor in the fall of 1915, leaving only Eugene Dotson as part of the 1915-winning Baylor College football program. But Dotson did not face any of his future Second Infantry teammates on the college field that season because Baylor did not play UT or A&M that year, and Dotson wasn't on the starting roster at the October 8 Baylor-Rice game in which he would have played against Bart Coan. It was the same when Baylor beat Southwestern by a score of 10-0 on October 23, a contest in which he would have faced Southwestern's Alfred Grady "Rats" Watson.

1915 Rice Season. The Rice University Owls were represented on the famous National Guard football team by one player, Bart Coan. Coan, who played his freshman year for Rice in 1914, was a first-string starter during the 1915 season. Rice that year was a member of both the TIAA and SWC and went 5-3 that season under former Southwestern University coach Phil Arbuckle. UT and Baylor both walked over the Owls by scores of 50 to 0 and 26 to 0, respectively, then in a surprise upset, the Owls beat Texas A&M 7-0.[42]

Bart Coan was a versatile player, playing tackle, guard, end, and was the team's punt returner. During the Longhorn's rout over the Owls, lineman Coan lined up across from Baker Duncan. In the November 8 Owl-Aggie game in Houston, right end Coan opposed left end Rip Collins for part of the game. He was probably unimpressed by A&M's right end, Jim Kendrick. While Coan's play in Rice's 7-0 victory over the Aggies that day was memorable, Kendrick had a rare bad day. His initial kickoff went out of bounds, he was penalized for off-sides, and fumbled a pass that would have evened the score.[43]

1915 Southwestern Season. Alfred Grady "Rats" Watson, one of the two Second Infantry starting quarterbacks, cut his football college teeth at Georgetown's Southwestern University. The Southwestern Methodists, later renamed the Pirates, played their first college ball game in 1908 under athletic director and coach Phil H. Arbuckle before his move to Rice. The team was a charter member of the TIAA and in 1915 was also part of the SWC. In its 1915 season, under coach J. Burton Rix, Southwestern went 4-3. The Methodists most lopsided game was a 45-0 drubbing by UT.[44]

Grady Watson would become a standout player on the Second Texas Infantry squad, then later at UT, and in the National Football League, but his college career did little to foretell his future achievements. In his first year at Southwestern in 1914 he was a scrub, and in 1915 was relegated to second-string for the entire season. Watson did not face off against any of his future Second Infantry teammates that year. He was not listed as a starter or a sub in either the Baylor or UT games, and the Methodists did not play Rice or A&M in 1915.

1916. After the 13-0 Longhorn loss to the Aggies in 1915, UT won the 1916 Thanksgiving Longhorn-Aggie match. Both teams, as well as every other Texas college sports program that year, had to scramble to put teams together, their rosters gutted by the May 1916 call-up of the Texas National Guard. Patriotic fever was running high, but not so high that the losing team of the Thanksgiving game, Texas A&M, publicly questioned when the Army planned to discharge its favorite performers. They would have to wait a long time.

Texas Intercollegiate Athletic Association president Dr. C.C Gumm was part of a lecture circuit that gave talks on college sports programs, such as one called "College Athletics and the Public," although in this ad for one his speeches, the writer misunderstood the title, substituting "Republic" for "Public." Modified from *Fort Worth Star-Telegram*, Oct 8. 1913.

The football team of the Texas University, or University of Texas, played its first game in 1893. Initially, the team was called the Varsity, but after the turn of the century, the Longhorn name made its appearance. Ellison Photo Company image donated by Russell Chalberg, *Portal to Texas History*, No. C02152, ark:/67531/metapth125124.

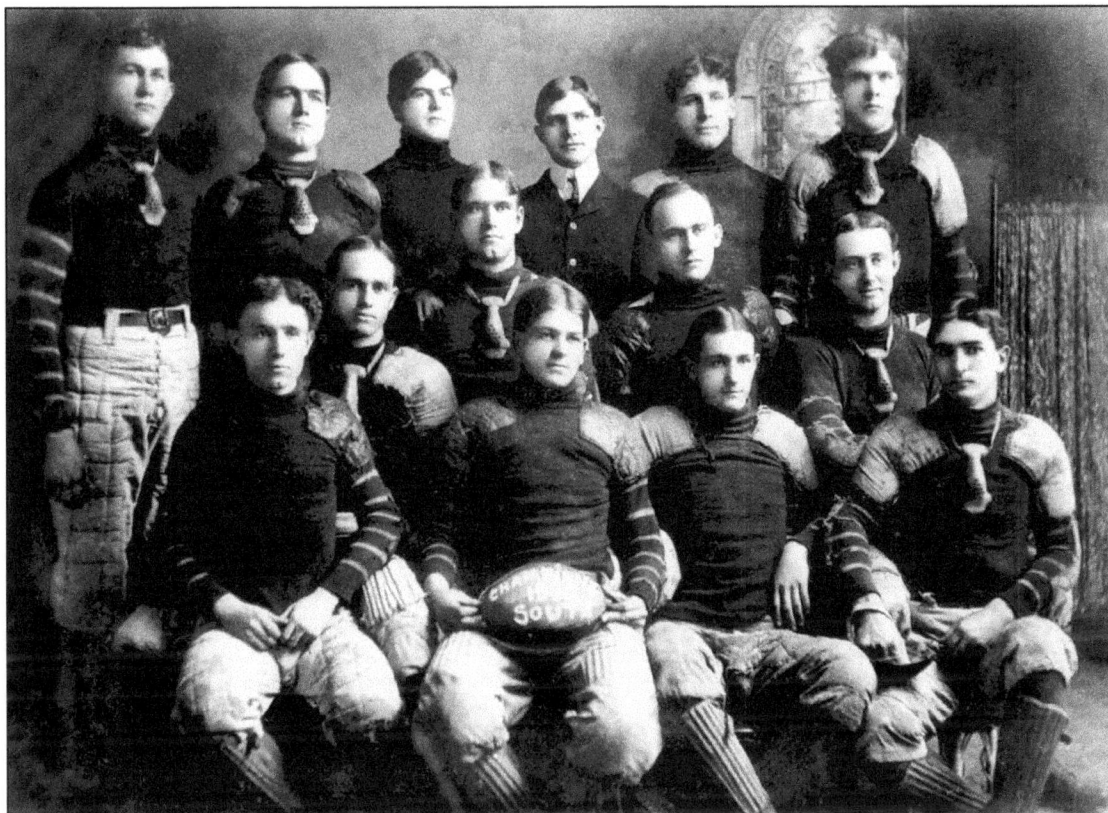

Top: An early image of the Texas A&M football team, probably 1909. The Agricultural & Mechanical College of Texas gridiron team was formed in 1894, its team first called the Cadets and the Farmers before the term Aggies began showing up in 1908 sports columns. *Texas A&M University Libraries*, Oak Trust, Cushing Collection, https://hdl.handle.net/1969.1/111118.

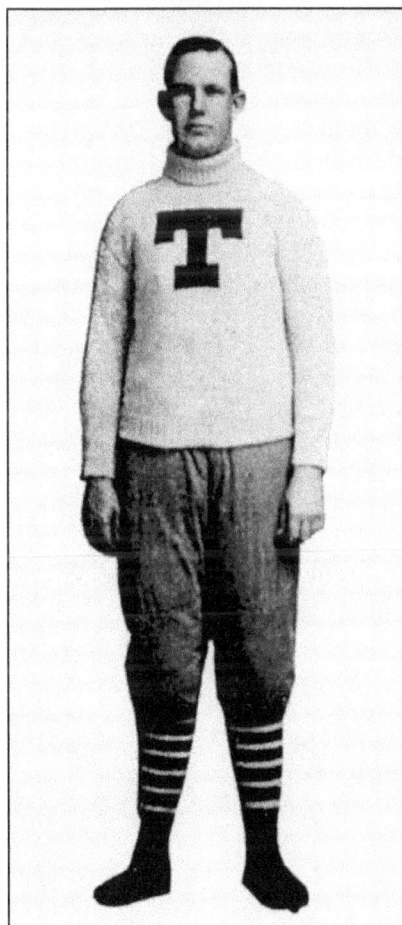

Left: A&M's Charles T. Schaedel, sporting his college block 'T' letter in 1911. Schaedel was one of the representatives selected from the Aggie faculty, team management, and student body to prepare a statement responding to UT's charges against Coach Moran and the Aggie football team. "1912 A&M Longhorn Yearbook," *Texas A&M University Libraries*, library.tamu.edu.

The 1910 State Champion A&M football team. Charles T. Schaedel is left of the team captain holding the football (first row, second from left). Ock Abbott is above and right of the team captain (second row, third from right). Between 1894 and 1907, UT and A&M faced off 15 times. During those 11 seasons, A&M College scored a total of 30 points to the Texas University Longhorn's 282. A&M managed just two ties and only one win – in 1902 – to UT's dozen. UT's dominance persisted into 1908, but its fortunes reversed when in 1909 and 1910, UT lost three matches to the Aggies by a combined 28-0 score. *Texas A&M University Libraries*, Oak Trust, Cushing Collection, https://hdl.handle.net/1969.1/124151.

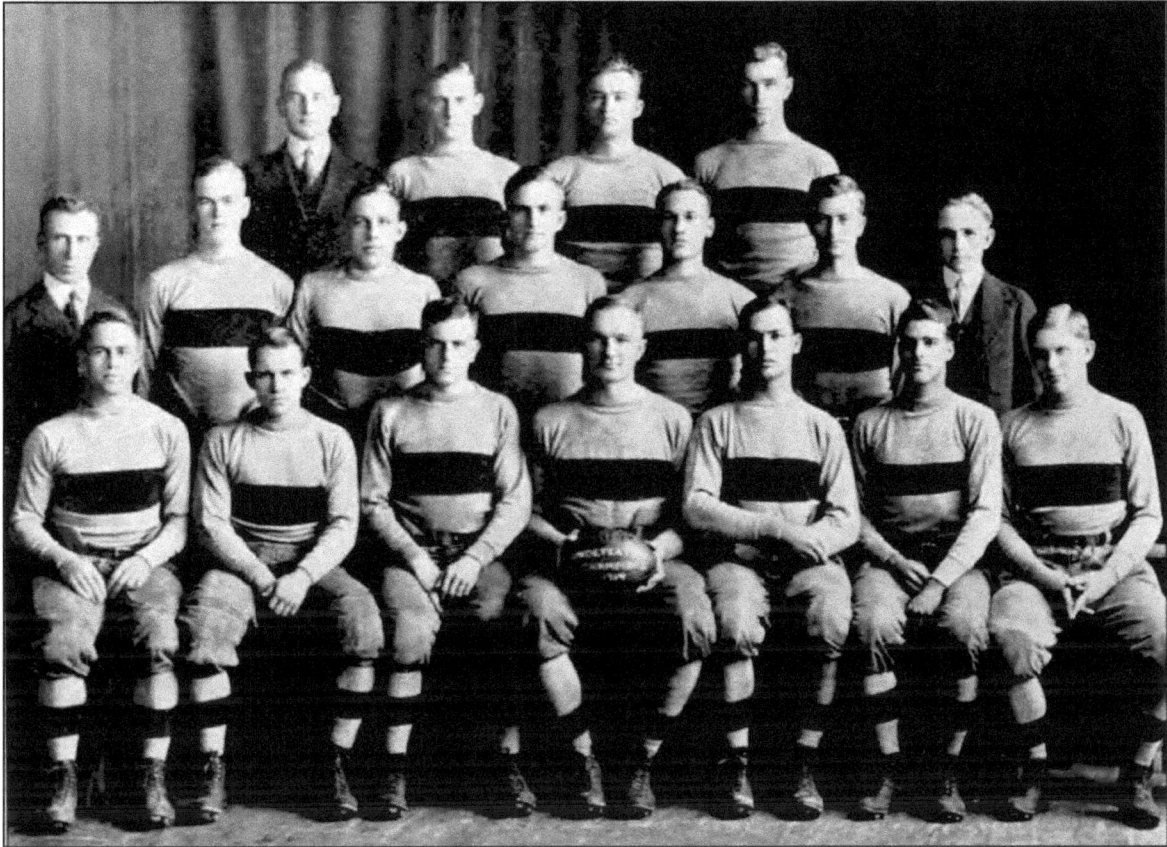

1914 State Champion Longhorn football team. Top row: Coach Dave Allerdice at far left, Berry at far right with Birge to his left. Bottom row: Charlie Turner is on far right. The 1914 Longhorn's went 8-0, outscoring their opponents 358 to 21. 1914 was the last year of the memorable UT and A&M feud, the two colleges restoring athletic relations in 1915. "1915 Cactus Yearbook," *Texas Scholar Works*, University of Texas Libraries, http://hdl.hande.net/2152/ 24283.

1915 Longhorn football team. Top row Dave Allerdice far left, Birge second from right. Second row from top has Baker Duncan third from right. On third row from top is Sylvan B. Simpson, third from left, and Captain K.L. Berry to his right. "1916 Cactus Yearbook," *Texas Scholar Works*, University of Texas Libraries, http://hdl.hande.net/2152/23763.

Left: Kearie Lee Berry. Berry was a three-letter man from UT. He enrolled at UT in 1911, starting his first season with the freshman "scrubs" but quickly moved to the regular lineup, playing both the backfield on offense and defensive lineman. He gained the honor of being included among "the Immortals" for his play during the 1911 6-0 UT triumph over A&M that ended the Aggie's two year, three-game winning streak. "Brig. Gen. Kearie Lee Berry," *Swhitesuela Family Tree,* https://www.ancestry.com/family-tree/person/tree/1206 3937/person/332061342350/facts.

Left: Bill Birge in a 1914 photo. "1915 Cactus Yearbook," *Texas Scholar Works*, University of Texas Libraries, http://hdl.hande.net/2152 /24283.

Right: Baker Duncan played center on UT's 1915 basketball squad and was a lineman on the Longhorn football team. In his senior year he was a tackle and was nominated to the All-State and All-Southwestern teams. "1916 Cactus Yearbook," *Texas Scholar Works*, University of Texas Libraries, http://hdl.hande.net /2152/23763.

Left: 1915 Longhorn's Sylvan Simpson. Simpson spent part of his first college year at Baylor, then transferred to UT for the 1915 spring semester. The next fall, he was eligible to play on the Longhorn scrub team, then moved to its first team as a versatile substitute, playing as an offensive and defensive lineman and, at the close of the 1915 season, as an end. "1916 Cactus Yearbook," *Texas Scholar Works*, University of Texas Libraries, http://hdl. hande.net/2152/23763.

Right: University of Texas end Charlie Turner in 1914. During his final collegiate season in 1915, Turner missed several games due to a strained ligament resulting from "bronco-busting during summer vacation." He still managed to rank as the state's third-best college scorer, racking up eight touchdowns for the Longhorns. "1916 Cactus Yearbook," *Texas Scholar Works*, University of Texas Libraries, http://hdl. hande.net/2152/23763.

UT Longhorn end Charlie Turner catches a pass during 1915 season. "1916 Cactus Yearbook," *Texas Scholar Works*, University of Texas Libraries, http://hdl.hande.net/2152/23763.

1915 Texas A&M-University of Texas Thanksgiving Day game at Kyle Field, the first time the two teams faced off since 1911. The Aggies beat the Longhorns 13-0. Many of the future Second Texas Infantry players were part of the memorable game. *Texas A&M University Libraries*, Oak Trust, Cushing Collection, https://hdl. handle .net/1969.1/110531.

Left: Warren "Rip" Collins in 1915 during his freshman year at A&M. "1916 A&M Longhorn Yearbook," *Texas A&M University Libraries*, library.tamu.edu.

Right: Jim Kendrick enrolled at Texas A&M where he played basketball and outfield on its baseball team. He was an end on the football squad in 1911, and again from 1913 to 1915. Kendrick was nominated twice to the Texas All-State roster. "1916 A&M Longhorn Yearbook," *Texas A&M University Libraries*, library.tamu.edu.

CHAPTER 4

South of the Border

*I*t took an unlikely series of events to pluck the young men from their hometowns and colleges and turn them into the Second Texas Infantry football team. Mexico had to implode, and America had to respond. Shortcomings in the readiness of the Regular Army needed to be recognized and then remedied by the National Guard. Germany had to precipitate a European conflict worrisome enough for America to keep the guardsmen in federal service, and the military had to post them in such a way that they all came together at a single location on the sandy bluffs of Corpus Christi. The first domino to fall was the Mexican Revolution.

The Mexican Revolution. The Treaty of Córdoba, signed in August 1821, proclaimed the new Empire of Mexico to the world. The nascent country quickly disposed of the European model of a king and monarchy, however, chartering a new course as a republic by 1824. The future of the retitled Republic of Mexico would be both a balance and a battleground between two competing factions, the federalists and centralists, for the next 100 years.

The federalists advocated a liberal platform with the dispersal of power to largely self-governed, autonomous states. Much of their popular support was from Mexican-born Spaniards, or *criollos*, and mixed-blood Indians and Mexicans, the *mestizos*. The conservative centralists, in contrast, were composed mostly of a ruling class of clergy and landowners, and favored a strong central government supported by the military. The ideological differences between the parties led to political cross-currents, intrigue, and divisions that threatened Mexico's stability for decades and, perhaps as importantly, put the country on a collision course with its northern neighbor.[1]

To the outside world, Mexico under President Porfirio Díaz in the late 1800s was gaining prestige as a player on the global stage. Although his was a dictatorial regime masked as a constitutional democracy, Díaz governed a Mexico for a quarter century that was, at least on the surface, politically stable. His was also a relatively prosperous economy that, for perhaps the first time in its history, wasn't mired in debt. Much of the financial vigor was from the influx of foreign capital that led to a period of modernization with infrastructure improvements to the country's railroads, bridges, mines, and irrigation.

But, like so many times in Mexico's turbulent history, beneath the Díaz façade of cohesion was a simmering cauldron of discontent. Detractors complained of corruption, social injustice, manipulated elections, and the concentration of land ownership and capital that enriched only a small number of Díaz loyalists or expatriates. Foreigners, for example, owned 100 million acres of territory while 90% of Mexican farmers owned none, and Americans held title to 97% of Mexico's mining interests. Mexico was ripe for change, and the disparate voices of nationalism and democracy began, during the first decade of the 1900s, to erode the 80-year-old president's support. The only question was whether the transfer of power would be smooth or tumultuous. It was the latter, and it was called the Mexican Revolution.[2]

In 1910, Díaz was challenged for the presidency by federalist Francisco Madero. Díaz responded by having him arrested. Madero, who learned of his political defeat from a cell in San Luis Potosi prison, escaped and made his way to San Antonio, where he claimed title to the Mexican presidency. Calling for an armed insurrection, guerrilla generalissimo Francisco Pancho Villa carried the exiled leader's banner, battling Díaz's troops in his home state of Chihuahua. It was the same in the state of Morelos, south of Mexico City, where Emiliano Zapata, as leader of a block of agrarian revolutionists, also dogged the Díaz army. After pro-Madero forces captured the border town of Ciudad Juarez across the Rio Grande from El Paso, Díaz's regime collapsed, and he fled to Paris in May 1911.[3]

Madero was elected president in October 1911, but the country immediately fell apart around him. Leaders and supporters of his party unceasingly plotted against him, and several announced they were in rebellion. Emiliano Zapata and his followers joined the revolt, promulgating a land reform plan that garnered support in several Mexican states. In February 1913, government troops in Mexico City openly mutinied, and its commander switched allegiances to Madero's rivals. Madero was arrested and later assassinated by a guard.[4]

Next atop the shifting sands of Mexico's politics was General Victoriano Huerta. Like Madero before him, the provisional president's detractors fought tirelessly to unhinge his rule and sway his conservative and military allies. The greatest threat came from Coahuila governor Venustiano Carranza, leader of the Constitutional Army, who had the support of both Zapata and Pancho Villa, and, tacitly, the support of the United States. In Harris and Sadler's *The Great Call-up*, the authors described how America influenced the course of events during Huerta's reign. The US refused to recognize him as the legitimate president of Mexico. It lifted the arms embargo on Mexico, which enabled Carranza's Constitutionalists to purchase weapons north of its border for use in their bloody campaign. Then, in a difficult-to-justify move, ostensibly over a diplomatic slight, the United States in April 1914 occupied the seaport town of Veracruz, naming General Frederick Funston as its temporary military governor. In November, Huerta limped into exile.[5]

Venustiano Carranza was installed as the next provisional president in 1914 and remained Mexico's "First Chief" for the next three tumultuous years, his tenure strained not only by the diplomatic chessboard of US relations but by a bloody civil war with his former supporters, Zapata and Villa. Convinced that Carranza was, among many things, a US puppet, Villa turned his wrath on the Carranza regime and eventually the United States. For years Villa, the self-proclaimed voice of the proletariat, avoided confiscating goods and money from foreigners living and working in Mexico. By 1914, he began targeting and killing them. What started with Villa's murder of Juarez rancher William S. Benton that year evolved into a personal vendetta. One of the most audacious attacks came in January 1916, when a Villa detachment stopped a train and executed 17 American mining engineers.[6]

The Mexican political drama spilled into the Rio Grande Valley when authorities in McAllen uncovered a manifesto called the "Plan of San Diego" outlining the intentions of a rebel "army of liberation" that named themselves the *Seditionists* to foment a race war in South Texas. Among its objectives was the annexation of Texas by Mexico and a threat to kill every white male over the age of 16. What followed was a period of unrest, suspicion, and fear as Mexican raiding parties harassed military posts, ranches, railroads, and towns across the border, then slipped back to safe refuge in northern Mexico.[7]

Between January and August of 1915, the bandits led mostly small raids. Then the boldness of the attacks increased. On August 8, 1915, about 60 armed Seditionists descended on the Norias Division of the King Ranch, between Brownsville and Corpus Christi. A spectacular shootout ensued at ranch headquarters in which eight cavalrymen and seven civilians repelled an invasion that left five raiders dead and wounded five defenders. On October 18, the Seditionists pulled the spikes from the tracks of the St. Louis, Brownsville & Mexican Railway at Tandy Station, north of Brownsville, and lay in wait. When the train derailed, they opened fire, boarded the wrecked cars, and robbed its passengers. Their attack left three dead: State Health Officer Dr. E.S. McCain and Pvt. Albert McBee, who were shot, and the train's engineer, who was crushed by the locomotive. Another four passengers were badly wounded. Three days later, some 75 *Seditionists* ambushed 15 sleeping soldiers near Mission leaving three dead and eight wounded cavalrymen and signal corpsmen.[8]

The US government began moving more troops into the region, and the Lone Star State responded with its Texas Rangers. Between the worst elements of the Rangers and local vigilantes, the Anglos unleashed their own brand of terror. By November, the guerilla warfare and the Texan response had claimed nine civilians, 11 soldiers, and some 200 bandits, although "a strict tabulation" of the number of Mexican dead, a Texas Ranger wrote, was not possible because "it is customary to bury the victims on the spot after an attempt at identification, and those killed in the brush are not found until the buzzards show the way."[9]

America was led to believe, or wanted to believe, that the Bandit War was a result of the Plan of San Diego, which was partly true, and that they were anti-Carranza guerillas, which was not. As early as mid-May there was evidence that Carranza and his supporters sponsored some of the violence. In August, intelligence proved that more than 1,000 Carranza Constitutionalist soldiers crossed into Texas and "were the cause of the raids of the past several weeks." Then, after the October raids, it was learned that Carrancistas furnished the Seditionists with guns and ammunition.[10]

The raids, it turned out, were a carefully crafted strategy on Carranza's part to secure US diplomatic recognition. Carranza showed his hand when he assured Washington that, if he was recognized as Mexico's legitimate president, he could "put an end to the deplorable border violence." After the US officially acknowledged him, Carranza's role in the Seditionist border raids largely ended. But not those by Pancho Villa. Furious with Carranza's new ally, Villa publicly declared that he would lead the next wave of raiding parties into the US. He made good on his promise. On the night of March 9, 1916, a Villa band of about 500 men attacked the New Mexico border town of Columbus and Camp Furlong, to its south. Buildings were looted and burned. Eight soldiers were killed, and ten civilians murdered. The garrison's 300 soldiers put up a stiff resistance, but Villa recrossed the border with over a hundred pack animals and 300 arms.[11]

The incident put both US President Woodrow Wilson and Mexican leader Carranza in a tough spot. Although Wilson had been reluctant to intervene in Mexico, Villa's was a blatant act of war on American sovereign soil. It was also an election year. Wilson had to counter. The legality of a US incursion into Mexico, however, was as tenuous as Carranza's position was delicate. Carranza needed the US as an ally, but if he tolerated US soldiers in Mexico, he risked losing popular support. The US and Carranza may have had a common enemy in Pancho Villa, but the next months were more about political brinkmanship than a concerted international attempt to exterminate the Villistas.

The Punitive Expedition. Wilson made the first move after the Columbus raid. On March 9, 1916, Brigadier General John "Black Jack" Pershing was ordered to organize an expedition of the Regular Army to capture Villa and disperse the guerrillas in their Chihuahua stronghold. Six days later, 4,800 men assembled at Columbus's Camp Furlong to wage a campaign into Mexico on foot, horseback, and in mechanized truck units. Called the "Punitive Expedition," they scoured the countryside for nearly a year in search of the elusive Villa, who always seemed able to erase himself in the difficult terrain of the high desert and Sierra Madre Occidental.[12]

President Carranza, throughout the Punitive Expedition, was uncooperative. He repeatedly demanded withdrawal of the American troops and refused access to Mexican railroads that would have allowed the American troops to expeditiously move men and supplies. Worse, it was rumored that the continued border raids – credited to Villa – were, once again, the work of Carrancistas. The turmoil extended to the battlefield. With what were now three belligerent armies in Chihuahua – Villa's, Pershing's, and Carranza's Constitutionalists – it was inevitable that US and Carranza forces would clash at some point. It happened at least twice, with the most bloodshed between the supposed allies occurring in the Chihuahua towns of Parral and Carrizal. At the latter, 45 Mexican troops were killed and nine US cavalrymen.[13]

By the spring of 1916, the American army had poured thousands of reinforcements into the Southern Department for its Punitive Expedition. But with the Bandit War continuing along its largely untamed 1,500-mile-long southern border – most recently an attack in May on the Texas town of Glenn Springs that was effected by Pancho Villa – Major General Frederick Funston and Army Chief of Staff Hugh Scott were running out of troops. They did, however, know where to find another 150,000 additional men. Now, it was their job to convince President Wilson, and the governors of three states, to call up the National Guard.[14]

After Carranza and Pershing's forces battled at Carrizal, Carranza repeated his warning that war between the two countries was becoming inevitable. President Wilson demurred, moving Pershing and the Punitive Expedition to the north and closer to the border, an act that prompted Pershing to challenge his superior by declaring that he should, instead, establish US military control over the region. His demand was ignored, however, and in July and August of 1916, the vexed general could only watch as Villa focused his raiders on Carranza strongholds in Chihuahua. Negotiations to remove the Punitive Expedition stalled for months during the fall of 1916. Germany and World War I rumblings hastened it along. On Christmas Eve, the US agreed to withdraw its forces, and on February 5, 1917, Pershing recrossed to the US side of the border.[15]

The Texas Militia. Citizen soldiers in Texas were called the Uniformed Militia and the Texas Volunteer Guard until the early 1900s, when they became the Texas National Guard. With a force in 1898 of only about 2,000 men, the necessity of organizing and increasing the number of militiamen was inevitable as friction increased during the

Mexican Revolution along the international border. On May 8, 1916, Generals Frederick Funston and Hugh Scott telegrammed President Wilson. The Regular Army along the border was stretched too thin to handle its defense, they advised, and urged that the National Guards of Texas, New Mexico, and Arizona be pressed into federal service in the Rio Grande Valley. May 9 marked the date of the first call-up. On June 18, 1916, a second call-up encompassed militias from the rest of the continental United States. Both call-ups produced a total of 156,414 guardsmen, of which Texas raised 4,755 troops.[16]

Several future Second Infantry footballers were members of the Texas National Guard before the May call-up. The team's champion, Lt. Colonel A.W. Mike Bloor, had been in the guard for 20 years and was second in command of the Second Infantry Regiment in 1916. Charles T. Schaedel, an A&M graduate from Bay City, was commissioned in Company G of the Third Texas Infantry as a second lieutenant in 1912. Louis Halphen, from Austin, joined the Second Infantry's Company E in 1913 and was promoted to corporal before the first call-up. First Lt. David R. Nelson volunteered before 1914. UT Law School student First Lt. Bill Birge, who had charge of Travis County's Company F, had also been in the guard since 1914. Schuyler W. Smith, also a UT law student, joined Company F in 1915. Waco native Jim M. Kendrick was a first lieutenant in Company G and Waco's George H. Lane, who joined Company K in 1915 after high school, was a sergeant. Austin's Victor Bintliff and Richard G. Lane enlisted in Company E the same year. A&M graduate and San Antonio native Oscar B. Abbott was a second lieutenant in the Second Infantry in 1916.[17]

The First Call-up. Camp Mabry, located west of Austin on a rolling prairie dotted with post oaks that edged limestone outcrops east of the Colorado River, was in the throes of a major expansion in early 1916. The 400-acre facility already had drilling grounds and rifle ranges, but as border tensions rose, Austin worked feverishly to modernize the camp for infantry and cavalry officer training. A two-story brick arsenal was completed in February, and the next month Governor Ferguson offered 29 state convicts clemency in return for clearing land and repairing buildings. By April, Brackenridge and Seton hospitals began training nurses for military hospital service at the facility.[18]

The National Guard's first officer's training school at Camp Mabry was scheduled from May 9 to May 18. Over 200 men selected for training from across Texas descended on the facility during the afternoon of May 8, the attendees including Lt. Colonel Mike Bloor, First Lieutenants David Nelson and Bill Birge, and Second Lt. Oscar Abbott. They had just completed their morning instruction the next day when, at noon, a telegram was read in the mess hall to a hushed crowd. President Wilson had ordered their units to the border, and they were to report to their respective guard units at once.[19]

Nearby, Austin guardsmen heard the news before the officers at Camp Mabry. That morning, at 10:30, the quiet was pierced by a prolonged whistle blast. The city's National Guardsmen responded, dashing to the armory at the corner of Tenth Street and Congress Avenue. It was a scene repeated across the Texas landscape as militiamen assembled at armories or other designated points in every major city.[20]

Lt. Birge hurried east from Camp Mabry to the Austin armory, where the senior law student was met by Dan M. Cook, Charles B. Stewart, and Walter F. Woodul, also from the UT Law School. Other UT students already on the Company F roster and mustering at the armory were Charley Ogden, Sylvan B. Simpson, John Erwin Stullken, and Charles E.

Turner. Kearie L. Berry waited a few days before he enlisted as a private in Company F. He was scheduled to compete in the Southwest Conference track and field meet, and after he set a new university shot put record, he hastily traveled to San Antonio to join Company F at Camp Wilson.[21]

Bill Birge remained busy with the induction of students and others from Travis County who signed up during the patriotic fever that marked the announcement. Future Second Infantry footballers and fresh Company F recruits included UT's Howard Davis, John Diller, Addison Baker Duncan, Tom Gambrell, and Tom Mitchell. Mitchell had only recently enrolled in UT's Law School after finishing his undergraduate degree at Baylor. Aggie student Warren "Rip" Collins, who left A&M after the winter semester and had been playing baseball in Austin's City's League, also enlisted with Austin's Company F. UT freshmen Phillip S. Clarke and Pleas B. Rogers joined Austin's Company E, along with Bertram E. Lenoir who had recently applied to the University of Alabama.[22]

That night, Companies E and F camped on the grounds of the Austin capitol, marching to the train station in the morning where a crowd of 2,500 well-wishers lined Austin's streets to cheer the 231 Company E and F volunteers as they boarded cars to mobilize at Camp Wilson, near San Antonio. In total, some 40 UT students answered that first call during the spring of 1916, the number reaching over a hundred by July.[23]

In Bryan-College Station, 21 Texas A&M students signed up for the Second Infantry on May 9, the first ten mustering out the next day. Charlie Brown, Lt. Jim Kendrick, and Sgt. George Lane, of Waco Companies K and G, left campus and rushed north to assist with the processing of nearly 120 recruits at the Waco city armory. Some were Baylor students and others were men who hurried to the city from across McLennan County. Late that afternoon, the Waco companies marched to Katy Station for their journey to Camp Wilson. Baylor student Eugene Dotson, from East Texas, volunteered with his hometown unit and probably signed up in Dallas.[24]

Two footballers initially joined the Third Texas Infantry Regiment. Bart Coan, who had just finished his freshman year at Rice University, joined the Houston Lights in Company A. Grady Watson, at Southwestern University, signed up in Orange for Third Infantry Company K. Charles T. Schaedel had been in the Third's Company G since his graduation from A&M in 1912.[25]

Camp Wilson. The future footballers boarded trains headed for Camp Wilson, a new training annex east of Fort Sam Houston. Originally the staging ground for Regular Army troops since the Spanish-American War, Fort Sam Houston was most recently headquarters for the Regular Army's Southern Division and General Pershing's Punitive Expedition. Located five miles northeast of San Antonio, Camp Wilson's flat, scrubby landscape was unbroken by hills or trees, and most recently it had been a cattle pasture and an occasional polo field. The Camp Wilson annex would become the main mobilization camp for militiamen from Texas, New Mexico, and Arizona, and by June, for guardsmen who answered the second call from across America.[26]

The grounds at Camp Wilson were buzzing with energy and anticipation. Their commanders, however, weren't as enthusiastic. The men scrambling before them were woefully unprepared for their border assignment. It took some volunteers a week or more to fully mobilize, the delay due to a rural population that had no way of rapidly receiving instructions or that was located far from Texas' railroad network. Only one Texas regiment had a machine gun company, and they were short on both weapons and bullets. Most men brought only civilian clothes, parading in a hodgepodge of outfits before uniforms were hastily ordered from textile factories in the East. There was also the issue of their training which superior officers thought would take at least six weeks. Instead, they were given just two.[27]

Equally troubling was the number of men rejected as physically unfit. During processing, a worrying percentage of Texas men were culled from the roster because of a lengthy list of maladies. At the top of the list was poor physique, followed by "defective vision," heart and lung disease, foot deformities, hernias, venereal diseases, bad teeth, and "amputations and deformities." A host of other causes were reported that impacted only a minority of the recruits.[28]

During their two weeks of drilling, Company F was comprised of 105 men and three officers, and Company E had 95 men with three officers. The numbers, however, would always be fluid as the National Guard brass implemented strategic personnel changes. Lt. Colonel A.W. Bloor, for example, moved temporarily from the Second Infantry to the Fourth Texas Infantry regiment, and Pvt. Walter Woodul was promoted to sergeant of the Laredo Milmo Rifles in Second Infantry Company I. Richard Lane, Pleas Rogers, and Charlie Stewart were assigned to a new machine gun company formed from Company E. In June, Charles Wesley Ogden and John Cabot Diller were at Fort Sam Houston in an officer's training program.[29]

On May 23, the Texas National Guard passed from state jurisdiction to federal and was renamed the "Organized Militia of Texas in the United States Service" or, less formally, the "Texas Brigade." The structure of the National Guard leadership that would be part of the future football decision-making included Lt. Col. Bloor, who was second in command of the Second Infantry Regiment, and Lt. Bill Birge and Lt. Jim Kendrick. Birge was second in command of Company F and Jim Kendrick was second in command of Waco Company G.[30]

On the Border. Brigadier General John Hulen, who had charge of the Texas Brigade at Camp Wilson, ordered the guardsmen to the border on May 24, 1916. Most of the Second Infantry troops boarded rail lines that headed south from San Antonio and connected to the St. Louis, Brownsville, and Mexico Railroad (SLB&M). Running parallel to the coast below Corpus Christi to Brownsville, the SLB&M also had an inland east-to-west track connecting Harlingen to Sam Fordyce. Towns and communities along this region of the lower Rio Grande Valley, termed the Brownsville Military District, were to be home to most of the Second Infantry's future footballers during the summer of 1916.

The city of Brownville and the town of Harlingen were nearest to the coast, situated 21 and 46 miles respectively from the mouth of the Rio Grande at the Gulf of Mexico. Upriver, to the west, the guardsmen shared the land with more cattle than people with postings in the Brownsville District towns, from east to west, of Mercedes, Donna, and Pharr, then the town of McAllen. Next was Mission, with Madero City to the south and closer to the Rio Grande, then Sam Fordyce, Rio Grande City, with the furthest upriver posting of the Second Infantry at Roma, some 100 miles from Brownsville.

From late May until September the Second Infantry relocated frequently as recruits from other states mustered in. During June, Company F was at Mission, Company E at Sam Fordyce, and Companies K and G at Pharr. During the next three months, the Austin company's postings included Madero City, Roma, McAllen, Donna, and Harlingen. Team business manager Walter Woodul was initially sent to Rio Grande City with Company I. In June, he ran for and was elected to the Texas House of Representatives, planning to take his seat the following January. Grady Watson with Company K of the Third Infantry was first at Pharr, and Bart Coan was stationed at Harlingen with the Third Infantry's Company A. Lt. Col. Mike Bloor spent time in the Brownsville District and served briefly with the Fourth Infantry in the Big Bend District.[31]

Other than the urban oasis of Brownsville, a city of about 11,000 in 1916, the land that paralleled the international boundary between the United States and Mexico was one of America's final frontiers. It had been a hard place to tame, known as a haven for outlaws, Civil War deserters, cattle rustlers from both sides of the border, and most recently, the setting for the bloody Bandit Wars. Even before Mexican insurgents began raiding across the border, Texas Rangers referred to it as the "lawless corridor." The first railroad, the SLB&M, reached the Rio Grande Valley just 12 years before the National Guardsmen moved in. Three years later, in 1907, the area saw its first automobile. It didn't get very far, bogging down in deep sand so often that Texas-born Mexican cowboys, called *vaqueros*, had to keep pulling it out with ropes they tied to their saddle horns.[32]

Harlingen, with about 1,500 residents, was the second-largest municipality in the lower Rio Grande Valley. Founded as a depot town when the SLB&M railway connected the region with the rest of Texas in 1904, it was little more than a mesquite thicket then, after the erection of a few houses and saloons, was named Six Shooter Junction and later renamed Rattlesnake Junction. Its founder, Lon C. Hill, had one foot in the Old West and one in the future. The two revolvers he wore wherever he went were not just for show. He was known to draw them, like in 1906 when he shot and killed a nemesis in the center of town.[33]

By 1910 the lawless reputation of the Rio Grande Valley was beginning to soften. A burgeoning new industry had taken shape in citrus fruits and vegetable farms, which were becoming as economically important to the region as cattle. The Valley's future in agriculture, cattle, commerce, and shipping had never seemed so bright. Then came the Mexican Revolution and the Bandit Wars.

The landscape of the far south part of Texas was nearly as alien to the Texans as it was to guardsmen from other states. The higher topography was a grassless landscape interspersed with cactus, sagebrush, and a few mesquite trees anchored on wind-blown sand deposits of the distal Coastal Sand Sheet. A common theme in letters written home by the guardsmen during the summer of 1916 was the ubiquitous "sand, sand, sand," including "burning sand" under the mid-day sun and "flying sand" that was composed of particulate matter picked up and sent airborne by pervasive onshore winds.[34]

The Rio Grande floodplain was a marked contrast to the mesquite-chaparral brush of the lower Coastal Sand Sheet. Here, the landscape was green and lush, in places dense with a canopy of ebony, hackberry, and ash trees. Distributary streams and ox bows spawned by the river, called *resacas*, were hidden deep in Tamaulipas thorn and mesquite-palmetto scrub. Scattered between the white sand of the high ground and the Rio Grande floodplain were curious-looking mounds and bluffs of orange and gray silt and clay deposits, called *lomas* and *potreros*.

The fauna was as diverse and unfamiliar as the landforms and flora. Long-eared jackrabbits and rattlesnakes of the Sand Sheet gave way to a diverse and abundant assemblage of wildlife along the Rio Grande Valley, its waterways profuse with bird life in colors of pink, white, blue, and purple and belonging to herons, spoonbills, ibises, and egrets. Thickets could explode with wild turkeys, quail, and the strange-sounding shrieking alarm calls of the equally odd-looking chachalaca. Then there were the predators of the night, such as ocelots, jaguars, and jaguarundi, their screams in the dark sending a chill up the spine of all but the most unflinching. Guard duty for soldiers in this foreign land was always tedious, but nighttime was their least favorite. The sounds of nature were disquieting, and the shadows cast by the moonlight could be anything from a wild animal to rumored guerilla raiders. Most eerie were the moving lights as Mexicans, ordered to carry lanterns at night to avoid being shot, shuffled to the river for water.[35]

The heat was unrelenting even when it rained. From May to early July, canvas tent camps sweltered in the sun. Then, in late July and early August, tropical storms brought monsoonal rains. The soldier's tents, bedding, and clothing took days to dry, but the worst were encampments adjacent to the silt and clay mounds and bluffs. When heavy rains eroded the *lomas* and *potreros*, they formed torrents of iron-stained mud that, if they didn't uproot everything in their downstream path, covered them in muck. Summer rains were followed by a plague of mosquitoes, every hospital tent filling with soldiers suffering from malaria.[36]

In mid-August, South Texas took a direct hit from the hurricane of 1916. In Laredo, "the tents of the various guardsmen were blown down, causing much discomfort and a great deal of hard work." It was the same in McAllen, where the soldiers were forced to take refuge in churches and other secure buildings. In Harlingen, one Second Infantry regiment rode out the tempest in the lee bank of a stream bed after every building was flattened and every tent blown down. Although one guardsman reported his company was "homeless but happy," border morale was justifiably sinking. Then, for the third time in just as many weeks, the Rio Grande left its banks, flooding the remainder of the camps that had survived the wind.[37]

Life in Camp. Shortly after their arrival on the border and with an eye on its readiness for the military future, Brigadier General James Parker, commander of the Brownsville District, ordered officers of the Regular Army to instruct guardsmen on the ways of the professional soldier. Noncommissioned officers would learn drill instruction, carrying out six to eight hours of drilling and marches of six to 12 miles each day. They were to follow a schedule of instruction prescribed in training documents that included such things as garrison duty, "close and extended order drills," bayonet exercises, trench digging, "knots and lashes," target practice, and were offered courses in mechanics, sanitation, and other requirements of a US Army infantryman in the field of battle. It was training they wouldn't use much on the border. Of the future footballers, only Company F saw any action. In July, an exchange of gunfire erupted at the ferry across the Rio Grande at Roma. It was a quick skirmish, the only near casualty an unnamed corporal who received a bullet through his hat.[38]

The Second Infantry devised innovative ways to alleviate their boredom when they weren't training. Company F's lawyers organized a legal team to handle guard infractions. Tom Gambrell was the lead prosecutor and Baker Duncan represented the defendants in three court-martials that summer, their legal sparring producing a record of two acquittals and one conviction. For most, the doldrum of camp life was punctuated by sports. Anything that could be used as a ball was thrown, kicked, or hit. Company E at Sam Fordyce, and Company F, in Mission, both organized baseball teams. Warren "Rip" Collins was the Company F coach, and after one or two lopsided games, none of the other companies posted nearby would play them.[39]

Another diversion was wildlife. Company E, in search of the ideal company mascot, captured a four-month-old javelina, an armadillo, raccoons, snakes, and terrapins. Phillip "Spitz" Clarke and Howard "Whitey" Davis even caught two young "wolves" that were likely either red wolves or coyotes. Animals that wandered into camp were also fair game, that list including a few stray dogs, a horse they taught to dance, and various goats. Of the menagerie, their favorite animals were the goats. One they adopted went by two names, Austin and Wilhelm der Grosse. Austin-Wilhelm traveled everywhere in camp "from the bottom of the storm cellar to the top of a table on the third-floor barracks." Famous for eating the wax from candles, the habit came to a halt when its nose discovered the flame.[40]

By a unanimous vote of the men, Company E settled on a second goat, named after Pvt. William Joe Parks, as camp mascot. William the goat escorted the men everywhere. He kept pace with them on their morning four-mile hikes, halted when the company halted, and "when we take up double time the goat increases his speed, accordingly, occasionally bleating his disapproval of the speed we make." After his marches, Pvt. Harry Stullken held him high in his arms to reach and eat leaves in the high branches of one of the few trees in camp. Between his military skills and intelligence, Company E expected William "to be made a corporal before long."[41]

William's reign, however, was short, when "after an illness of two days, he passed away on July 24." His obituary was posted in camp and read like that of a respected Texas leader, and William was given a military funeral. His procession was formed in columns that marched from the front of the barracks to a newly prepared grave. Buglers played a funeral march as pallbearers, led by Phillip Clarke, conveyed the wooden casket accompanied by the company chaplain. They sang as the "body was lowered into the grave" followed by a rifle volley and taps.[42]

Promotions and Rumors. The men of the Second Infantry played hard and worked harder, and many demonstrated their leadership skills on the border. In Company E's Machine Gun Company, Pleas Rogers was made first sergeant in May, and by September, Charlie Stewart was quartermaster sergeant and Richard D. Lane a sergeant. Company F's Baker Duncan and John Diller were promoted from privates to corporals in July. Jim Kendrick was promoted to first lieutenant in August and given command of the 24-man Company G then encamped at Mission and Madero City.[43]

That June, when law students Bill Birge, Baker Duncan, Tom Gambrell, Schuyler Smith, and Charles Stewart were unable to complete their degrees at the end of their final semester, UT Regents gave them credit for National Guard duty and conferred degrees in absentia. Those who had not finished their collegiate programs were eager to return, and as fall football rosters were being decided in early July, university towns cast their eye to the border. The Longhorns were anxious for the return of all three 1915 team captain players Kearie L. Berry, Charlie Turner, and Sylvan Simpson. A&M seemed certain that Jim Kendrick would return "in fine trim." University athletic directors were assured that an effort would be made to discharge some of the young men if "border conditions continue to improve." Their optimism was misplaced.[44]

Camp Scurry. Every Rio Grande Valley town was eager for the economic boost of hosting America's Regular Army or its National Guard. But during the spring of 1916, Corpus Christi was not on any list of military encampments, and although the town was 200 miles from the border its mayor, Roy Miller, chafed. In early July, Mayor Miller and other leading city leaders contacted General Funston to extoll the virtues of their city on the bay. Corpus Christi wanted to host the guard, they said, and the city would provide the land and pay for improvements to construct a post. The Army began to look at the offer seriously in mid-summer, their reasons political, logistical, and partly for morale.[45]

One of the pressing political issues was that Washington policymakers were hearing from constituents who complained that the border emergency had passed, and it was time to bring the boys home. There was truth to their words. There had been no significant border warfare since the Glenn Springs raid in May, and it certainly appeared that the troops had restored "peace and security" to residents "on the international line." The logistics consideration, from a military perspective, was that it was easier to provision a larger number of troops at a single location than fewer men in scattered encampments distributed throughout the sparsely settled Valley. Then there was the issue of morale. War with Germany was likely, and it looked as if the National Guard was to remain in federal service for the long haul. There would be less reason for grumbling at the seaside tourist resort of Corpus Christi. A hurricane nearly unraveled their best-laid plans.[46]

On August 16, the National Weather Service warned that a "West India hurricane" had entered the Gulf of Mexico. During the morning of the 18th, the Corpus Christi weather office barometer was in freefall, a red flag with a black rectangular center raised to signify the approach of a major storm. The hurricane made landfall that afternoon 40 miles south of Corpus Christi at Baffin Bay with wind gusts of 132 miles per hour. While the only loss of life in the immediate Corpus Christi area was at sea, the city's power, telephone, and telegraph poles were shattered. Miles of railroad tracks were damaged and part of the causeway across Nueces Bay was swept away. The Corpus Christi beachfront at the planned guard encampment was entirely underwater, its sand bluffs scoured and eroded by wind-driven currents and seething waves. Just nine days later, the order to relocate some 3,350 men from the border was given anyway. The military, it seemed, was now as intent on Corpus Christi as the city was on the army.[47]

Despite the storm damage, the city was able to deliver on its promise to build a "model camp" that would be "the envy of thousands of soldiers" posted elsewhere in Texas, the success credited to Mayor Miller, the office of the City Engineer, Corpus Christi City Council, Commercial Club, and the Rotary Club. After they procured a 200-acre cattle pasture south of the city on a bluff facing the Gulf of Mexico, hundreds of city employees were tasked with clearing brush, digging drainage ditches, extending water pipes to the site, and completing two oyster shell roads. Contracts were signed for electricity, telephone lines, and an extension of the streetcar line to camp. Wood and coal-heated hot water baths were planned for each company that required thousands of feet of underground pipes to deliver water at a "pleasant temperature" and "any degree of heat." Workmen were only a little behind schedule on some of the planned 40 buildings and the 24 mess halls.[48]

Not only was Mayor Miller's city on the military map, but it had also been chosen as the Texas Brigade headquarters, home to the entirety of the Texas National Guard apart from the Texas Field Hospital unit and two batteries. The first of the Texas Brigade from the Third Infantry departed Harlingen on September 6 for the 132-mile journey to Corpus Christi. Townspeople gathered to gawk at the spectacle of 1,380 soldiers, 125 officers, 200 horses and mules, 27 wagons, four ambulances, and other equipment disembarking at the rail depot. From there the men marched the one-mile distance to camp, accompanied by their regimental band and followed by 20 wagons drawn by teams hauling tents, armaments, and other gear. Two days later, the Second Infantry arrived from Donna and Pharr.[49]

In just days, the camp swelled to about 1,500 troops of the Third Infantry, 1,715 from the Second, and 205 from Battery A of the Texas Field Artillery. For a city of 16,000, the arrival of nearly 3,500 soldiers not only swelled the population but also provided an economic boost and a diversion from the routines of daily life. Thousands of townspeople thronged the camp during the excitement of that first week, their welcome ceremonies including a reception for the guardsmen held by "the women of Corpus Christi" who delivered "5,000 bottles of ice-cold soda water and hundreds of baked cakes."[50]

Until now, the guard camp was known by the locals as Camp Alta Vista, its name derived from a once majestic but now abandoned hotel located on the bluff south of the town and camp. In a formal ceremony during the first inaugural weeks, Brig. Gen. Hulen officially named the post Camp Scurry in honor of the late Gen. Thomas Scurry, a major in the First Texas Volunteer Infantry during the Spanish-American War. The choice of the name may have been suggested by Colonel Bloor, who served under Scurry and attended the popular general's retirement ceremony in 1903, where he was presented with a chest bearing the letter 'S' engraved on its top and filled with silver pieces.[51]

Located about a mile from the business district at the end of South Broadway and 3rd Streets, Camp Scurry was essentially an extension of the city. The luxurious Nueces Hotel downtown became the de facto headquarters for military dignitaries, politicians, and businessmen who came to review Camp Scurry troops and attend guard events. Hundreds of people came from town to observe routine drills, marches, rifle and bayonet practice, and to watch guard parades and sports. Field days, in which the regimental companies competed in dashes, relay races, broad jumps, pole vaulting, sack races, and arms drills were popular events held on the second and fourth Saturdays of each month.[52]

At Camp Scurry's completion over 500 tents, with wooden floors and screens, were erected in orderly rows. Each tent held eight men, and with just 16 feet square of living space, folding cots were erected with their headboards against the canvas walls, leaving just two feet of narrow walkway in the center. Every company had its own mess tent, which was screened to allow for cooling breezes and to keep insects out. There was a well-stocked commissary store, called the Canteen. An Army YMCA was constructed that, by October, was the center for camp social activities with its library and club rooms for meetings. Chaplains held daily devotionals, and in the evening, entertainment included "movie picture shows" and musical programs, put on by both soldiers and the people of Corpus Christi, like one in January sponsored by Mrs. Roy Miller. The civilized nature of the camp was evident when Lt. Col. Bloor and other guard officers were permitted to bring their wives to live on the base.[53]

It didn't take long before Corpus Christi thought of the men at Camp Scurry as "our boys." Thanksgiving was a good example. The Corpus Christi Rotary Club and the local Western Union office made plans to distribute cakes to the regiments. For weeks, they ran a *Corpus Christi Caller-Times* advertisement proclaiming the affair, adding that "as the majority of the Rotarians are not expert cake bakers, they solicit the assistance of the ladies." Both the town and the army provided a large assortment of food for the holiday feast, and the soldier's wives and children were invited to camp. Colonel Benjamin F. Delameter, commander of the Second Infantry, permitted Companies E and F to take a four-day furlough to attend the UT football game in Austin. The special train of the San Antonio & Aransas Pass Railroad bulged with an estimated 200 guardsmen plus the Second Infantry band, and the rail company provided a private car for Lt. Col. and Mrs. Bloor. When the train converged on Austin, the guard companies paraded from the depot to the capital. After the game, Austin's Mayor A.P. Wooldridge hosted a Thanksgiving dinner for the traveling party.[54]

Christmas that year was equally festive, and equally a partnership between the Army and its host city. Mayor Miller was the self-titled "Chairman of the General Committee for the Municipal Yuletide Festival," and with the Commercial Club, City Council, Rotary Club, and City Federation of Women, planned an elaborate holiday celebration for "its boys." Mayor Miller telegrammed every city in the state, inviting the guardsmen's friends and family to visit the city during the festivities and encouraging them to send Christmas gifts that he offered to collect and distribute. The Wells Fargo Express Company, he added, would offer steep shipping discounts. In all, some 15 tons of community gift boxes made their way to Camp Scurry, the bounty including a yearling calf shipped by an East Texas rancher to Texas Brigade commander General Hulen for the Yuletide officer dinner. A tall Christmas tree was procured and decorated in the city's Artesian Park, with three days of holiday celebration planned for townspeople and soldiers. The army's selection of Corpus Christi, with the hope of improving morale, was by the end of 1916 appearing to be a wise choice.[55]

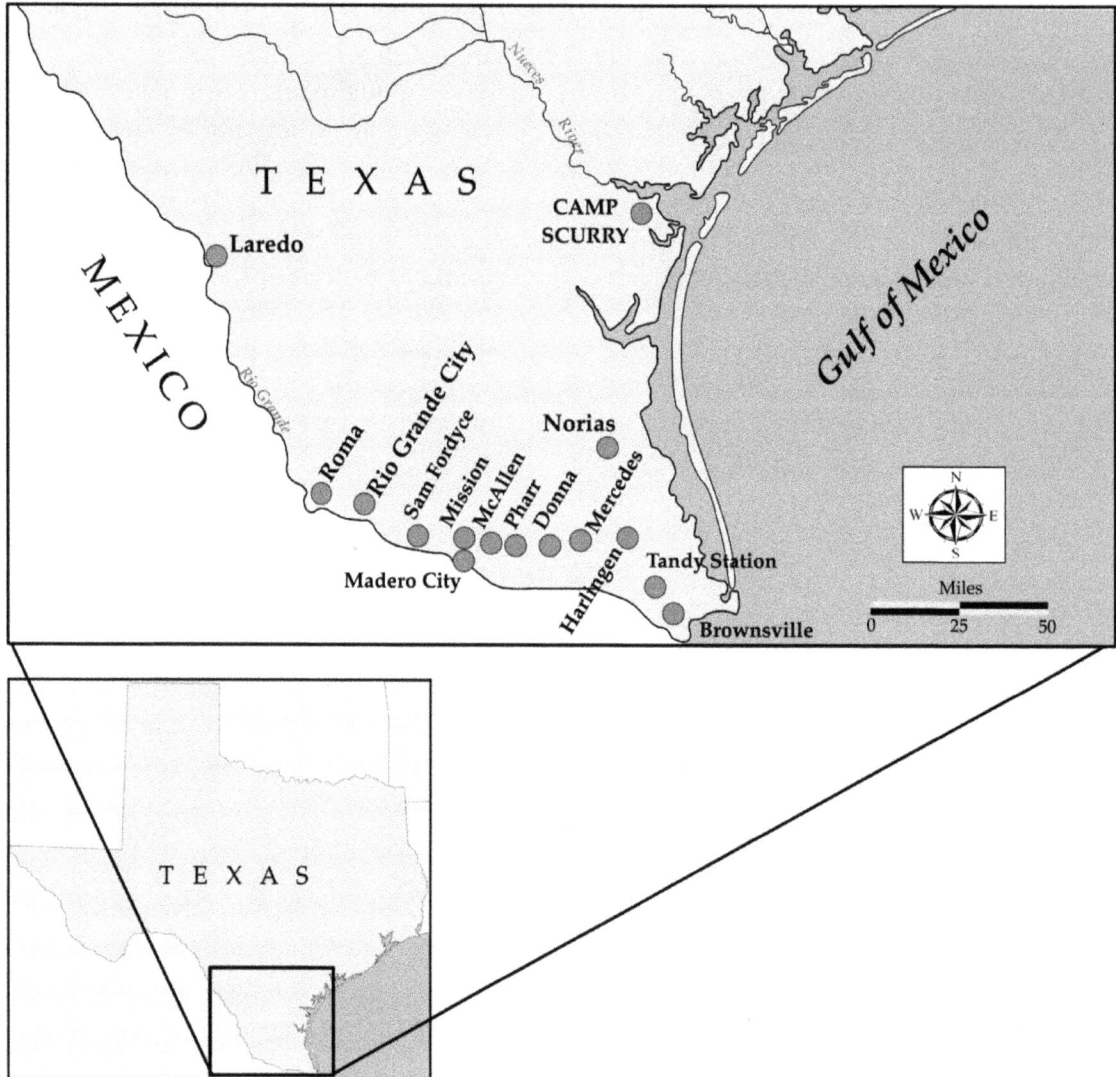

Map showing location of Camp Scurry in Corpus Christi, and the South Texas towns of Brownsville and Laredo. The location of the Norias Ranch and Tandy Station border raids are also shown. The towns that parallel the Rio Grande are where the 36th Division of the Texas and Oklahoma National Guard companies were posted during 1916 and 1917, and followed the track of the St. Louis, Brownsville & Mexican Railway. Drawing by R.K. Sawyer.

On August 8, 1915, some 60-armed Seditionists descended on the Norias Division of the King Ranch, the ensuing shootout leaving five raiders dead and wounding five defenders. Norias ranch headquarters (top) and "The Six Defenders" bottom. Collection Jim Moloney.

Top: The wreck of the St. Louis, Brownsville & Mexican Railway at Tandy Station, north of Brownsville. The Seditionist bandits boarded the wrecked cars and robbed its passengers, their attack leaving three dead and another four passengers badly wounded. Shown in the photo is Texas Ranger John R. Peavy. Collection Jim Moloney.

Bottom: The bandits burned the railroad bridge about a mile north of the train wreck to slow the pursuit of law enforcement. Photographs by Robert Runyon. Collection Jim Moloney.

General Francisco "Pancho" Villa in 1914 with Raul Madero, brother of former Mexican president Francisco Madero. That year Villa and his supporters murdered Juarez rancher William S. Benton. Published by Bain News Service, *Library of Congress Prints and Photographs Division*, Washington, https://www.loc.gov/item2014695367.

Top: Pancho Villa in Chihuahua, 1911. *Library of Congress Prints and Photographs Division,* Washington D.C., No. LC-USZC4-129.

Bottom: Villa shown holding a Hotchkiss machine gun with rifles that are probably Mauser 1912s. *Library of Congress Prints and Photographs Division,* Washington D.C., No. No. LC-B2-2377-5.

President Woodrow Wilson with his fiancée Edith Galt at the Army-Navy football game in New York in 1915. After Pancho Villa's raid on Columbus, Wilson ordered Brigadier General John "Black Jack" Pershing to organize an expedition of the Regular Army to capture Villa south of the border. Called the "Punitive Expedition," by the spring of 1916 the Army had poured thousands of reinforcements into the Southern Department and were running out of regular troops. President Wilson responded by mobilizing the National Guard. *Library of Congress Prints and Photographs Division*, Washington D.C., No. LC-LC-DIG-ggbain-20517.

Aftermath of Pancho Villa's raid on Columbus, New Mexico on March 9, 1916. G.G. Bain Collection, *Library of Congress Prints and Photographs Division*, Washington, D.C., No. LC-B2- 3784-7.

Left: General John Pershing during the 1916 Punitive Expedition. *Library of Congress Prints and Photographs Division*, Washington, D.C., No. LC-USZ62-89218.

Top: Army camp at Columbus New Mexico in 1916, with a truck supply train preparing to leave as part of the Punitive Expedition. *Library of Congress Prints and Photographs Division*, Washington, D.C., No. LOT-7729-14.

Bottom: The National Guard's First Officer's Training School at Camp Mabry, in Austin. "Camp Mabry," No. PICA 16347, *Austin History Center*, Austin Public Library.

Promotional poster for National Guard. *Library of Congress Prints and Photographs Division*, Washington, D.C., No. LC-USZC4-7549.

Top and bottom: Destruction of the Texas Brigade National Guard camp at the border town of Pharr from the August 18, 1916, hurricane. Collection Jim Moloney.

The Missouri National Guard camp at Fort McIntosh in Laredo, digging out after the August 1916 storm. The Second Texas Infantry football team played two contests against the Missouri team between November and December. In the bottom photograph, one can almost sense despair in the soldier's demeanor. Collection Jim Moloney.

Devastation at Corpus Christi after the August 1916 hurricane. Just nine days after the storm, the order to relocate some 3,350 men from the border to Camp Scurry was given anyway. Top photo: A view of Water Street at the edge of Corpus Christi Bay filled with debris from piers and wharves destroyed by the storm. Bottom photo: Bridges over Hall's Bayou to North Beach at the northern edge of Corpus Christi that were washed out by the storm. Collection of Jim Moloney.

Top: An aerial view shows Corpus Christi in the foreground and Camp Scurry's rows of tents towards the Gulf of Mexico. Collection Jim Moloney.

Bottom: Transportation at Camp Scurry was by mule and horse carts, although automobiles were becoming more common. The bottom photograph was taken by Corpus Christi lensman Karl Swafford. Collection Jim Moloney.

More scenes from Camp Scurry. Top: Hospital tent in the left foreground. Bottom is one of the company's dining tents. Collection Jim Moloney.

Second Texas Infantry Company E at Camp Scurry, top and bottom, was one of the two Austin militia organizations. Some of its members were football players Victor Bintliff, Spitz Clarke, Tige Halphen, Dick Lane, Mullie Lenoir, and Pleas Rogers. Photographs taken by Karl Swafford, ca. 1916-17. Collection Jim Moloney.

Top: Richard Lane, Pleas B. Rogers, and Charlie Stewart were assigned to the Second Texas Infantry Regiment machine gun company formed from Company E. Collection Jim Moloney.

Bottom: Lt. Jim Kendrick was second in command of Waco's Company G. Photographs taken by Karl Swafford, ca. 1916-17. Collection Jim Moloney.

CHAPTER 5

Play Ball

Sports consumed any spare time the guardsmen had while posted in Texas. Wrestling, boxing, and rifle contests were popular, as was baseball. In October, Brownsville District commander Brigadier General James Parker authorized regiments under his auspices to organize a football league. Following the same structure used for guard baseball, each Brownsville District regiment was encouraged to create and enter a team in the league. The plan was for the winning "regimental gridiron eleven" of each Texas district to compete for the National Guard championship title at the end of the season.[1]

The Second Texas Infantry didn't wait for the official order. Just days after they arrived in camp, the regiment announced it was organizing "a real fast football eleven." Colonel A.W. Bloor was divulged as the team's athletic director and Lt. Bill Birge its captain. Some 80 men hurriedly signed up for tryouts, and 26 were quickly selected for the squad. The players cleared brush in a pasture next to camp, raked the silty clay into a makeshift field, and started practice immediately, drilling every day from 10:00 in the morning until 5:00 in the afternoon, and sometimes twice a day. At first, they wore jerseys from their colleges if they had any at all, and it wasn't until the first game that they were issued gray jerseys split by an infantry blue stripe with matching brown pants. Despite their rag-tag appearance, word quickly spread that they were "a force to be reckoned with."[2]

The team that evolved from the palmetto scrub on the edge of Corpus Christi Bay played a tough brand of football. They played both offense and defense, without the luxury of specialty teams for such things as conversions or punt returns. As a result, they were on the field for the entire contest, the only exception when substitutes were brought in for a particular play or because the score was so lopsided they were assured of victory. Players never considered leaving the field with an injury unless it was severe enough to require emergency medical care, and even then, they resisted it. Only a few wore shoulder pads, and none had helmets or headgear.

But there were perks to being on the team. Second Texas Infantry commander Colonel Delameter excused all players from regular training and military duty so they could dedicate their time to practice. K.L. Berry remembered that "we did nothing much militarily except stand inspection on Saturday." The players were given a separate mess. Bill Birge recalled how he once spent all morning trying to locate substitute quarterback Watson, and when he was escorted to his tent, found him "being served breakfast in bed by the cook."[3]

The Second Infantry were keen competitors, and tired of practice. They wanted a game. Their first opponent was supposed to be the Third Infantry at Camp Scurry in early October but, according to legend, "those fellows took one look at us and refused to play." With no other games forthcoming from their regimental officers, Charlie Stewart and Bill Birge arranged a game between the Second Infantry and Texas A&M at College Station for October 22. The only hitch was that they neglected to inform their superior officers.

General James Parker's directive was clear – National Guard teams would play other National Guard teams, not Lone Star State universities or colleges. As the team boarded the train for their first game, the order was passed from Camp Wilson to Camp Scurry to cancel the match.[4]

Walter F. Woodul and Game One. Walter F. Woodul organized what would be the Second Infantry's first game. Woodul, who later refined his negotiating acumen in the halls of Texas politics, was hesitant to go through proper military channels but demonstrated his ability to get things done without, somehow, ruffling many feathers. He had been with the gridiron team briefly at Camp Scurry and knew its boys wanted to play ball. Elected to represent Laredo and Webb County in the Texas House of Representatives in the summer of 1916, he was equally anxious to support his new legislative district and his native Laredo. He combined both worthy objectives with a plan to organize and promote a contest between the Camp Scurry and the Missouri guard companies stationed at Laredo's Fort McIntosh.

Woodul's scheme faced two obstacles. First was authorization from the military brass, which he thought would be characteristically slow to respond. The other was that the Missourians didn't have a football team. Woodul overcame the first challenge by going around formal military approval channels, enlisting instead the support of an obliging press. In a letter published in the *Laredo Weekly Times* in late October, he phrased his wording as if the game was already scheduled, likely reasoning that once the contest was in print, it would be awkward for the military to retract. For any other soldier, the move was both bold and unwise, but Woodul risked little wrath. He had just been discharged from the guard after winning his seat in the Texas House and was a week away from returning home to Laredo.

As for the inconvenient reality that the Missouri guardsmen had no organized football team, spin master Woodul wrote in his *Laredo Weekly Times* missive that the remarkable Second Infantry could "challenge anything in the South," but that the players thought the Missouri athletes were their only worthy adversary. While completely fiction, it was a carefully crafted appeal to Missourian manhood that Woodul figured they wouldn't ignore. But before he even gave the Show-Me-State guardsmen the chance, the local paper answered the challenge for them, editorializing that the Missourians would have little trouble forming "an invincible football squad" because they had "some of the best college and university talent in the whole country." Still not waiting for a reaction, the correspondent, with notepad in hand, went directly to the commander of the Missouri Field Artillery for his answer. He was trapped. Yes, Missouri would accept the challenge. Now they had to scramble to form a team.[5]

Not willing to lose the momentum, Woodul waited a week and then sent another telegram to the *Laredo Weekly Times*. This time he advised the paper that he was travelling to Laredo to finalize details for the Second Texas Infantry-First Missouri Artillery game. Most likely, it was the first time the Missouri officers ever heard about any meeting.[6]

Mayor Miller and the Gulf Coast Exposition. Woodul was as determined to see the coming game played in Laredo as Corpus Christi mayor Roy Miller was in hosting it at Camp Scurry. The hopes of Laredo businessmen, who viewed the contest as "a great drawing card" that would attract "several thousand excursionists" were dashed. Miller and other Corpus Christi business leaders had gone to great lengths to see the game played on

Monday, November 20, the first day of the city's much-heralded Second Annual Gulf Coast Exposition. Miller wisely offered an olive branch to Woodul by suggesting a second game in December at Laredo.[7]

The Gulf Coast Exposition planners worked as hard as Miller to exploit the opportunity. The fairground was relocated from its original location to within a block of Camp Scurry and, like the guard camp that emerged from the scrub just a month earlier, the city poured its resources into its preparation. During October, exhibition buildings and livestock sheds were erected, an athletic field was constructed from 300 loads of oyster shells that were crushed and smoothed with rollers, and a stadium was built for the occasion, called "the big grandstand," with seating for 3,000.[8]

On the eve of the Gulf Coast Exposition, several hundred Missouri National Guardsmen, accompanied by their regimental band and supporters, boarded a special train for Corpus Christi. The city that greeted them was in a festive mood. Mayor Miller watched from the Nueces Hotel as the fair kicked off with an impromptu parade that started when Camp Scurry's Second and Third Infantries, returning from maneuvers, marched into the city where they were joined by city citizens on foot and in automobiles, six brass bands, wild and tame animals from Backman's Carnival, and uniformed Boy Scouts. In all, nearly 3,000 people joined the improvised parade that marked the Expo's opening.[9]

Fairgoers wandered the grounds the morning of the game, occupied by its hundreds of exhibits of corn, cotton, and native wood products, a chicken and livestock exhibit, and a home economic program that included floral displays and home-canned vegetables, preserves, and pickles. The National Guard sponsored band concerts, track and field meets, and the Second Infantry even entered the cow pony races with a second-place finishing pony named Shorty. At 3:00, the grounds were mostly emptied as the Second Infantry took to the field in what the *Corpus Christi Caller-Daily Herald* touted as the "biggest football game ever played south of San Antonio."[10]

First Missouri Artillery Game. Jim Kendrick opened the first game of the Second Texas Infantry football season with a kick to Missouri. Four minutes later Texas scored its first touchdown, with Kendrick missing the extra point. At the end of the first quarter, the 6-0 score did not reflect the Lone Star teams' dominance. The ball never crossed into Texas territory. Collins' kickoff opened the second quarter, the Missourians gaining ground in two running plays and pushing their way to the opponent's 12-yard line. Then they fumbled. With the ball in Texas' possession, backfielder Spitz Clarke immediately found a hole in the Missouri line for a gain of 24 yards, and fullback Berry carried the ball over the line on the next down for a halftime score of 13-0.[11]

The third quarter was scoreless until Kendrick, tackled on an end run, tossed a lateral to Rip Collins who took it across the goal line. In the final quarter, Collins intercepted a Missouri pass – still novel enough to clarify it as a "forward pass" to differentiate it from a lateral – and gained 30 yards. On the next play, halfback Spitz Clarke made the score. After left end Charlie Turner ran for a touchdown in the game's last minutes, the final tally was 33-0.[12]

Nothing the Missouri team attempted in its clash with the Second Infantry succeeded. In the first half, they relied mainly on "line plunging" but lost yardage on almost every play. Still convinced that the key to winning at football was player weight over skill, one post-game analyst maintained that the Missourians were defeated because they "were too light." Except for Kendrick's two missed extra points – a 50% average on conversions was a good record in early games – the Second played flawless football. If they had developed any of the "special plays" they were noted for later, they refrained from using them. Instead, the team played "earnest old-style football," with one post-game pundit adding that "the game was clean throughout, and the absence of rough work was appreciably noted."[13]

First Wisconsin Infantry Game. The second Texas Infantry gridiron match was arranged mostly by Mayor Miller, who convinced the guard brass of the benefits of hosting a game on Saturday, November 25, to coincide with the closing day of the Gulf Coast Exposition. Less than a week after their Missouri Field Artillery game, the Second Texas Infantry was scheduled to face the First Wisconsin Infantry, stationed at San Antonio. The First Wisconsin Infantry team arrived in Corpus Christi on the morning of the game on its special train accompanied by 550 fans and a 32-piece regimental brass band. The Nueces Hotel was headquarters for visiting dignitaries, with an enthusiastic Roy Miller as toastmaster. Turnout at the fairgrounds more than doubled from its opening day to 6,200, with an increase in the football game attendance from 2,000 to 2,500.[14]

Texas scored in the game's first three minutes when halfback Rip Collins carried the ball through a wall of defenders. Collins' kick then bounced off a Wisconsin blocker, the ball recovered by alternate fullback Dotson who evaded all comers to score again. Collins made the extra point. On Wisconsin's next possession, they drove deep into Texas territory then bobbled the ball in the end zone. It was recovered by Texas, the team marching the length of the field for another six points. The Texas defense continued its assault on the opposition's offense, causing another Wisconsin fumble that led to another quick score when Abbott connected to Collins. Runs by Rip Collins and K.L. Berry, who scrambled 50 yards through the defense on one play, counted for two more scores in the second quarter. At halftime, the game was a lopsided 54 to 0.[15]

The remainder of the contest was given to the Second's substitutes. Dick Lane came in at tackle, Nelson at center, Pleas Rogers at guard, and George Lane at right end. Quarterback duties, shared during the first two quarters between starter Spitz Clarke and Ock Abbott, were turned over to Rats Watson. Years later, it was learned that Watson played that game with a foot so swollen from a tarantula bite that the shoe he wore on his left foot was four sizes larger than his normal seven-and-a-half-size cleat.[16]

With the Second Infantry team filled with substitutes from their second and third strings, the final half was a more evenly matched contest. Still, Wisconsin was unable to move the ball against the Texas defense, and the game concluded the celebrated Corpus Christi Gulf Coast Exposition with a score of 60-0.[17]

First Missouri Artillery "All-Stars" Game. The third Second Infantry game was on the docket for December 9, a Missouri rematch at Laredo. The Missourians adopted town of Laredo – the "Gateway to and from Mexico" – was bustling in the early 1900s. Two railways reached the town from major Texas cities, and it boasted a rich Mexican culture as unfamiliar to the Show-Me-State boys as it was captivating. The artillerymen were encamped at Fort McIntosh on a bend in the Rio Grande at the edge of town, and drilled at Caliche Field, aptly named for its iron-rich limestone and alluvial grit. Linesman Charley "June" Ogden remembered that the sand-sized particles were six inches deep, and "every time you hit the ground you would have to dig the sand out of your mouth with your fingers."[18]

On the official National Guard roster, they were called the First Missouri Artillery but dubbed themselves the Missouri All-Stars after they were encouraged to select any player for their squad from Fort McIntosh's 10,000 guardsmen. Anxious to restore their damaged pride from the 33-0 loss in their initial contest, among the hand-picked lineup changes announced for the Laredo home game were the addition of player-coach Chuck Wilson, and replacements in the backfield and line. As to the changes, a spokesman for the Second Infantry remarked that he hoped the strengthened lineup "will at least give us a better tussle than in the first game."[19]

Walter F. Woodul, organizer of the third game, traveled between Corpus Christi and Laredo to attend to its every detail, even arranging for three bands to greet the Texas boys at the train depot. The Second Infantry left Camp Scurry on December 8 for the ten-hour journey to the border city on a chartered train filled with over 300 militiamen and civilian fans. But no bands and no crowd were there to meet them. Laredo business leaders later apologized and blamed the early hour and extreme cold. Whether a deliberate snub or an unintentional blunder, the Texans ignored the oversight, heading quickly to the Fort McIntosh practice field while their traveling party, adorned with ribbons, pennants, and banners of the Second Infantry's gold and white colors, wandered the town's quiet streets.[20]

The National Guard regimental bands of both teams took to the field before the game, the tone for the contest set when one bulldog mascot pounced on another canine mascot, nearly killing it. The 3,000 fans who showed up far exceeded the field's seating capacity. Crowding the sidelines at game time, a section of park fence gave way under the "pressure of numerous soldier-spectators."[21]

In their first possession, the Second gained good field position on two dazzling runs by fullback Berry and Charlie Turner took the ball over the line. The Texans scored again on their next possession. Less than five minutes into the game the score was 13-0. Both touchdowns, a result of "fake plays" that put the Artillerymen off guard, seemed to assure that the contest would be another Texas rout. It wasn't.[22]

Emotions climbed as penalties stacked up on the Texas side, but none were called on the Missouri All-Stars. Each time the Second advanced, another penalty was called. They changed their strategy and took to the air, with mixed results described by one post-game pundit as "the forward pass was used several times successfully" but "failing on numerous [other] occasions." In the final quarter, with the ball on the Missourian's one-yard line, the Texans threatened again. Penalties kept them from scoring. The game ended with its first-quarter total of 13-0.[23]

The Missouri rematch was the lowest-scoring game of the Second's eight-game football season. The reason wasn't publicly discussed at the time, but it came up later. In Charley Ogden's 1956 letter to Associated Press sports editor Harold Ratliff, he fell short of accusing the officials, all of which were affiliated with the Missouri team, of rigging the game. But he did write that they were the "lousiest, blindest, or the most prejudiced bunch I ever saw." Ogden was then an official of the Southwest Football Officials Association, and his carefully chosen words were understandable.

Former Second Texas gridiron star K.L. Berry, who was by the time of Ratliff's interview a decorated combat veteran of two World Wars, was not as guarded. He said the Texas Eleven competed against a team of 14 Missouri players – eleven footballers plus their three extra men – the officials. "We threatened repeatedly to score," the major general told Ratliff, "but the three extra men kept us from doing it. We caught them napping a couple of times, however, and scored before they could think up a violation."[24]

Curiously, when the *Laredo Weekly Times* reported on the game in 1916, the paper felt impelled to note "that the referee's decisions were impartial." It was an odd admission, as was their comment that it was a "clean game" throughout. The Second Texas Infantry remembered that differently. It was more like "boxing instruction," according to Ogden, and "the fun started" after the Texan's second touchdown. "When the ball was snapped, seven fists would come up in our faces [and] the holding made the game look like a wrestling match." Team captain and player-coach W.S. Birge consoled his teammates with: "Remember, we are Texans, and we don't play dirty."[25]

By the second half the game was a slugging match. Birge called in the referee and the opposing team's captain for a consultation. So far, he was able to prevent retaliation, Birge counseled, but if the slugging continued, he'd turn the Camp Scurry boys loose. On the next play, Birge's words of conciliation were met with a punch in the nose by a Missouri lineman. The Texans played the remainder of the game without the bloodied Birge, and with only ten men on the field, all of whom "spent the rest of the game guarding their faces."

Still an Uncertain Schedule. The Second Texas Infantry players were convinced they could take on any team in football after the Missouri rematch, and they cajoled Bill Birge, Charlie Stewart, and Walter Woodul to canvas the countryside and find worthy opponents to fill their schedule. Birge and Woodul successfully organized the next game on their calendar, with the First Virginia Artillery. Stewart, for his part, posted an advertisement in Pennsylvania newspapers challenging any Eastern Seaboard football team to a duel. Stewart's challenge was mainly aimed at the Penn State Eastern Collegiate Champions, who didn't rise to the bait. But it did catch the attention of former Syracuse University All-American Red Wilkinson, who was posted in the Valley with the First New York Cavalry. Wilkinson was itching to put the Texans in their place. He and Stewart carried on a dialogue for several weeks, tentatively arranging a game date in January.[26]

First Virginia Artillery Game. Walter Woodul arranged the financing and planning for the First Virginia Artillery game, traveling between Corpus Christi and Camp Wilson to coordinate with Captain Walt Johnson, chairman of the Army football tournament committee in San Antonio. It would be Woodul's crowning organizational achievement. Woodul and Johnson convinced the Army brass to allow thousands of guardsmen from Camp Wilson and Fort Sam Houston to attend the event, and Woodul with Mayor Miller planned for many more visitors from Corpus Christi and Camp Scurry.[27]

With a crowd assured, Woodul took the financial risk of renting San Antonio's League Park instead of playing the game at Fort Sam Houston. The modern, larger venue meant no more Camp Scurry crushed oyster shells or Laredo red dirt playing fields, and no more standing room only. League Park provided the comfort of manicured sod adjacent to grandstands, boxes, and bleachers, the latter important so that "fans of the fair sex will be enabled to see the contest in comfort."[28]

Both teams had perfect records going into the contest, and neither had allowed an opponent to cross its goal line. One Texas paper gushed that "few football games outside of intercollegiate competition" had ever attracted "anything like the widespread interest" of these "football giants." Another described the match in titanic terms, as "nothing of [this] sort has ever been attempted before in the history of football." The writer explained that "its scope is national in interest," a battle between East and West and a clash between hand-picked All-Star teams with their different playing styles, "football systems, and football brawn."[29]

The play of the Virginia team was said to eclipse that of "even the best university elevens." Early on the Virginians were favored, with betting odds of four to three against Texas. Pre-game analysts observed that the Second Infantry might have the weight advantage, but Virginia had the speed, including the 165-pound and always menacing "line-plunger" Dodson from Randall Macon College. They were, as well, "a very shifty team," capable of "slipping something over at any moment."[30]

The First Virginia Artillerymen arrived at the Gunter Hotel several days before the game to practice. The Second Infantry came by train on the morning of the game, December 16, parading from the San Antonio & Aransas Pass depot through the city's streets behind its regimental band with "a choice assortment of natural history specimens as mascots" in tow. These were the animals collected and raised by the Second Infantry during their various border postings and included the team goat, bobcat, javelina, coyote, and an adopted parrot. Military bands played in a relay all day. Pre-game ceremonies featured Virginia's two bands that marched onto the field while its entourage of 800 rooters made for the stands. A thousand fans from Corpus Christi came north for the game, as well as rooters from across Texas.[31]

There were a few player changes to the Second Infantry roster in the First Virginia Artillery game. Left end Charlie Turner missed this and the next two games, tending to an ill father in New Mexico. He was replaced by George Lane and Bart Coan. John Diller, Spitz Clarke, and Jim Kendrick were injured, but played part of the first half anyway, although Kendrick's kicking duties went to Eugene Dotson. Abbott started at quarterback, then shared receiving duties with Lane and Coan, turning the quarterback helm over to Rats Watson.

The Second Texas Infantry received the kick and maintained possession of the ball for the first four minutes. At fourth and ten, halfback Spitz Clarke sailed downfield 25 yards on a fake kick. Their next play was a double lateral in the backfield that ended with an end around by Kendrick who gained another 25 yards for the touchdown. Texas scored again in the first quarter when Rats Watson "hurled an aerial" to halfback Rip Collins. The play was more elegant in print than it was on the field. The Second had been penalized, again, and it was fourth down with long yardage. The team was in a "short punt" or shotgun formation, and when substitute center David Nelson snapped the ball to Watson, it soared over Watson's head. He scrambled to chase it down and made a hurried toss to Collins, who ran 40 yards. After another touchdown run by Clarke, the first half ended with a score of 20 to 0.

Texas opened the second half by regaining possession after an onside kick, then lost their field position to another holding call. Watson threw to wide receiver Kendrick for 20 yards and then Collins, who ran through, over, and around the defenders for another 25-yard gain and the team's third TD. On their next possession, Abbott was back as quarterback and ran the ball around the left side of the line for a gain of 20. A 30-yard pass to Kendrick put Texas on the goal line. Clarke hurled over the Virginia defensive line for another score. The Second scored their last touchdown of the third quarter on a 30-yard catch by Kendrick, bringing the score to a lopsided 40-0.

In the fourth quarter, Texas brought in their second and third-string roster, and they played as well as the regulars. The Texas defense never allowed the Virginians to slip into Texas territory, and the offense scored two more touchdowns in the final quarter. Watson ran 20 yards and Dotson scored on two more running plays. Abbott was again at the helm at the end of the quarter and danced his way through "the whole Virginia team" for a 40-yard score. In the final moments, Kendrick ran 40 yards to within striking distance of the goal when the game was called. The Second Texas won it by a score of 53 to 0. Halfbacks Clarke and Collins scored twice on runs and right end Kendrick scored twice on a run and a pass completion. Quarterback Abbott and substitute fullback Dotson each crossed the goal line once. Most post-game summaries credit the Second Infantry with eight touchdowns and four extra points for a score of 52-0. But the official team record and a few later articles listed the score at 53-0, and this is believed to be the most accurate tally.[32]

By the time they faced the Virginia team, the Second Infantry offense had almost exclusively adopted a variation of the modern-day shotgun or open formation, called during the time a "kick formation," configured with the quarterback in the backfield and split ends on the line. Abbott, from his drop-back throwing position, threw more passes than in the previous three games, "shooting his long spirals like a rifle bullet" his "whirling spiral passes" connecting with a high percentage to receivers Kendrick and Collins for substantial downfield gains. It was the same for Watson. When Collins was forced to punt, nearly always because of penalties, it didn't matter what field position Texas had, he always put the ball neatly between the goal and the 10-yard line. Some of his kicks soared the full length of the field with one booted "so far it took about $8 to get it back by parcel post."[33]

The Second's defensive play was equally brilliant. In four quarters, the Virginia running game produced only one first down. Even the menacing Dodson, one the best college fullbacks playing in the National Guard, couldn't penetrate the Texas defensive wall. Much of the credit went to Baker Duncan, "the lanky lad in left tackle" who played brilliant defense, "interrupting and smearing more plays than any forward on either side."[34]

Texas sportswriters were beginning to notice the Second Infantry's contests, with one newsman calling their performance against Virginia "one of the biggest, fastest, and cleverest football games that ever cleated the grass on a Texas gridiron" and "an exposition of high-class football. There were no stars – all were stars." Still another wrote that "it is a team in which the value of its stars is retained, and at the same time teamwork perfected." Virginian coach Jeffries remarked that "Texas outclassed us all the way around," adding that, even in a rematch, he didn't think he'd ever beat them. They were simply "one of the most wonderful teams I've ever seen."[35]

Buried in the Virginia game's fine print were names that would soon have a big impact on the Second Infantry football program. D.V. "Tubby" Graves was a referee during the Virginia game, and two weeks later became the Second Infantry's head coach. The game's umpire, Walt C. Johnson, would organize the team's game against the 12th Division All-Star team in January, and Austin High football coach Howard Goodman, the Virginia game field judge, also had a role in the Second's All-Star match. The future coach of the 12th Division All-Stars was originally listed as one of the Virginia game umpires, but he had to cancel. His name was Dwight D. Eisenhower.[36]

Fourth Nebraska Infantry Game. By the time their fifth game was played on December 21 at Camp Scurry, the Second Infantry was described in glowing terms such as "the famous football machine" and the Second Infantry "steam roller," as well as other innovative titles reflecting their gridiron dominance. Played against the Fourth Nebraska Infantry stationed on the Rio Grande at Llano Grande, the contest would surpass even the Second's expectations of their playing prowess. The Thursday match was played on a cold day with a strong north wind, the weather making the game "disagreeable" for the small crowd in attendance. But it had no effect on the Second Infantry. The Nebraska team hardly knew what hit them.[37]

In the first quarter, left end starter Bart Coan fielded the ball on a kick that bounced off a Nebraska receiver and Coan carried it downfield. Halfback Collins took it across the goal line. The score at the end of the first quarter was 7-0. The most memorable play of the second quarter was a fake pass by starting quarterback Rats Watson that he turned into a long run for a touchdown. At the close of the half, the Texan's racked up 34 points to Nebraska's zero.

The second half was hardly different. Collins in the third quarter made an interception that he ran across the goal line, and in another possession, quarterback Abbott scored on a "straight line plunge." Then, Nebraska managed to do what few had done before them – they marched across the field to the Texas five-yard line and threatened to score. Nebraska quarterback Logan threw an interception. Spitz Clarke made the nab, then ran the length of the field for a 95-yard touchdown. The Second continued to score until the final whistle, winning the game 68-0. It was their highest-scoring game to date.[38]

In total, the Second scored ten touchdowns and kicked eight extra points. Rip Collins was the high scorer of the day with 36 points from four touchdowns and he successfully booted all eight extra points. Spitz Clarke made three touchdowns, Rats Watson two, and Ock Abbott made one. One post-game analyst wrote that the Nebraska team "put up a good fight" and "tried to keep the score down as low as possible." It was faint praise. Evidently bored with the matchup, the *Austin American* carried but two lines summarizing the lopsided contest, concluding that the game "lacked exciting features."[39]

More Schedule Negotiations. The next game on the Second Infantry's calendar was supposed to be against the First Florida Infantry on Christmas Day, in San Antonio. The opposing team, however, surprised everyone in mid-December by canceling. Bill Birge, Charlie Stewart, and Walter Woodul scrambled to reschedule, finding a willing adversary with the Fourth Minnesota Infantry. Scheduled in Corpus Christi, Mayor Miller was only too happy to roll out the red carpet of his city by the sea for what he knew would be a great seasonal attraction. On game day, the Second Infantry was on the Exposition Park ballfield when Minnesota sent a telegram that they, too, were cancelling because they were granted a furlough for Christmas week. Negotiations with Red Wilkinson's First New York Cavalry were progressing, but with just one more game against the 74th New York Infantry left in their season, the Second Texas Infantry was looking hard for other suitable opponents.[40]

74th New York Infantry Game. The headlines were brutal, with words like "crushed" and "swamped" followed by commentaries such as "Lone Star gridiron veterans' toy with Empire State bunch at will" for "the most one-sided score of any game played on the border this season." If there were any doubts about the Second Infantry's football proficiency, they evaporated after the team met the 74th New York Infantry on New Year's Day in front of 3,000 fans in Exposition Park at Camp Scurry.[41]

Rip Collins recalled how the New Yorkers bragged they would run up only 40 points before sending in their substitutes so as not to "ruin the morale of our club by scoring too many points against us." The Second Infantry got even. As the points piled up during the first quarter, the Texans passed the word to go for "a hundred or bust." They succeeded, rolling over the New Yorkers 102-0.[42]

Texas scored 15 touchdowns and 12 extra points. Halfback Spitz Clarke and fullback Eugene Dotson scored three times, and right end Jim Kendrick and substitute quarterback Ock Abbott scored twice. Defensive lineman John Diller crossed the goal twice on pass interceptions. Starting quarterback Rats Watson and left end George Lane each scored once. Out of 15 possible extra points, Jim Kendrick kicked eight and Rip Collins went for four. The score might have been higher if the game hadn't been called in the last few minutes of the final quarter. The New Yorkers ran out of players, having exhausted their starting roster and the entirety of their bench.[43]

No One Left to Play. When the football series started in the fall of 1916, it was structured such that the winning "regimental gridiron eleven" of each Texas military district would compete for the National Guard championship title. Technically, the Second Texas Infantry should have played against the First Wisconsin Infantry, the winner of the 12th Division series. But they previously drubbed them 60-0 during their November game. They had also trounced every other team in the Brownsville District, and found other opponents wherever they could. According to the organization of the Army football series, their regular season was over, and they faced the real possibility there was no one left to play.

The Second Infantry's management traveled to San Antonio to discuss their options with Army football tournament director Walt C. Johnson. There was talk about organizing a match with the winner of the Army-Navy game, but the assembled men agreed it would be a one-sided contest – the Second Infantry would walk over whichever team won. On Johnson's suggestion, they decided the only challenging contest would be against a team of All-Stars picked from the "entire roster of teams at Fort Sam Houston and Camp Wilson." Johnson took charge of organizing the All-Star team from the 16 ball clubs in San Antonio's 12th Division and, with Woodul studying for the bar and preparing for his move as a legislator to Austin, it was left to Stewart and Jim Kendrick to begin negotiating venues.[44]

Promotion for the Gulf Coast Exposition and the first Second Texas Infantry football game against the First Missouri Artillery. Modified from *Corpus Christi Caller and Daily Herald*, Nov. 21, 1916, University of North Texas Libraries, Portal to Texas History.

Walter F. Woodul organized what would be the Second Infantry's first game, played at Camp Scurry at the Gulf Coast Expedition, November 20, 1916, against the First Missouri Artillery football team. Shown is the Missouri football team on the sidelines during a match they lost 33-0. Collection Jim Moloney.

Top: Huddle of the First Missouri Artillery football team at the Gulf Coast Expedition contest in Corpus Christi. Collection Jim Moloney.

Bottom: The Second Texas Infantry (left) lined up opposite the First Missouri Artillery football team (right). Visible in the background are tents of the Gulf Coast Exposition. Collection Jim Moloney.

Several hundred Missouri National Guardsmen, accompanied by their regimental band and supporters, attended the game in Corpus Christi. Here they are shown parading for their team in what was called "the snake dance." Collection Jim Moloney.

Promotion for the December 16, 1916, football match with the First Virginia Artillery, played at Camp Wilson in San Antonio. The Texans won it 53-0. Modified from *San Antonio Express*, Dec. 16, 1916, University of North Texas Libraries, Portal to Texas History, crediting Abilene Library Consortium.

Top: From left to right is end Big Jim Kendrick, halfback Rip Collins, and halfback Spitz Clarke during their Camp Scurry days. Modified from Ratliff, Harold V., *The Power and the Glory: The Story of Southwest Conference Football* (Lubbock: Texas Tech Press, 1957).

Left: Texas Eleven starter and lineman Baker Duncan during his time with the Second Texas Infantry. *Ancestry.com*, https://www.ancestry.com/mediauiviewer/collection/1030/tree/48549124/person/27785991532/media/4a2e8415-708c-4f40-adaacb.7b75c7d9a2.

CHAPTER 6

They Can't Be That Good

By January 2, the Second Infantry's negotiations were bearing fruit. They had arranged three more games, the first organized for January 7 with Walt Johnson's 12th Division All-Star at Camp Scurry's Exposition Park in Corpus Christi. After Charlie Stewart inked the First New York Cavalry team for January 13, Jim Kendrick took the train to the Bayou City to arrange logistics, signing a contract to host the venue at the Houston Buffaloes 4,000-seat West End Park. The final game, against the Texas Field Artillery, was on the calendar for January 20 at Corpus Christi. Then everything changed.[1]

During their first six games, the Second Infantry was entirely responsible for their schedule, arranging their game logistics, and raising money from within their regiment to pay for travel and venues. After their final district game against the 74th New York Infantry, however, they belonged to the Army, or more specifically to Walt C. Johnson. It was Johnson who conceived of a round-robin tournament between the Second Texas Infantry and the 12th Division All-Stars, and it was Johnson with a host of Regular Army higher-ups who now took control of the final weeks of the schedule. Second Infantry managers Bill Birge, Jim Kendrick, and Charlie Stewart found themselves benched.[2]

Names that had never been associated with any Second Infantry football contest were coming out of the woodwork now. Austin High School football coach and self-proclaimed promoter James Goodman, with Johnson's blessing, announced that he had closed arrangements for the 12th Division All-Star game at Austin's Clark Field, rather than Corpus Christi, on January 6. W.E. Long, secretary of the Austin Chamber of Commerce, furthered Johnson and Goodman's efforts with a letter-writing campaign to generals Funston and Hulen. In his reply on January 9, Funston agreed to an Austin venue, then added: "as long as there is no expense to the federal government." Captain William L. Culberson of the Texas Brigade and UT's Athletic Director L. Theo Bellmont – two names absent in Second Infantry football circles to this point – signed the contract designating Austin's Clark Field three days later.[3]

Pre-game jockeying for the First New York Cavalry match was just as divisive. With a contract already in place, Houston had every reason to believe it would host the Second Infantry's final game. The Houston promoters had collected signatures from hundreds of Houstonians on a petition requesting Texas Brigade commander Hulen to hold the game in the Bayou City, and after Kendrick's visit, Houston Baseball Association Secretary Doak Robertson immediately began adding seating at West End Park. Local business leaders had also completed arrangements for "a grand parade," and game day tickets were already printed and on sale at Camp Wilson and Fort Sam Houston.[4]

The deal appeared to be done, but Houston underestimated the influence of another new entry into guard football promotion, Major Charles Tobin of the First New York

Cavalry. Tobin, who called both San Antonio and New York home, snubbed earlier preparations made by the Second Infantry, announcing instead he was sponsoring the New York game in San Antonio. Leaving little to chance, he brought in a publicity manager, Stuart J. Saks, who "set about advertising this game as no game in this section ever before was advertised." The effusive Saks peppered newspaper dailies with a litany of San Antonio advantages, including tempting the Alamo City with visions of two days of festivities sponsored by the New Yorkers that would include bands, parades, cheering, and their play and minstrel show, the "Cavalry Frolics," replete with a cast of a hundred performers and an orchestra.[5]

It seemed everyone had charge of the two big games and at the same time, no one did. In an interview with a *San Antonio Light* correspondent, Walt C. Johnson attempted to quell the confusion. He was less than genuine, however, in his admission that the game dates and venues were still undecided and that the early speculation was "a bit premature." Johnson had, in fact, already worked through the chain of command, and the deals were done. Finally, in an air of mock transparency, the *San Antonio Express* declared that the entire matter was taken for resolution to General Funston who, after "considerable discussion" selected January 16 for the All-Star game at Clark Field in Austin and January 20 as the date for the First New York match in League Park, San Antonio. The Texas Field Artillery game, originally scheduled by the Second Infantry management for January 20 at Corpus Christi, was entirely lost in the jockeying.[6]

Walt C. Johnson may have played logistical hardball, but he deserves credit for recognizing the public relations value of the larger-than-life Second Infantry and how to capitalize on it. Without his vision, it's likely the Texas team would have closed the season with its final game on January 1 and then been largely forgotten. Instead, Johnson pitted them against players from the royalty of America's college and regional pro football programs, and who in many instances were mentioned as Walter Camp All-American contenders. Now, the Texans were taking to the field in the two biggest football games ever played in the South. The main beneficiary of Johnson's farsightedness was the Lone Star State, until now largely ignored in national gridiron circles.

12th Division All-Stars Game. Tryouts for the 12th Division All-Stars were announced in December under the auspice of Walt C. Johnson, chairman of the Army football tournament committee in San Antonio, and his assistants Lt. James Dunbar and R. Scott Israel. Creating the team for "the sole purpose of defeating the Second Texas," they had the pick of 20,000 guardsmen from 16 teams that had competed in the Army series, and who hailed from America's premier gridiron colleges and universities.[7]

Lt. Dwight D. Eisenhower was the choice of head coach from the beginning. Born in Denton Texas, the future US president was appointed to West Point in 1911 and played football for two seasons until he was sidelined by a knee injury. The next year he coached the West Point freshman team. After his transfer to Fort Sam Houston in 1915, he umpired San Antonio area high school games and, as the coach for the Peacock Military Academy, was credited for turning its sports program around. By 1916 he was a coach at San Antonio's St. Louis College. After he accepted the All-Star nod, Eisenhower added Lt. Walmsley as a second coach and Robert Hyatt, the 1911 West Point team captain, as assistant coach.[8]

The Second Infantry made only one adjustment as they prepared for the All-Star contest. During the first week of January, the Texans brought in D.V. "Tubby" Graves, who had recently finished his assistant coaching duties for the Aggie football season. Right end Charles Turner returned for the final two games after a furlough to visit his father in New Mexico.[9]

Before the game, the usually opinionated sports columnists held their tongue. They didn't know what to expect. The resumes of the All-Stars were breathtaking, but the Second Infantry were proven performers. No side seemed favored. The pre-game hype was frenzied, and promoter Walt C. Johnson had every reason to expect that the All-Star game at Clark Field would attract the largest crowd ever to "witness such an event in the Southwest." The game coincided with Texas Governor Ferguson's inauguration, with politicians descending on the city from across the state for the occasion that would be marked by parades and an inaugural ball. General Greene of the 12th Division called for a military holiday and was joined at game time in his private box by Major General Frederick Funston, commander of the Southern Department.[10]

Trains to Austin ran from every Texas city. Ticket sales to students and the public, and advance rail tickets, suggested that attendance would top 3,000 spectators. More than 1,800 Fort Sam Houston soldiers were given passes to the game, and another 300 soldiers from Corpus Christi were expected to accompany the Second Infantry. But, in the end, the response was muted. Only about 2,500 fans were on hand to brave the conditions of a "beastly" cold front that brought rain, ice, and snow. The weather wasn't the only blow to attendance. Most of the Texas Brigade boycotted the game in protest to the involvement of "private promoters" – Johnson and Goodman – who were responsible for moving the All-Star game from Corpus Christi to Austin. Less than 200 Camp Scurry supporters accompanied the team and, to bring further attention to their grievance refused to march in Governor Ferguson's inaugural parade.[11]

The Second Infantry arrived the day before the game to mist and sleet, then went directly to the slippery, muddy field to practice. On game day, January 16, the weather turned worse. Alternating between a mist and downpours, a gusting north wind blew sheets of rain from vertical to horizontal. With the temperature dropping below the 30-degree mark, ice covered the goalposts, and the rain that froze on the field was churned into a muddy slush under the cleats of the combatants.[12]

Rats Watson started behind the center for the Second against Harvard quarterback Robinson for the All-Stars. Right end Jim Kendrick opposed University of West Virginia player J. Willard Ironmonger, who also played against the Second Infantry with the First Virginia Artillery in their fourth game. Baker Duncan at right tackle opposed Catlin, from Wisconsin, and right guard Bill Birge was across from Loos, the 6-foot, 210-pound left guard and a three-year man from the University of Illinois. John Diller opened for the Second Infantry as center, opposing Weidman from Ripon College. On the left side of the line, guard Berry faced Illinois' Lanham, tackle Sylvan Simpson was across from Marquette's R. Johnson, and returning left end Charlie Turner lined up against team captain and West Point star Joseph Merit Tully. In the backfield were Spitz Clarke and Holy Cross' Carmody at right half, Dotson and Northwestern's E. Kuesener at fullback, and at left half Rip Collins and W. Johnson.[13]

The All-Stars won the toss, and the Second Infantry's Collins kicked off. Four downs later Texas had the ball. Watson tossed a short pass to Kendrick who gained 20 yards, but Texas used up its downs and was forced to punt. On their next possession, Watson scrambled across the goal line and Collins kicked the extra point. Watson, Dotson, Clarke, and Collins continued to run over the All-Star defense, their combined running performance ending the first half with the score at 28-0. Although the All-Stars managed two pass interceptions, their offense never made a first down.[14]

In the third quarter, Abbott waltzed across the goal on short yardage, and Collins missed his only extra point of the day. Ahead by 34 points, coach Tubby Graves pulled most of the starters and sent in the reserves. During the final quarter, the Second's replacements fumbled a punt return on their 35-yard line. Sportswriters followed each detail of the only touchdown ever scored against the Second Infantry and the only highlight of the All-Star performance. Substitute Bob Sims, of Washington and Lee, ran a pair of first downs, then carried the ball another 13 yards to within a yard of the goal. Texas held them for two downs until Sims did what no one else had ever done before. Powering through the left side of the line between the center and guard, he crossed the Texan's goal line. Kuesener missed the extra point. The final score was 34-6, and the All-Star's six points marked the only time a team scored against the Second Texas Infantry. Most of the Texas Eleven never forgot that their second and third teams were the ones who allowed the single touchdown that tarnished their perfect record.[15]

Over 35 players were on the All-Star roster at game time, and they hailed from such celebrated football programs as Harvard, Illinois, Northwestern, Virginia, Washington and Lee, West Virginia, Wisconsin, and West Point. The All-Stars did their best at subterfuge. They constantly shifted formations, paid little attention to the formality of positions, and brought in substitutes for specialized plays. In all, they rotated 23 players through the game, including three of their four quarterbacks. The unstoppable Bill Birge forced the All-Stars to exhaust their entire bench strength of five offensive right guards, including the 240-pound, three-year Army man Warden. The Second Infantry played conservative football. Conditions hardly favored a passing game, the mainstay of the Second Infantry with their open offense. Instead, they turned to a running game and their famous "ten-man interference."[16]

That evening, the "Football Special" pulled out of Austin at 7:30 bound for Camp Wilson and San Antonio, with other trains running until late in the night. The players and management of both teams remained until the next day to attend a banquet at the Driskill Hotel hosted by former UT Longhorn football manager and Orange timber baron H.J. Lutcher Stark. The remarkable Second Infantry had just four days to prepare for their final game.[17]

First New York Cavalry Game. Football legend Walter Camp had traveled to Corpus Christi on Christmas Day to observe the attention-grabbing Second Infantry in their contest against the Fourth Minnesota Infantry. He was joined by Red Wilkinson, who was regarded as one of the greatest football players in the world – a two-time All-American and a member of Jim Thorpe's renowned Canton Professionals football team, his play commanding $400 a game. When the game was canceled, Camp returned home while Wilkinson remained in town to do a little New York-style pre-game promotion. Holding court in the lobby of the Nueces Hotel, Wilkinson discoursed on the upcoming First New York Cavalry game. The New Yorkers wanted to organize a side bet, he pronounced, and for every dollar the Second Infantry put up on the game's outcome, they would put up $20. "I have a firm conviction," he crowed, that "they don't know high-class football in the South."[18]

Wilkinson's comments quickly reached Camp Scurry, and he got the desired results when two Second Infantry footballers came for a visit. They took the bet, and with the New Yorker's anteing up $10,000, the Second stood to make a pile of money. For the regular betting public, the odds started at three to one for New York, then shifted to two to one in favor of the Second Infantry after they walloped the 12th Division All-Stars. The margin probably would have reversed in favor of the New Yorkers if the public knew the seriousness of the injuries Jim Kendrick sustained during the All-Star game. Kendrick, after three days, was still in the Camp Scurry field hospital and being treated for a kidney injury. He wanted to play against the New Yorkers so badly, however, that he snuck out and joined his team on the train to San Antonio.[19]

Like the 12th Division All-Stars, the First New York Cavalry football team was put together for the sole purpose of extinguishing the Second Texas Infantry. Its coaches had the pick of any player from each of the New York National Guard companies. The list was daunting. During the previous July, as they mobilized for the border, a writer noted that some 2,000 "athlete members" had enlisted in the New York National Guard. They covered a wide range of sports, including track and field, wrestling, baseball, cycling, rowing – and college and semi-professional football. Many were "topliners," holding Olympic, national, and Gotham City titles in their chosen sports.[20]

When Red Wilkinson announced the formation of the team at McAllen in late December, 60 men tried out, with 40 making the squad. Although the Cavalry had less than a month to whip its team into shape, supporters felt certain that the disadvantage would "be offset by the superiority of the individual men who will comprise the team."[21]

The Cavalry played its first and second games against the 74th New York Infantry – the same beleaguered squad the Texans walloped 102-0 on New Year's Day. In its January 6 match at Pharr, the McAllen squad bested the 74th Infantry by a score of 25-7. The second match was played on Jan. 16, and again they trounced the hapless Infantrymen. Three days later the Cavalry faced off against the Third Iowa Infantry in a contest they won 39-6. Spirits were high as they headed for the rail depot after the game. They would meet the Second Infantry "steam roller" the next day.[22]

Before the match, the press advertised the contest as a clash of styles, pitting "Eastern football," with its strong defense, against the Texas brand of football described with its "open offense." Neither team openly discussed its game strategy. The blustery Red Wilkinson came closest, offering that "we are going to tear in at the whistle, rush Texas off her feet, and drive home a victory before the Infantrymen know the game has started." Later, Wilkinson admitted to Rip Collins that he had instructed his team to keep Collins, Kendrick, and Watson "on the ground" throughout the game. But, as Collins quipped, "his plans went wrong. He had forgotten about Berry, Duncan, Birge, Diller, and Simpson."[23]

The university and college names of the starting and alternate New York players were a who's who of intimidating football programs. Four were from Syracuse, two from Cornell, with a sprinkling of Harvard, Princeton, Buffalo, Pennsylvania, Dartmouth, Indiana, Williams, and even a New York pro football player. The rules of the game were written in some of these blueblood institutions, and their players dominated the All-

America All-Star selections of Yales' legendary Water Camp year after year. There is no evidence that the Second Infantry was nearly as enthralled by their gridiron resumes as the press.

Starting quarterback Rats Watson was listed at 150 pounds instead of his usual 145, but either weight was diminutive compared to the 178-pound, three-year Cornell starter and All-American nominee Eddie Butler. At the end positions, right end Jim Kendrick had a 10-pound advantage over Princeton's player-coach and 1912 All-American Hamilton Andrews. Left end Charlie Turner faced Nathaniel Duffy, of Buffalo, both at 155 pounds. On the right side of the Texas line, tackle Sylvan Simpson opposed Jordan, from Indiana, their weights about even. It was right guard Bill Birge versus Dartmouth freshman Russell Potter, and center John Diller faced Syracuse veteran Ben Forsythe. K.L. Berry, at left guard, was across the line from Bill Canlon, a New York professional footballer, and left tackle Baker Duncan faced Keith Driscoll of Syracuse. The backfield was a match between left halfback Spitz Clarke at 155 pounds and 1914-15 All-American Red Wilkinson at 180, the 210-pound Eugene Dotson overshadowing the 166-pound Syracuse fullback Walter Glass, and right halfback Rip Collins, at 195, faced 186-pound Granny Miller of Cornell.

On the management side, Mike Bloor's equivalent was athletic director Bill Donovan, "the old Columbia star." The New Yorker player-coach was Princeton's Cpl. Hamilton Andrews, and the New York team captain was Sgt. Red Wilkinson, who never used his given name, Marcus E. Wilkinson.[24]

With the eyes of the nation on San Antonio, preparations for the January 20 contest started early. The Menger Hotel was the first stop for Cavalry team manager Edwin H. Lee, publicist Stuart Sachs, and Everett Wood, the director of the Cavalry Frolics, who booked every room for the First New York Cavalry headquarters. Then they checked on preparations for the reserved boxes, grandstands, and the extra bleachers added at San Antonio's baseball field at League Park, called the "old Block stadium."[25]

It was to be a grand affair. General and Mrs. Funston, General Parker and his staff from McAllen, First New York Infantry commander Colonel C.I. De Bevoise, General Hulen and Mayor Roy Miller from Corpus Christi, and every army officer from Camp Wilson and Fort Sam Houston announced their plans to attend. Most in San Antonio's high society regaled more in the ambitious social calendar than the game itself. An elaborate Army dinner and dance was planned at the Menger Hotel for the "hostesses and the young ladies who planned society's welcome to the soldiers," and New York delivered with two Cavalry Frolics shows on Friday and Saturday night at the Empire Theatre.[26]

The day before the game, 900 New York guardsmen and 300 rooters filled 28 cars at the McAllen depot, making it the longest "sleeper train" ever to roll into San Antonio. The Second Infantry was accompanied by 700 Camp Scurry guardsmen, pulling into San Antonio in 18 cars later that evening. On game day, another train brought more fans from the Rio Grande Valley, a second train rolled in from Corpus Christi with another 500 spectators, and still other trains descended on the city from across Texas. There were likely about 15,000 fans who attended the game, although estimates varied from a low of 6,000 to a whopping 25,000.[27]

The New York supporters wore orange arm bands, and most brought megaphones to amplify their game-time cheers and songs. Their fans paraded from the rail depot to their respective hotels, then at game time marched from the Menger Hotel to the field with several bands. At the games' start and at half time, the flashy New Yorkers paraded and exhibited special cheers and stunts they had practiced for the occasion. Their mascot, a Great Dane, appeared more regal on the sidelines than the Second's assemblage of donkeys, dogs, coyotes, and another dozen or so favorite animals from their entourage.[28]

Rats Watson received the kick and ran it to the Texas 20-yard line. The Texans threw the defense completely off guard in their first possession by running four fast plays without calling a signal. On first down, Watson gained 33 yards on a wide scramble around the left end. Fullback Dotson then followed in his footsteps for more yardage, and on third down, another end run by Watson went unchecked. With the ball on the goal line, Dotson plunged into the end zone – the hurdle called a "line buck" in those days – for the TD. Collins kicked the extra point. Texas was up 7-0 on their first possession.

The second quarter opened with Texas on the New York 17-yard line. Dotson and halfback Clarke whittled away at yardage until Dotson carried it over, with Collins booting the extra point. On New York's next possession, end Charlie Turner intercepted a toss by Ham Andrews and ran it 35 yards for a touchdown. Four New York downs gave the Texans the ball again, and Dotson "made a circus baseball catch of a forward pass" for a fourth touchdown. Collins finally missed an extra point. At halftime, the Second Texas Infantry was leading 27-0.

The Texans scored twice in the third quarter on runs by Kendrick and Clarke. With two more successful kicks by Collins, the Texans led 41-0 when the quarter ended. In the final quarter, Watson connected to right end Kendrick for another score, then Watson scrambled across the goal line to give them a 55-point lead. Ock Abbott came in for Watson and continued the assault with a quick handoff to Clarke for another touchdown. Passing and running plays gave the Texans good field positions twice more, with fullbacks Dotson and Berry making critical short ground gains for another pair of touchdowns. The Second Infantry tallied ten touchdowns with only one missed extra point, the final score 69-0.[29]

It was a stunning outcome. Offensively, there was little question that quarterback Watson played his best game ever, running fearlessly with support from the Second's "magnificent, machine-like interference." The Orange High School football star ran through the entire New York team twice for touchdowns and his broken-field kick returns were so unstoppable that the New Yorkers began punting the ball out of bounds to keep him from fielding it.[30]

Defensively, the Second Infantry allowed New York only one completed pass and just three first downs. Their line was "like a rock" and "from under every other scrimmage was dragged an injured New Yorker, attesting to the power of the drive they were sending to futile slaughter." For the first time in his career, Red Wilkinson was forced to leave the game early because of an injury. Later, a contrite Wilkinson told reporters his injury resulted "not of dirty football, but of the hardest football I ever saw played."[31]

Post-game headlines across America heralded the news of the Texans crushing performance, but it was Texas papers that carried the most coverage. One newsman wrote that the game "was the biggest football day the state of Texas ever saw" and another gushed that "Texas has brought out into the limelight the greatest team ever assembled in the South and one of the greatest the country ever knew." Several San Antonio articles allocated space to praise the New Yorkers, who not only organized the social program but won the hearts of the Alamo City "by their attitude and the game manner in which they took the reverse," and who "showed their real sportsmanship and were every bit the gentlemen afterward." That was also true of Red Wilkinson, who reportedly said: "It is a pleasure to have watched such an Eleven in action even though [we were] beaten by it in decisive style."[32]

It Ends. Texas and America never really discovered the world's best football team until its last few games, the team not hitting the peak of its rock star-like reputation until after Christmas. Once the public found them, they couldn't get enough. After the New York Cavalry rout, Walt C. Johnson and the Camp Wilson All-Stars declared a rematch and preliminary talks started for a ninth game on January 27. Laredo, too, was organizing a game between the Second Infantry and Second Florida Infantry for its three-day Washington's Birthday festival in late February. A "flattering offer" was made just days after the New York game for the Second to participate in a two-month playing tour against various colleges and universities in the North and East for the next fall. America had indeed taken notice, but none of the plans would come to fruition.[33]

Few of the followers of the gridiron sport were ready for the Second Infantry season to end. The *San Antonio Express* knew the answer but asked the rhetorical question anyway in its headline: "Will America's Greatest Football Machine Ever Play Again?" The answer was no. The Second Infantry was given a 30-day furlough after the New York game, and on February 17, 1917, General Funston ordered the demobilization of the National Guard, scheduling it to begin in early March and to be finalized by March 26.[34]

The last huddle of the famous Second Infantry would be their return trip on the San Antonio train bound for Corpus Christi on January 21. When they returned to camp, most quickly packed their gear and headed home. The Corpus Christi Elks Lodge had arranged a social program to honor them on January 24 but canceled it when they learned that only Bill Birge, Spitz Clarke, and Pleas Rogers were still in camp.[35]

A farewell banquet was hosted for the players after their furlough on March 8, 1917, at the Nueces Hotel. Although Mike Bloor, Charlie Brown, Bart Coan, Rip Collins, Dan Cook, Whitey Davis, Eugene Dotson, Charley Ogden, Charles Schaedel, and Harry Stullken were unable to attend, the team was well represented. Besides the players, the invitees included Brigadier General John A. Hulen and his staff, and various politicians, businessmen, and others from Corpus Christi and South Texas. The banquet was remembered as a "wild, boisterous night of corks, speeches, awards, and cheers." Toasts were made to their accomplishments, and hopes were expressed for the future. Team members raised a glass while recounting their season with anecdotes and praise. Few of their words, however, were preserved for posterity. Near its conclusion, the Texas Eleven were presented with lapel-sized, diamond-studded football fobs embossed with their game scores and the word "undefeated." Management also bought each player a blue wool sweater and a matching wool blanket, the sweaters bearing the words "Second Texas Infantry, Army Football Champions."[36]

What Made Them So Good? Texas never forgot the Second Texas Infantry. The often team resurfaced in sports columns until the 1960s, and occasionally until as recently as 2013. Most writers explored, and tried to put into words, what made them so much better than their rivals. Teamwork and leadership surfaced in their articles. The journalists also agreed that the team was ahead of its time and had "played a new kind of offense." We must take them at their word. Little that they revealed described precisely, or even generally, what the Second Infantry did differently from other teams of the era.

We know that, on offense, they adopted an open formation characterized by split ends with the quarterback situated in the backfield. Called the kick formation or short punt formation, it is more popularly known today as the shotgun. Their offensive line configuration is unknown other than it consisted of split ends, with both their ends and backfielders eligible pass receivers.

Rats Watson noted that they sometimes switched between the short punt and a "box" offense formation. He didn't elaborate, but it was probably a variation of the Notre Dame "box" or "shift" formation. A later description implies it incorporated an "unbalanced" line geometry to adjust for the defense's perceived strengths and weaknesses. As both the short punt and box formations were already popular with several college teams and not unique to the Second Texas Infantry, the offensive reviews are useful but still shed little light on how the Second Infantry consistently confounded its opposition.[37]

Perhaps it was, in part, because they invented nearly all their own plays. Most were developed by innovative UT engineer Charlie Turner, and it was left to line coach Baker Duncan to figure out what the line had to do to make his designs work. The team debated every new play, then practiced it. Rats Watson said: "We'd get into an argument about a play and to settle it we'd go out to the field, use half of the line against the other half, and run that play until we either proved it would work or found out it didn't." Watson added that although the team's play inventory was small, they executed them perfectly.[38]

Charlie Ogden offered some insights on the running game. He explained it was built around "our unusually fast backs" – the Austin duo of Rip Collins and Spitz Clarke – and relied on the power of backfielders K.L. Berry and Eugene Dotson. Ogden said they executed a lot of "wide end sweeps" in which the guards, instead of protecting the pocket, rushed the defense and immediately went "into interference." For Red Wilkinson, that interference was a crucial part of their offensive success. "Up in my section," he said, "we think a team that has only two men running interference for the ball carrier is poor, one that has three in the interference is fair, while one with four is good. But how are you going to stop a team that gives one man the ball and puts ten men in interference!"[39]

Vic Cook, in his 1937 account, also made a stab at explaining what made the Second Infantry great. For him, it was a combination of their ten-man interference and speed. In his words, the "secret to [their] success" was that, on the snap, the offensive line rolled up into "an entire forward wall." He added that "their broken-field runners were fast," and their "backs could outrun anybody coming from behind, so they concentrated on taking care of those out in front in the offensive lineup."[40]

Another factor was that they kept their opponents on the opposite side of the line entirely off balance with quick turnarounds between downs. A 1955 sports writer remarked that they rarely bothered to call plays, and if they did, they called them on the line. He surmised that the strategy worked only because they knew each other, and the game, exceptionally well.[41]

Was the Texas Eleven a fortuitous collection of the best athletes in the nation? Maybe. Some players were farm boys gifted with athletic ability and hardened by their labor. Others were city boys who developed their skills and countenance in organized sports programs. Sports analysts at the time did not keep it a secret that they thought Rip Collins was the best kicker in America. He didn't have just distance and accuracy but put a spin on the ball that returners simply couldn't field. Later that technique would be called "kick breakaway," and at the time, Collins and Jim Thorpe were the only players who mastered it. Some thought John Diller made more defensive tackles than the "whole team combined," but that was speculation, as no one of that era compiled any statistics. Included in the press list of unparalleled talent were Spitz Clarke, Eugene Dotson, and Big Jim Kendrick.[42]

It was rare for the players to gloat about one of their own. The exception was their universal praise for Rats Watson. Rip Collins recalled that "he would try anything on the field." And he was fast. "When Rats hit an open field," Rip continued, "it was like dropping a cottontail on a stove." Bill Birge was succinct in his admiration. Watson, he said, was "the greatest quarterback who ever cleated a Southern gridiron."[43]

If anyone should have been able to answer the greatness question it was coach D.V. Tubby Graves. He offered his thoughts in a 1959 letter to *Corpus Christi Caller-Times* Sports Editor Louis Anderson, but like those before him, couldn't put his finger on it. His comments were interesting anyway. He said he couldn't take any credit for the success of the team, because "they did not need coaching." Amusingly, he thought what they did need was a mediator. He recalled that "morale was not too high, and they quarreled among themselves," and attributed this to the fact that they hailed from so many different college programs. Graves said his most important contribution was listening to their ideas for offense and defense, then shaping their strategy during the game as he observed the opposing team. In closing, he said his time with the Second Texas Infantry "was a privilege and an honor."[44]

One For the History Books. Joseph E. Chance, author of the *Texas' Greatest Football Team: On the Border with the Texas Second Infantry, 1916-1917* remains convinced that the team's innovative offensive strategies strongly influenced those that followed them. Dr. Chance says that "they did not just overpower their opponents with muscle, they bewildered them as well with plays heretofore unseen on the playing field." The historical record, unfortunately, is so vague that we may never be able to document what, exactly, they did.[45]

Maybe, in the end, it wasn't just one thing but a combination that made the Second Infantry so good. Regardless of how they accomplished it, what's not in question is that the Second Texas Infantry broke entirely new football ground – and put Texas on the American football map. Not just a Lone Star State phenomenon, they fought "interstate and intersectional" gridiron battles and contests that pitted North versus South and East versus West. One sports commentator effused that, after the final game with the New York Cavalry, the Second closed "one of the most spectacular seasons in the history of the game, playing a brand of ball that attracted nationwide attention." Ten years after their last game, commentaries still flowed with words like "the Second Texas Infantry team was a pioneer in Texas' bid for national football fame. It was the outstanding Texas team of 1916, [and] one of the greatest teams in the country for the year and perhaps *the* greatest."[46]

For a time, the Second Texas Infantry name became part of the lexicon of American football. Walter Camp secured its place in sports fame when he declared it "the greatest football team on the American gridiron." America's most renowned football programs also came to respect the name. Famed footballer Knute Rockne, as Notre Dame's coach in 1926, was drawing a play that he thought was impossible to execute and concluded that "even the Second Texas couldn't do that." Yale football spokesman and fullback Ted Coy acknowledged that the Texas Brigade had "the biggest, best disciplined, and most perfectly working piece of football machinery I've ever seen." Red Wilkinson agreed, saying it was "the greatest football team" that he, too, had ever seen."[47]

Sportswriter Homer Olson in 1943, still enamored by the team a quarter century after its final contest, asked Rip Collins if, despite the passage of time, he thought the Second Infantry was still America's greatest football team. Collins settled the debate, at least in his opinion, when he declared that, despite fine performances by other "football elevens" over the years, our "outfit is still the greatest of them all." One reason, he said, was that "the opposition in 1916 was tougher. They wore baseball cleats on their shoes back in those days. And put horseshoes in their shoulder pads." He went on to apologize for the single touchdown made by Bob Sims in the 12th Division All-Star game, explaining to the correspondent that: "The game was played in a blizzard, and they scored against us when we had the fourth string in."[48]

There is no telling how far the 1916-17 Second Texas Infantry football team might have gone if it had another season to play. Given that it had already beaten the best footballers in America, however, perhaps there were no more mountains to climb. In just a single season, the players made sports history, leaving a legacy as a team that AP writer Harold Ratliff, in his immutable style, summed up as "one of the greatest gridiron machines that ever cracked a rib."[49]

Advertisement for the 12th Division All-Star game in San Antonio. Modified from *San Antonio Express*, Jan. 15, 1917, University of North Texas Libraries, *Portal to Texas History*, crediting Abilene Library Consortium.

Below: Promotion for the Menger Hotel festivities celebrating the Second Texas Infantry match against the 12th Division All-Star game in San Antonio. Modified from *San Antonio Express*, Jan. 20, 1917, University of North Texas Libraries, *Portal to Texas History*, crediting Abilene Library Consortium.

Above: Advertisement for the Second Texas Infantry and First New York Cavalry game. Modified from *San Antonio Express*, Jan. 19, 1917, University of North Texas Libraries, *Portal to Texas History*, crediting Abilene Library Consortium.

Left: Early use of celebrity names in advertising (left), in which Harrell's of Austin mentions the Second Texas Infantry in their sales promotion. Modified from *Austin American*, Jan. 15, 1917, University of North Texas Libraries, *Portal to Texas History*.

119

FOOTBALL

BIGGEST ATHLETIC EVENT EVER

HELD IN THE SOUTH

REAL CLASSIC OF THE GRIDIRON

SECOND TEXAS INFANTRY

VERSUS

FIRST NEW YORK CAVALRY

All-Star Southwestern Eleven Against
All-American Selections—Each
Team Undefeated

TODAY LEAGUE PARK 3 P. M.

BIG YELLOW TICKET at $1.00 each entitles bearer to grandstand seat with unobstructed view of the entire field of play. Field now runs diagonally with stands, giving side view of gridiron's entire length.
Tickets on sale at Gunter, St. Anthony and Menger Hotels and at League Park entrance at 1:30 p. m.

400 SIDELINE SEATS AT $1.50 EACH ON SALE TODAY

Promotion for the Second Texas Infantry and First New York Cavalry game, the "biggest athletic event ever held in the South." Modified from *San Antonio Express*, Jan. 17, 1917, University of North Texas Libraries, *Portal to Texas History*, crediting Abilene Library Consortium.

AMUSU THEATRE Today
Matinee 10 Cts.
Night 20 Cts.

Football Returns

From three to five this afternoon we will show at the Amusu bulletins from the football game to be played between Second Texas Infantrymen and First New York Cavalrymen this afternoon at San Antonio.

NO ADDITIONAL CHARGE FOR THIS SERVICE.

Fans who were at the movie theatre in Corpus Christi during the January 20 game could keep abreast of the score with the Amusu Theatre's use of bulletins posted on the big screen, free of charge. Modified from *Corpus Christi Caller and Daily Herald*, Jan. 20, 1917, University of North Texas Libraries, *Portal to Texas History*.

Some of the Texas Eleven starting lineup in the Second Texas Infantry's final game. Upper four players, left to right: K.L. Berry, Rats Watson, Rip Collins, and John Diller. Bottom row three players, left to right: Baker Duncan, coach D.V. Graves, and Charles Turner. Far left: Eugene Dotson. Far right: Sylvan Simpson. Modified from *San Antonio Express*, Jan. 21, 1917, University of North Texas Libraries, *Portal to Texas History*, crediting Abilene Library Consortium.

Some of the players of the Second Texas Infantry ball team during its final two games in 1917. Top row (left to right): Rip Collins, Bill Birge, John Diller, Harry Stullken, Sylvan Simpson, K.L. Berry, Baker Duncan, Charley Ogden, and Victor Bintliff. Front row: Dick Lane, Bud Smith, Rats Watson, Spitz Clarke, Charley Turner, and Whitey Davis. Ock Abbott, Eugene Dotson, Jim Kendrick, and George Lane from the first squad are not pictured. Collection Jim Moloney. Below: The final tally of the Second Texas Infantry football team.

Game	Date	Venue	Opponent	Texas Score	Opponent
1	Nov. 20, 1916	Exposition Park, Corpus Christi	First Missouri Artillery stationed at Laredo	33	0
2	Nov. 25, 1916	Exposition Park, Corpus Christi	First Wisconsin Infantry Regiment stationed at San Antonio	60	0
3	Dec. 9, 1916	Caliche Park, Fort McIntosh, Laredo	First Missouri Artillery "All-Stars" stationed at Laredo	13	0
4	Dec. 16, 1916	League Park, San Antonio	First Virginia Artillery stationed at Camp Wilson	53	0
5	Dec. 21, 1916	Exposition Park, Corpus Christi	Fourth Nebraska Infantry stationed at Llano Grande	68	0
6	Jan. 1, 1917	Exposition Park, Corpus Christi	74th New York Infantry stationed at Pharr	102	0
7	Jan. 16, 1917	Clark Field, Austin	12th Army Division All-Stars, from Camp Wilson and Fort Sam Houston in San Antonio	34	6
8	Jan. 20, 1917	League Park, San Antonio	1st New York Cavalry from McAllen	69	0
			Total	**432**	**6**

	Name	Game 1	Game 2	Game 3	Game 4	Game 5	Game 6	Game 7	Game 8	Total Games
The Texas Eleven	Abbott, Oscar Bergstrom, "Ock"	QB	Sub QB	QB	QB	Sub QB	Sub QB	Sub QB	Sub QB	8
	Berry, Kearie Lee	FBK	FBK	FBK	FBK	Sub FBK	FBK	FBK	LG & FBK	8
	Birge, William S., "Bill"	RE	RG	LT	RG	LG	LG	RG	RG	8
	Clarke, Phillip Soloman, "Spitz"	HBK	QB	RE	HBK	HBK	HBK	HBK	HBK	8
	Collins, Warren, "Rip"	HBK	HBK	HBK	HBK	HBK	HBK	HBK	HBK	8
	Diller, John Cabot	Center	Center	Center	Sub Center	Center	Sub Center	Center	Center	8
	Dotson, Eugene Malcolm	Sub FBK	HBK		Sub FBK	Y FBK	Sub FBK	LG	FBK	7
	Duncan, Addison Baker	LT	LT	Y RG	LT	RT	RT	LT	LT	8
	Kendrick, James Marcellus, "Big Jim"	RE	RE	HBK	RE		RE	LE	RE	7
	Lane, George H.		Sub RE		LE	Y RE	LE	Sub RE	Sub RE	6
	Ogden, Charles Wesley, "Charley" and "June"	LG	LG	LG	LG	Y RG	Sub RG	3rd string FBK		7
	Simpson, Sylvan Blum	RE	RT	RT	RT	LT	LT	RT	RT	8
	Turner, Charles E., "Charlie"	LE	LE	LE				RE	LE	5
	Watson, Grady, "Rats"		3rd string QB		Sub QB	QB	QB	QB	QB	6
Second Squad	Coan, Bart				Sub LE	LE				2
	Gambrell, Tom				2nd string			3rd string HBK	2nd string	3
	Lane, Richard, "Dick"	2nd string	Sub Tackle		2nd string		RG	Sub FBK		5
	Lenoir, Mullie						Sub LG	2nd string	2nd string	3
	Mitchell, Thomas D.						Sub HBK	Sub HBK	2nd string	3
	Nelson, David R.	2nd string	Sub Center		Center		Center		Sub Center	5
	Rogers, Pleasant Blair, "Pleas"		Sub Guard		2nd string			Sub RT	2nd string	4
	Schaedel, Charles T.								2nd string	1
	Stullken, John E., "Harry"				LT					1
Other Players	McConnell		2nd string End							1
	Smith, Schyuler W,. "Bud"							2nd string		1
	Brown, Charlie									0
	Halphen, Tige									0
	Bintliff, Victor									0
	Davis, Howard H., "Whitey"									0
	Stein or Steen, D. or B.							2nd string HB	2nd string	2

Compilation of the Second Texas Infantry football team game and position record,1916-17.

Walter Camp, pictured in 1924, seven years after the Second Texas Infantry played its last game. Football legend Camp had traveled to Corpus Christi on Christmas Day, 1916, to observe the attention-grabbing Camp Scurry footballers in their contest against the Fourth Minnesota Infantry, but the game was canceled. Camp wrote in a letter years later that they were "the greatest football team on the American gridiron." Courtesy *College Football Hall of Fame*, Atlanta, Georgia.

LOST AND FOUND

LOST—RIBBON WATCH FOB, WITH GOLD PLATE CONTAINING FOOTBALL SCORES OF 2ND TEXAS INFANTRY; GOLD FOOTBALL WITH DIAMOND SET; A BLUE "T," 1916, AND MILITARY CHAMPIONS UNDEFEATED ENGRAVED ON BALL, K. L. BERRY ENGRAVED ON BACK, REWARD IF RETURNED TO P. S. (SPITZ) CLARKE, COACH MAIN AVE. FOOTBALL TEAM, HANCOCK HOTEL, OR CALL PHONE 6589.

At the team farewell banquet in March 1917 at the Nueces Hotel, the Texas Eleven were presented with lapel-sized, diamond-studded football fobs embossed with their game scores and the word "undefeated." It was evidently a little hard for some of the players to keep track of them.

Top: K.L. Berry lost his in 1921 when was a captain in the Regular Army and posted as infantry commander at Fort Sam Houston in San Antonio in 1921. He had reconnected with Second Infantry teammate Spitz Clarke when he played against Clarke in the Army-All-Star football game. Likely out of the city on assignment, it was Clarke who posted the advertisement for his lost fob. Modified from *Austin American*, 1921.

Bottom: After his years at UT, Rats Watson returned to Orange in the spring of 1921 to coach at Port Arthur High School when he lost his fob in 1922. Modified from *Orange Daily Leader*, July 13, 1922.

LOST: Diamond set gold football. Return to Grady Watson and receive reward.

CHAPTER 7

The Lost Year

*T*he dizzying 1916-17 football season was over. The Second Texas Infantry expected to return home at any time, but in early February they were still posted at Camp Scurry and still had organized sports on their minds. The soldiers received permission to form a polo team, and matches were being discussed with teams from Camp Wilson and Brownsville. Among the organizers were David Nelson and Pleas Rogers, who had prepared a practice field and were in negotiations to purchase eight polo ponies.[1]

Jim Kendrick took the lead in organizing a baseball team with former footballers Rip Collins, Eugene Dotson, Tom Gambrell, George Lane, and Mullie Lenoir. A field was constructed on the Exposition Grounds, and exhibition games were planned, including one with the Houston Buffaloes with ticket sale proceeds dedicated to the Nueces County Red Cross. The Second's baseball team played a game against the St. Louis Browns, who were in Corpus Christi for spring training. Rip Collins pitched four innings, the Browns winning the match 8-4 in front of 2,000 spectators.[2]

Organization of the new sports teams was abruptly halted when, on February 17, 1917, General Funston ordered the National Guard to muster out, beginning in early March. The 3,100 men of Camp Scurry's Texas Brigade quickly began scattering to their homes to resume civil life. The last of the Corpus Christi activities for the Texas Brigade was a farewell dinner hosted by Corpus Christi businessmen and master of ceremonies, Mayor Roy Miller, to honor the Camp Scurry troops and General John A. Hulen.[3]

Second Texas Infantry Companies E and F left Corpus Christi on March 24. Arriving at the Austin depot, they were greeted by a thousand supporters before marching up Congress Avenue to stack arms in front of the Driskill Hotel. Texas A&M coach Dana Bible wasted no time, meeting Jim Kendrick, Rip Collins, and Spitz Clarke at the Austin train station to let them know that, if they signed up for the remainder of the 1917 spring semester, they would be eligible for the fall Aggie football season. The guardsmen's freedom was short-lived. A week later, on April 1, 1917, Austin newspapers carried the headline "Texas Guardsmen Recalled to Service." America declared war on Germany five days later.[4]

Every town in Texas was struck with patriotic fever and Austin, where the greatest number of young men eligible for wartime service were enrolled in college, was at its epicenter. Several Second Infantry footballers were greatly involved in the University of Texas war preparations. Bill Birge volunteered for campus recruiting and had charge of Austin's citizen's training camp, starting in that role just three days after he arrived home from Camp Scurry. When he drafted a petition with 55 law school student signatures requesting the university permit students to attend officer training programs, the faculty went a step further, sanctioning substitution of military training for regular academic classes. UT had a formal military readiness program, and two of its student body leaders were Dan M. Cook of the university's law program and Sylvan B. Simpson of the Arts and Education Department. Clark Field was converted into a military training camp, where Simpson took charge of drilling a hundred men each morning at 6:00.[5]

Ock Abbott, Kearie L. Berry, Dan Cook, John Diller, Tom Gambrell, Jim Kendrick, Sylvan Simpson, and Charlie Turner were discharged from the guard in late March. Most signed back up before the ink was dry on their papers. Abbott, Berry, Gambrell, and Simpson re-upped in the Regular Army, and the others were back with Companies E and F when they collected in Austin during the first week of April. Company E camped at Fifth and Guadalupe Streets, and Company F at Pease Park before they mustered out in early April. About 3,000 well-wishers bid them off from the train station to Camp Wilson, where the Texas Brigade started their wartime training. There were exceptions, but most of the Second Infantry spent their spring at Camp Wilson and by summer, about half of the former footballers were reposted on the border at McAllen.[6]

While the Texas soldiers sweltered in the summer sun, the War Department was busy reorganizing the National Guard into a numerical structure without reference to the guardsmen's home states. Nearly all the Texas and Oklahoma National Guard was rolled into the 36th and 90th Divisions. The Texas Brigade moniker, on paper at least, was relegated to history when the Second Texas Infantry Regiment became the 36th Division's 141st Infantry Regiment of the 71st Brigade, and the Seventh Texas and First Oklahoma Infantry were combined to form the 142nd Infantry of the 71st Brigade. The Third Texas Infantry Regiment and part of the Fifth Texas Infantry were merged into the 143rd Infantry and assigned to the 72nd Infantry Brigade. Two newly organized machine gun battalions, the 132nd and the 133rd, were assigned to the 71st and 72nd, respectively.[7]

With the Army reorganization complete, the footballers who remained in the National Guard were posted during late summer at either Fort Worth's Camp Bowie as part of the new 36th Division or in the 90th Division at San Antonio's Camp Travis, the new name for Camp Wilson. Both Rats Watson and Rip Collins were absent from the guard's muster roles in 1917. Watson was enrolled at UT for a few months, then rejoined the guard in December. Collins was at Texas A&M during the 1917 fall semester and back on its football team. He played in A&M's 7-0 win over UT in November, then "mysteriously" disappeared from campus. The faculty lost its patience when he would not explain his hiatus, unceremoniously dropping him from the Aggie squad and the college. After a stint in the spring of 1918 in amateur baseball, Collins enrolled at Camp Mabry's School of Auto Mechanics during the summer.[8]

The National Guard soldiers organized football teams during early fall. No one in the press was ready to retire the Second Texas Infantry name, but with most of the former footballers dispersed between McAllen, Camp Bowie, and Camp Travis, there was little of the gridiron rosters that resembled the former Second Infantry. It didn't matter. The pressmen used the name with abandon when covering football matches, and for the first time, they were met with disappointment. The first mention of a so-called Second Texas Infantry gridiron team was during September, when Bill Birge, Spitz Clarke, George Lane, David Nelson, and Pleas Rogers, organized a squad at McAllen. Jim Kendrick was the player-coach, and Victor Bintliff, Tige Halphen, and Bud Smith were on the second team. Every organized football squad at Camp Bowie and Camp Travis expressed an interest in facing them, but before they could, the McAllen guardsmen were transferred to Camp Bowie.[9]

Camp Bowie. Home to the 36th Division, Fort or Camp Bowie covered ten square miles on the high prairie overlooking Fort Worth at Arlington Heights between the West Fork and Clear Fork of the Trinity River. Summers were as brutally hot and dry as winters were cold, the place more hospitable to coyotes and cattle than a base for 18,000 to 27,000 military men. As fall turned to winter in 1917, a remarkable six to 12 soldiers died each day at camp, mainly from pneumonia, measles, and meningitis, and 2,000 men a day filled the base hospital. Contributing to the health problem was that the soldiers lacked overcoats, blankets, socks, and tents until Major General Greble, the Camp Bowie commander, ordered an additional 2,000 tents and dispersed over 100,000 wool socks and 28,000 overcoats and gloves.[10]

The military spared no expense in recreating battlefield conditions at Camp Bowie. Trench school entailed five miles of ditches bounded by wire entanglements that its students captured and recaptured in practice drills 20 times a day. Artillery rocked the long-gun range, machine guns rattled, and the rifle range popped with bolt-action Enfields. The guardsmen practiced hand-to-hand combat and fought in mock battles. The men trained eight hours a day except for Saturday and Sunday, and at the end of each day, officers attended leadership training, French language instruction, and absorbed stacks of War Department literature.[11]

Camp Bowie Football. The roster of the reorganized McAllen team at Camp Bowie, in addition to six starters from the former Second Infantry, was filled with players from other Texas locations and some from other states. Although the football team they organized was technically the 141st Infantry gridiron team, the media still called it "the famous Second Texas." The team began practicing in a field "strewn with rocks" and although they had little equipment, "the way those boys hit each other and the ground in their bare arms and undershirts provided that the spirit is there."[12]

The 141st won their first two games, then opened the Dallas State Fair in October in a game against the First Texas Field Artillery. They won their third match 21-0, although it was a "rough game, with numerous suspensions on both sides." The 141st then won its fourth game against Texas Christian University at Panther Park in November. In their 14-7 victory, Jim Kendrick scored one of the touchdowns and kicked both extra points.[13]

Still unable to accept that the 141st Infantry was not the same team as the Second Texas Infantry, sports headlines announced that the famous Second Infantry "met with grief" in its first-ever loss to Waco's Camp Mac Arthur by the lopsided score of 19-0. Then on Thanksgiving Day, the 111th Engineers defeated the 141st with a drop kick through the goalposts that decided the contest by a score of 3-0. According to sports analysts, it was the end of an era.[14]

Camp Travis. The 90th Division trained at Camp Travis on 18,290 acres located northeast of downtown San Antonio and adjacent to Fort Sam Houston. The first troops arrived in late August and by mid-October numbered about 31,000 officers and men. Originally composed of Texas and Oklahoma guardsmen, by 1918 it was represented by soldiers from other states. In addition to instruction in trench warfare and rifle practice, the 90th Division established specialized training in gas defense, signaling, physical exercise, and field sanitation, and its officers studied French. Like Camp Bowie, illnesses plagued the camp. The 90th Division was also challenged by the number of men who were transferred to other commands to fill their wartime quotas. Eugene Dotson, Dick Lane, and Sylvan Simpson, for example, were reassigned to the 36th Division at Camp Bowie in 1918, and Capt. John Diller was transferred to Camp Grant in Rockdale, Illinois as an instructor before rejoining the 36th in Europe.[15]

Camp Travis Football. The 90th Division at Camp Travis also formed a football team during the fall, its roster composed of players from nearly every Texas college, and players from Alabama, New York, and Virginia. Four former Second Infantry footballers were represented at most of their games, including John Diller, Eugene Dotson, Dick Lane, and Sylvan Simpson.

The 90th Division built a stadium at Camp Travis, scheduling a much-publicized contest with the Kelly Field Aviators in San Antonio for Thanksgiving Day. Some 20,000 fans, in a mix of military drab with the colors of civilian life, packed the stands and sidelines. Airplanes circled the stadium, then flew low over the field dropping footballs with bomber-like accuracy. When the Camp Travis Eleven mascot goat was paraded to the Aviator's side the stands erupted, with fans swarming the field to seize it. It took a squad of military police to restore order, the coveted but confused goat remaining under police protection for the duration of what was a well-played, close contest.

Camp Travis won in the last minutes of the game 12-7. Fullback Eugene Dotson played brilliant ball and contributed to both touchdowns. It must have reminded John Diller of his days at UT when Gus Dittmar took the first squad center honors, with Diller moving to right guard.[16]

Despite the hyperbola around its four celebrated players, the Camp Travis 90th Division Eleven lost games. One was in early November against the Camp Mac Arthur Eleven, a game that was neck and neck until a fourth-quarter safety that broke the 7-7 tie, giving the Mac Arthur team a 9-7 victory. Still infatuated by the great Second Texas Infantry football team, the *San Antonio Express* headlines for the Fifth US Engineers football match against Camp Travis, scheduled at Camp Scurry for New Year's Day, carried the news that Eugene Dotson, "star of Second Texas Infantry, will be in the lineup." They lost 14-3.[17]

Training for War. Between their induction into the National Guard and eventual mobilization to the Western Front, members of the Second Texas Infantry football team were recognized with promotions, and many were nominated to the venerated three-month officer training program at Camp Stanley in Leon Springs. Of the team management, athletic director Mike Bloor was promoted to colonel of the Seventh Texas Infantry in the summer of 1917 and given command of the 142nd Infantry at Camp Bowie. Manager Dan Cook and business manager Charlie Stewart attended Leon Springs officer training and were commissioned as captains. Capt. Stewart was reassigned to the 90th Division Headquarters, Infantry Reserve Corps, as an OTC instructor at both Leon Springs and Camp Travis. Walter F. Woodul resigned his seat in the Texas House of Representatives to join the newly formed First Texas Cavalry as a First Lieutenant before he was promoted to major and designated as the 36th Division Assistant Adjutant General stationed at Camp Bowie.[18]

Of the 14-member Second Infantry starting football squad, 12 were promoted to captains. Oscar Abbott was commissioned as a captain in the Regular Army and spent

1917-18 at Fort Sam Houston. Captain Bill Birge was given command of Company D of the 141st Infantry and was second in command of Camp Bowie. Other captain promotions during 1917 and early 1918 were awarded to Kearie Berry, Rip Collins, John Diller, Eugene Dotson, Baker Duncan, Jim Kendrick, Charley Ogden, Sylvan Simpson, Charlie Turner, and Rats Watson. Spitz Clarke and George Lane were both promoted from second to first lieutenants. Former first-squad footballers Birge, Clarke, Kendrick, George Lane, and Simpson were assigned to the 36th Division 71st Infantry during the summer of 1918. Diller, Dotson, Simpson, and Turner were moved to the 90th Division. When Collins and Watson returned to the National Guard, Collins served in the Mechanics Brigade and Watson in the 36th Division 61st Field Artillery.[19]

Whether they were in the National Guard or Regular Army, the Second Texas Infantry leaders on the football field brought their leadership skills to the war. Besides those who commanded regiments and companies, several former first squad players were assigned as trainers and recruiters. Capt. Berry was an instructor in the 141st and was also assigned intermittently to the Fort Sam Houston training program before he was commissioned in the 21st Infantry, Regular Army, at San Diego. Capt. Birge had charge of recruiting and the citizen's training camp in Austin and oversaw the guard's civilian training program at Camp Mabry from May to June in 1917. Capt. Duncan transferred from Camp Travis to the Army Training Center at Fort Lee, in Petersburg Virginia. Charles Ogden was commissioned in the Regular Army as an instructor in the 57th Infantry Division at Camp Logan in Houston. In February 1918, Lt. George Lane and Lt. Spitz Clarke were in Austin as recruiters.[20]

Of the nine-member second team, Capt. Tom Gambrell, Lt. Dick Lane, and Lt. David Nelson received officer commissions at Leon Springs. Nelson, who transferred from the 141st to Bloor's 142nd, was a recruiter at the Brenham National Guard office. In 1918 he received a captain's promotion and was named as a Leon Springs instructor. Pleas Rogers and Tom Mitchell were promoted from Second to First Lieutenants at Camp Bowie in December 1917. Both were initially assigned to machine gun companies, with Lt. Rogers reassigned to General Henry Hutchings' Brigade Headquarters Battalion at Camp Bowie as an aide-de-camp. John Erwin Stullken was commissioned as a lieutenant in the Regular Army's Sixth Division, 52nd Infantry, at Fort Bliss. Bart Coan, who was in the 143rd Infantry at the beginning of the war before transferring to the 144th, earned his first sergeant stripes.[21]

Victor Bintliff, Charlie Brown, Whitey Davis, Tige Halphen, and Bud Smith of the third squad can also be tracked through their military service before and during World War I. Second Infantry Company E Private Victor Bintliff was promoted to sergeant when he joined the 36th Division's 71st Brigade 141st Infantry Regiment. Private Charlie Brown was at Camp Bowie with the 36th Division, 61st Field Artillery in the 131st Field Artillery Regiment. Whitey Davis was promoted to first lieutenant and in the 141st Infantry. Bud Smith was also in the 141st Infantry and was selected as an artillery instructor at the Third Officers Training Camp at Camp Bowie. Tige Halphen would be the Second Texas Infantry's first casualty.[22]

It was a blow to the UT faculty and student body when the *Austin American* reported the death of substitute player Cpl. Louis "Tige" Halphen in 1918, one of eleven soldiers killed when a trench mortar exploded during a gunnery drill at Camp Bowie. The newspaper was wrong. The San Marcos native had narrowly survived but lost an eye and an ear. From his Fort Worth hospital bed three weeks later, the 141st Brigade sergeant had two requests. One was to trim his good ear to match the prosthetic one, that now stuck out "like an elephant's." The second was that he desperately wanted to remain in active service. He got his wish on the ear surgery, but the military medical examiners ruled he was no longer fit for overseas duty. They did advise him, however, that he could remain as an instructor, with one officer remarking: "We would rather have you with one eye than lots of fellows we have with two."[23]

Gathering Clouds. Sandwiched between headlines of football scores and tensions with Mexico from 1914 to 1916 were the key events that would precipitate America's involvement in World War I. In June 1914, Austro-Hungarian Archduke Franz Ferdinand and his wife were assassinated by a Bosnian Serb nationalist. The next month, Austria-Hungary declared war on Serbia. By August, the Central Powers of Germany, Austria-Hungary, and Bulgaria were at war with the Allied Powers of Great Britain, France, Belgium, Russia, Romania, Canada, and Japan. Within a few months, the Ottoman Empire entered the war on the side of the Central Powers with Italy joining the Allied Powers. On May 7, 1915, a German U-boat torpedoed the British luxury passenger liner *Lusitania*. Of its 1,959 passengers, 1,198 drowned, the death toll including nearly 200 Americans.

Although US President Woodrow Wilson won a second term in 1916 on a neutrality platform, it was clear America was on a collision course with the Central Powers. Pressure from the Allies to join the conflict was enormous. Germany had proposed an alliance with Mexico, opening a wound only recently beginning to heal after the Punitive Expedition and Bandit Wars. Then, on April 1, 1917, German torpedoes sunk the American cargo ship *Aztec*, killing 28 Americans. The next day, Wilson called a joint session of Congress requesting the Senate and House pass a resolution declaring war with Germany. On April 6, 1917, America was officially at war but hardly prepared. The Regular Army numbered just 130,000 officers and enlisted men and the National Guard about 180,000. Another 2,800,000 men would be drafted over the next 19 months.[24]

The order directing the 36th Division to Europe came on July 2, 1918, and on July 3rd an advance party left Camp Bowie for the foreign theatre. The movement of the main body of the division occurred between July 8 and July 26, 1918, with most of the regiments embarking from Halifax, Hoboken, and Newport News for Brest, France. For most of the 36th, it was the first time they'd ever seen the Atlantic Ocean and the first time they had ever been at sea. As the coastline of North America disappeared in their wake, a long year had passed since the footballers were recalled to the National Guard, and it had been 18 months since they played their final game as the Second Texas Infantry.

TEXAS

CAMP BOWIE
Ft Worth

Neches
River

Brazos
River

Trinity
River

CAMP MABRY
Austin

San Jacinto
River

Colorado River

Houston

CAMP LOGAN

CAMP STANLEY
(Leon Springs)

FORT SAM
HOUSTON
CAMP TRAVIS
(Camp Wilson)

San Antonio

Guadalupe

La Vaca River

Navidad River

River

San Antonio River

Nueces

River

Rio Grande

CAMP
SCURRY

Gulf of Mexico

McAllen

Miles
0   25   50

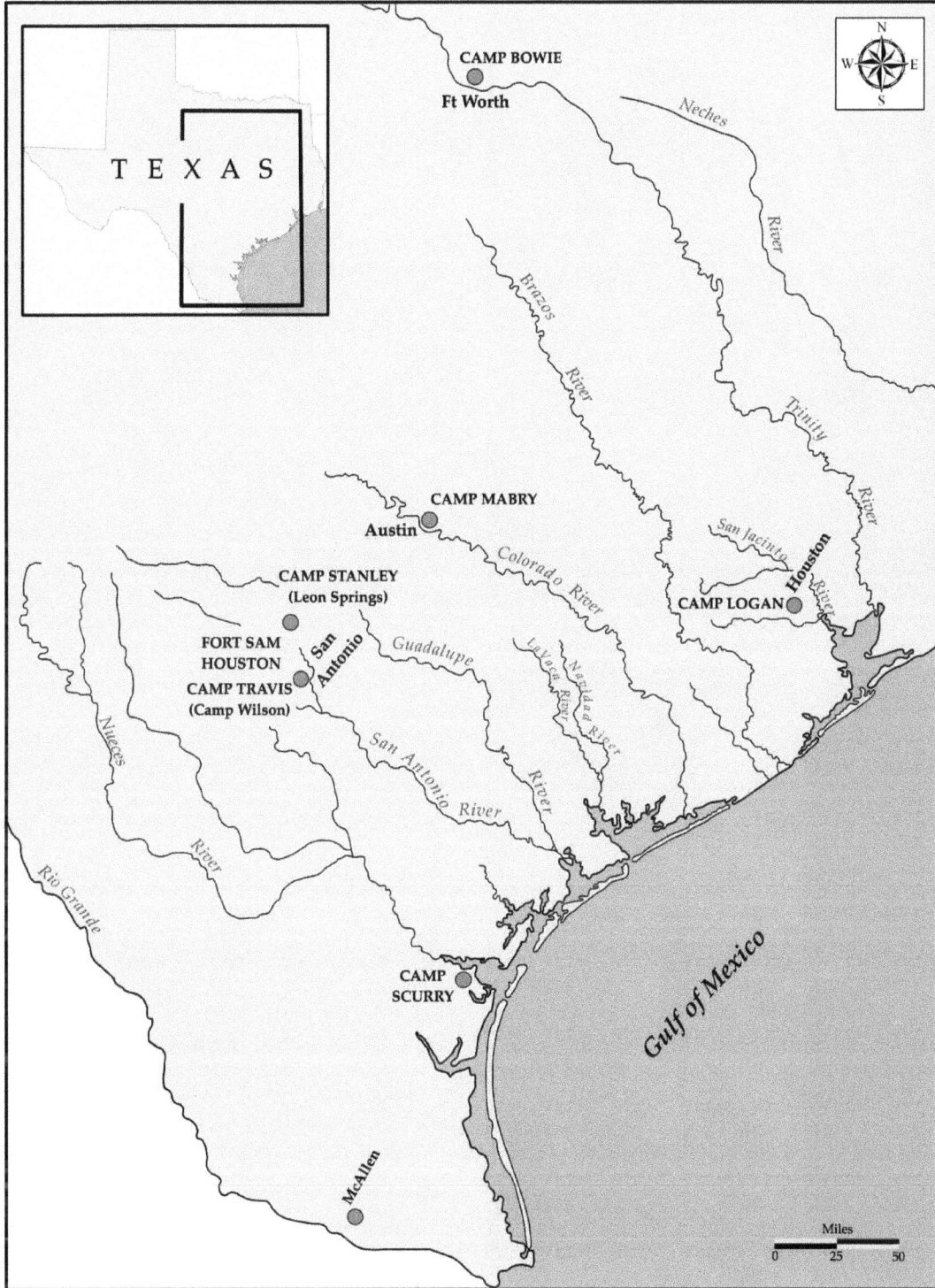

Location of the main National Guard and Regular Army encampments where the Second Texas Infantry, reorganized as part of the 36th Division, received combat and officer training during 1917 and early 1918. Camp Travis was the new name given to what was Camp Wilson. Drawing by R.K. Sawyer.

133

After his National Guard border posting, Kearie Lee Berry attended officer training school and was commissioned in the Regular Army. "Brig. Gen. Kearie Lee Berry," *Swhitesuela Family Tree,* https://www.ancestry.com/family-tree/ person/ tree/12063937/person/332061342350/facts.

Second Texas Infantry center John Diller attended Leon Springs officer training school, received a captain promotion, and was transferred to the 90th Division before World War I. "John Diller Family Tree," *Ancestry.com*, https://www.ancestry.com/ mediaui-viewer/collection/1030/tree/6955720/person/1194662746/media/e52566d7-a90f-4792-beac-44874080 4b58.

Charles W. Ogden Jr. was commissioned in the Regular Army as an instructor in the 57th Infantry Division at Camp Logan in Houston. "Margaret Ogden Welch Family Tree," *Ancestry.com*, https:// www. ancestry.com/mediauiviewer/collection/1030/tree/193 79203/person/292010061444/media/ea3997d8-542e-4689-8514-f285e952e805.

36th Division, 61st Field Artillery, 131st Machine Gun Battalion at Camp Bowie, Fort Worth, 1917-18. Substitute player Pvt. Charlie Brown was assigned to the 131st Regiment. *National Archives and Records Administration*, No. 165-WW-149C-11, NARA 31476101.

Top: Artillery drill at Camp Bowie, 1917-18. "The WW I Era, Mobilizing for War, April-Nov. 1917," *US Army Center of Military History*, www.history.army.mil.

Bottom: Bayonet practice at Camp Bowie, 1917-18. "The WW I Era, Mobilizing for War, April-Nov. 1917," *US Army Center of Military History*, www.history.army.mil.

Top: Members of the 143rd Regiment washing dishes after mess at Camp Bowie, 1917-18. Charles Schaedel was assigned to this regiment. "The WW I Era, Mobilizing for War, April-Nov. 1917," *US Army Center of Military History*, www.history.army.mil.

Bottom: Fire drill at San Antonio's Camp Travis, 1917-18. "The WW I Era, Mobilizing for War, April-Nov. 1917," *US Army Center of Military History*, www.history.army.mil.

Lt. Colonel A.W. "Mike" Bloor was second in command of the Second Infantry Regiment in 1916 and had charge of the 142nd Regiment during the Great War. "The Gateway to Oklahoma History," *Oklahoma Historical Society*, https://gateway.okhistory.org/ark:/67531/metaD.C.1616856.

Louis "Tige" Halphen while he was a private in the Second Texas Infantry National Guard. During "the lost year" Cpl. Louis "Tige" Halphen was badly wounded when a trench mortar exploded during a gunnery drill at Camp Bowie. Collection Jim Moloney.

	Name	College Before 1916	1916 Guard Regiment	1916 Guard Company	1917 Posting	1918 Posting	WW I Division	WW I Brigade	WW I Regiment	Served
The Texas Eleven	Abbott, Oscar Bergstrom "Ock"	Texas A&M	Second TX Infantry	Unknown	Leon Springs-Transferred to Cavalry	19th Infantry, Fort Sam Houston	Regular Army, Fort Sam Houston			Stateside
	Berry, Kearie Lee	UT	Second TX Infantry	F	Leon Springs-ORC	21st Infantry, San Diego	Regular Army, Camp Kearny			Stateside
	Birge, William S., "Bill"	UT	Second TX Infantry	F	Camp Mabry-McAllen-Camp Bowie	Camp Bowie	36th	71 Infantry	141 Infantry	Meuse-Argonne
	Clarke, Phillip Soloman, "Spitz"	UT	Second TX Infantry	E	McAllen-Camp Bowie	Leon Springs-Camp Bowie	36th	71 Infantry	141 Infantry	Meuse-Argonne
	Collins, Warren, "Rip"	Texas A&M	Second TX Infantry	F	A&M	Camp Mabry-Leon Spings	36th	Auto Mechanics Brigade		Unknown
	Diller, John Cabot	UT	Second TX Infantry	F	Leon Springs	Camp Travis	90th/36th	180/71 Infantry	141 Infantry	Meuse-Argonne
	Dotson, Eugene Malcolm	Baylor	Second TX Infantry	Unknown	McAllen-Camp Travis	Camp Travis	90th/36th	180/71 Infantry	345 MG/132[1]	Meuse-Argonne
	Duncan, Addison Baker	UT	Second TX Infantry	F	Waco Home Guards-Leon Springs	Camp Travis	Fort Lee, Virginia			Army Training Center
	Kendrick, James Marcellus, "Big Jim"	Texas A&M	Second TX Infantry	G	McAllen-Camp Bowie	Camp Bowie	36th	Fifth Artillery Observation School		AEF Division HQ
	Lane, George H.	Texas A&M	Second TX Infantry	K	McAllen-Camp Bowie	Camp Bowie	36th	71 Infantry	141 Infantry	Meuse-Argonne
	Ogden, Charles Wesley, "Charley" and "June"	UT	Second TX Infantry	F	Leon Springs-Camp Bowie	Camp Logan	Regular Army, 57th Infantry			Stateside
	Simpson, Sylvan Blum	UT	Second TX Infantry	F	Leon Springs-Camp Bowie-Camp Travis	Camp Bowie	Regular Army, 85th Infantry, 165th Depot Brigade			Stateside
	Turner, Charles E,. "Charlie"	UT	Second TX Infantry	F	Leon Springs-Camp Bowie	Camp Bowie	90th	180th Infantry	345th MG	Meuse-Argonne
	Watson, Grady, "Rats"	South-western	Third TX Infantry	K	UT-Camp Bowie	Leon Springs-Ft Sam Houston	36th	61 Field Artillery	111 Engineers	St. Mihiel & Meuse-Argonne

This page and the next: Summary of the Second Texas Infantry players, noting their university affiliation before the National Guard, 1916 guard regiment and company, posting during "the lost year," and World War I service.

	Name	College	Regiment	Co.			Div.			Location
Second Squad	Coan, Bart	Rice	Third TX Infantry	A	Camp Travis	Camp Bowie	36th	72 Infantry	144 Infantry	Meuse-Argonne
	Gambrell, Tom	UT	Second TX Infantry	F	Leon Springs	Camp Bowie	Infantry ORC			Stateside
	Lane, Richard, "Dick"	None	Second TX Infantry	E	Leon Springs-Camp Travis	Camp Travis	90th/36th	180/71 Infantry	345 MG/132[1]	Meuse-Argonne
	Lenoir, Mullie	None	Second TX Infantry	E	Unknown	U of Alabama; Camp Bowie	36th	71 Infantry	141 Infantry	Unknown
	Mitchell, Thomas D.	Baylor	Second TX Infantry	F	McAllen-Camp Bowie	Camp Bowie	36th	71 Infantry	132 MG	Meuse-Argonne
	Nelson, David R.	None	Seventh TX Infantry[1]	HDQ	McAllen-Camp Bowie-Leon Springs	Officers Traning Camp	36th	71 Infantry	142 Infantry	Meuse-Argonne
	Rogers, Pleasant Blair, "Pleas"	UT	Second TX Infantry	E	McAllen-Camp Bowie	Camp Bowie	36th	71 Infantry	141 HDQ	Meuse-Argonne
	Schaedel, Charles T.	Texas A&M	Third TX Infantry	G	Unknown	Unknown	36th	72 Infantry	143 Infantry	Unknown
	Stullken, John E., "Harry"	UT	Second TX Infantry	F	Fort Bliss	Fort Leavenworth	Regular Army, 64th Infantry, 21st Machine Gun Battalion			Meuse-Argonne
Other Players	Bintliff, Victor	None	Second TX Infantry	E	McAllen	Camp Bowie	36th	71 Infantry	141 Infantry	Meuse-Argonne
	Brown, Charlie	Texas A&M	Second TX Infantry	K	Camp Bowie	Camp Bowie	36th	61 Field Artillery	131 Field Artillery	Artillery Training Camp
	Davis, Howard H., "Whitey"	UT	Second TX Infantry	F	Camp Bowie-ORC	Camp Bowie	36th	71 Infantry	141 Infantry	Meuse-Argonne
	Halphen, Tige	None	Second TX Infantry	E	McAllen	Camp Bowie	36th	71 Infantry	141 HDQ	Stateside
	Smith, Schyuler W,. "Bud"	UT	Second TX Infantry	F	McAllen-Camp Bowie	Leon Springs	36th	71 Infantry	141 Infantry	Meuse-Argonne
Management/Coaches	Bloor, Alfred Wainwright, "Mike"	A&M and UT	Seventh TX Infantry[2]	HDQ	Camp Bowie	Camp Bowie	36th	71 Infantry	142 Infantry	Meuse-Argonne
	Cook, Dan	UT	Second TX Infantry	F	Leon Springs	Camp Bowie-Camp Travis	36th	71 Infantry	141 Infantry	Unknown
	Stewart, Charles B.	UT	Second TX Infantry	F	Leon Springs OTC Instructor	Camp Travis OTC Instructor	90th	HDQ	Infantry Reserve Corps	Unknown
	Woodul, Walter F.	UT	Second TX Infantry	F, I	1st Texas Cavalry	Texas Asst. Adj. General	36th	Texas Asst. Adj. General, Camp Bowie		
	Seay, James B.	UT	Second TX Infantry	Unknown	Camp Bowie	Base Hospital No. 84	Army Surgeon's Offfice			AEF

1. Dotson, Lane, and Mitchell's 132nd Machine Gun Battalions served with Bloor's 142nd Brigade.
2. The Seventh Texas Infantry was formed during the summer of 1917 after it was disbanded at the end of the Civil War.

CHAPTER 8

From Gridiron to Battlefield

*W*hen America entered the Great War, the Western Front of occupied France extended from near the Belgian-French border on the English Channel to the France-Germany boundary close to the Rhine River, a distance greater than 300 miles. For four long years, the Allied forces had fought the advance of the Central Powers along this crescent-shaped boundary. The United States began putting boots on the ground on the Western Front in the spring of 1918 under former Punitive Expedition leader John J. "Black Jack" Pershing.

Most of the former Second Texas Infantry footballers would serve in France as part of General Pershing's American Expeditionary Forces, or AEF, when the Allies initiated a series of joint attacks along the entirety of the Western Front in late September called the "Grand Allied Offensive." The sector under American command was termed the Meuse-Argonne where, for 47 days between September 26 to November 11, 1918, over one million AEF soldiers participated in what was, up to that time, the largest and bloodiest battle in US military history. The seven-week campaign cost American Gold Star mothers 26,277 dead sons and another 95,786 who were wounded.[1]

The Footballers on the Front. After their Atlantic crossing the guardsmen of the 71st and 72nd Brigades were sent to the 13th Training Area at Bar-sur-Aube, southeast of Paris. Here they readied for battle from mid-August until September 26, 1918, their training cut short by the start of the Meuse-Argonne Offensive. The First American Army initiated the AEF's offensive along a line bounded by the Argonne Forest on the west and Verdun on the east. The 71st and the 72nd Brigades were with the French Army Group Centre (GAC) in the Champagne region and positioned on the left flank of the First American Army. On October 6, the 36th Division was ordered to push an offensive and extract the Germans from St. Étienne village and the heights of Blanc Mont north of St. Étienne.[2]

Battle of St. Étienne. The 141st Infantry was commanded by Major Edwin G. Hutchings with Captain Bill Birge second in command. The 142nd was under Colonel Mike Bloor. With the 141st on the right and the 142nd to its left, the 71st Brigade advanced towards St. Étienne in the early hours of October 7. Hutching and Birge's 141st took a dirt road towards the Army's Second Division during the night. With no food or water, they slept as best they could as artillery fire exploded between them. On the morning of October 8, they "went over the top," scrambling forward through the mud, searching for any foxhole or dugout to avoid being cut down by the incessant machine gun fire. As they advanced, they were hit with a concentrated barrage of shelling of live and gas rounds. The first casualty was commander E.G. Hutchings, who was killed by an artillery fragment. Bud Smith, who was next to him when he died, was wounded minutes later. The 141st dug in on the edge of St. Étienne, where Captain Birge assumed command of the regiment.[3]

Mike Bloor's 142nd was on the left flank during the St. Étienne advance, and he provided a detailed account of the 36th Division during the Meuse-Argonne campaign in a series of articles published in 1919. On the road to St. Étienne, he wrote, the Texas and Oklahoma guardsmen faced an enemy ensconced in wooded hills, trenches, a cemetery, and a landscape laced with wire entanglements. Although the Germans were deeply entrenched and resisted their push with heavy machine gun fire and artillery, his 142nd succeeded in taking a tree-lined hill and then the cemetery. They continued towards St. Étienne, but sniper fire from the church tower and machine gun nests and rifle fire erupting from trenches fortifying the town checked their movement and forced a retreat by nightfall.[4]

On the first day of the St. Étienne battle, the 71st Infantry Brigade suppressed 75 machine gun nests and captured over 600 prisoners, but it was the deadliest day of the campaign. The 141st and 142nd suffered casualties of 66 officers and 1,227 enlisted men – between a quarter and a third of its fighting strength. One marine summed up the battle with: "They were green untried troops who charged in reckless ignorance and won. They paid a price in taking Saint-Étienne." Bloor, who thought the carnage that day was avoidable, disagreed.[5]

Colonel Bloor alleged that, when the 36th Division was ordered to engage the enemy, it inherited a badly organized battle plan with poor preparation. Sector maps were unavailable and the guides they relied on for reconnaissance got lost, forcing the 71st to march and counter-march through the night on the eve of the battle. Orders were late in arriving and communication was hindered when the signal platoon also got lost. The expected artillery support missed their targets. Of the French tanks sent to support the position, only six made it to the field. But the French officer in command of the tanks was killed, and the other five were either crippled by enemy fire or withdrew.[6]

The 143rd and 144th Regiments of the 72nd Brigade entered the fight on October 10 and, pushing ahead of the 71st, managed to finish dislodging the Germans at St. Étienne. The 72nd then fought a rear-guard action between St. Étienne and Machault as the Germans retreated on October 11, the withdrawing enemy moving north to occupy a new defensive line on the south bank of the Aisne River east of Attigny. Reorganized and resupplied, the 71st marched east of Machault in the wake of the 72nd through a countryside that was a smoking ruin of enemy wire, bombed bunkers, and buildings reduced to stone and wood rubble. At dusk the 71st bivouacked in a valley southeast of Dricourt with no shelter or blankets, spending a cold, sleepless night in a steady rain. As Bloor looked over his regiment, he was shocked by its losses.[7]

Battle of Forêt-Ferme. By October 13, the 143rd and 144th took a position between Vaux Champagne and Attigny south of the Aisne River and west of the German stronghold at Forêt-Ferme. During their advance, the 144th Regiment took the brunt of the casualties, with 207 officers and men killed or wounded. Bart Coan, a first sergeant in the 144th, described what his regiment endured in the Aisne Valley to a *San Angelo Morning Times* reporter twenty years after the battle. With no shelter from machine gun fire or bursting shells, the 144th dug trenches in a cabbage field as their numbers were whittled away by enemy fire for over ten days. His depiction of the "men's fear and courage and reactions" within "a thunderous world" was particularly poignant, as well as his account of how he refused to leave the battlefield, despite his wounds, because he was the only officer remaining to lead the badly shot-up outfit.[8]

The 71st Brigade moved to the east of the 72nd through the rolling hills of Chargeny and into open terrain dotted with farms and the small villages of Chufilly and Mery. On the night of October 18, they dug into a new position on the flank of the 72nd directly in front of the German line. Four days later, on October 22, Bloor and the 142nd relieved the French on the right, leaving the 141st positioned to its left. They waited five days while the 36th commanders pored over maps and developed their plan. The shortcomings that plagued the St. Étienne battle a little over two weeks earlier would be corrected before the battle of Forêt-Ferme.

The German's Aisne River position was well defended, extending from Forêt-Ferme, on the west meander of the Aisne River, for a mile to the east river bend. They had cut trees to improve their field of fire, and stretched three rows of barbed wire, each about 20 feet thick, that now separated the German line from the advancing Allies. Trenches that were fortified by concrete bunkers and artillery ran most of the way between the river meanders. More than thirty machine gun nests defended the high ground. Across the river, German artillery rained alternating volleys of mustard gas shells and live rounds with deadly accuracy from the hilltop town of Voncq.[9]

In historian Peter Larsen's 36th Division compilation, on the day of the attack, October 27, the weather was sunny and clear. Allied assault troops had moved forward into the front line before sunrise. German positions were closely monitored for any changes to their routine that might indicate the enemy was expecting their advance. In the late afternoon, five German planes flew over American lines. Nothing they saw caused alarm. Shadows were lengthening over the Aisne River Valley when, at 4:10 a single cannon fired from the Allied side, signaling the beginning of a devastating barrage of "masterfully placed" artillery fire concentrated on the enemy position. Smoke shells formed a black curtain around the bend in the river to obscure the German field of fire. The mortar battery started firing, and French artillery pounded German observation posts on Voncq and other vantage points. German artillery opened on the Allies but was mostly ineffective.

Larsen wrote that the 71st left their trenches at 4:30. Engineers crawled forward, cutting barbed wire while the infantry advanced under a cover of Allied machine gun fire directed just above their heads. The smoke screens continued to reduce the accuracy of the German machine gunners and artillery, allowing machine gun teams to carry their weapons forward through the wire barriers and closer to the enemy's concrete bunkers. Infantrymen leaped into German trenches with grenades and fixed bayonets, followed by fire teams that moved through the maze, reducing the threat in every corner.[10]

According to Colonel Bloor, the Forêt-Ferme fight lasted just 30 minutes. During that short, intense time, his 142nd reduced 16 bunkers and took 108 prisoners at a cost of 24 men killed or wounded. It would be the last engagement of the 71st. On October 28, after three weeks of service on the Western Front, the 71st Brigade was relieved by the French Army and counter-marched 150 miles to join the US First Army Reserve. The 72nd Brigade was held in reserve for the final Meuse-Argonne assault, but Germany was withering after seven weeks of combat. Between late September and November 11, the Grand Allied Offensive had pushed the Germans back as much as 60 miles along 200 miles of the Western Front. Occupied Western France was now Allied territory. Germany signed the Armistice that ended the Great War on November 11, 1918.[11]

A Different Type of Score. No one was any longer counting touchdowns, field goals, or extra points. They were keeping a different score now. After 20 days of fighting during the Meuse-Argonne Offensive, the 36th Division captured 813 prisoners, three field artillery guns, 17 trench mortars, 277 machine guns, and munitions and materials. The success came at a cost to the Texas and Oklahoma National Guardsmen of 2,601 casualties. Of them, 21 officers and 469 enlisted men were killed in action, another four officers and 70 men died later from their wounds, and the remainder were wounded, gassed, or missing in action.[12]

At least 16 of the Second Texas Infantry footballers were part of the 71st and 72nd Brigades and fought in the Meuse-Argonne campaign, including Eugene Dotson, Dick Lane, and Tom Mitchell of the 132nd Machine Gun Company, who were assigned to Col. Bloor's 142nd Regiment during the fighting. Charlie Turner was with the 90th Division 345th Machine Gun Regiment that saw combat in the last weeks of the Meuse-Argonne offensive. Rats Watson probably spent the most time of any former gridiron star in the combat arena as part of the 111th Engineers Regiment of the 61st Field Artillery Brigade. His brigade was assigned to the First American Army Corps and was on the front at both St. Mihiel and the Meuse-Argonne from September 12 until early November.[13]

None of the former footballers were killed in battle, but at least seven were wounded. Sgt. Victor Bintliff, Lt. Whitey Davis, Lt. Spitz Clarke, and Major Bud Smith of the 141st were wounded on the first day of fighting during the initial attack on St. Étienne. Bintliff took machine gun fire to his leg during the attack, his sister receiving a letter from him two months later from a Red Cross hospital in France. He was walking with a cane after repeated surgeries for gangrene. Lt. Whitey Davis was severely wounded during the same battle as Bintliff. Shipped stateside, Davis was still recovering at the Fort Sam Houston base hospital five months later. Spitz Clarke, who was also wounded on October 8, waited 24 years to receive his Purple Heart. Schuyler "Bud" Smith received shrapnel to his ankle and was gassed after he fell. He was in a French hospital for several months.[14]

Bart Coan, of the 144th, was wounded during the Aisne Valley assault in mid-October. Eugene Dotson, who was assigned to the 132nd Machine Gun Battalion under Colonel Bloor's command, received a throat wound during the Meuse-Argonne campaign. It eventually contributed to his death in 1937 at 38 years old. Rats Watson of the 61st Field Artillery was gassed in the same offensive and spent three months recovering in an Army hospital.[15]

Not all the players saw combat. Charlie Brown was part of the 61st Field Artillery Brigade Regiment that remained for the war's duration at the Artillery Training Camp in Coetquidan, France. Jim Kendrick was also in France, assigned to training at AEF Division Headquarters. Ock Abbott, K.L. Berry, Baker Duncan, Charley Ogden, Sylvan Simpson, Tom Gambrell, and Walter F. Woodul were assigned to stateside military administrative or training positions.[16]

Promoted to captain, Abbott spent part of the war at Fort Sam Houston and, ironically, was back along the US-Mexico border at El Paso and Arizona. Berry was assigned as an instructor at Camp Kearny in San Diego. Duncan was at the Fort Lee Army Training Center in Petersburg Virginia. Tom Gambrell was stationed stateside as a captain in the Army Infantry Office Reserve Corps. Charley Ogden was in the Regular Army's 57th Division as an instructor at Camp Logan. Sylvan Simpson was part of the 85th Infantry, 165th Depot

Brigade and posted mainly at Camp Travis. Woodul remained in Texas as Assistant Adjutant General of the 36th Division. Rip Collins was also posted in Texas, and depending on the source, was either an auto mechanic or a bayonet instructor. Cpl. Louis "Tige" Halphen, who was wounded by a trench mortar during training at Camp Bowie, remained stateside as an instructor.[17]

Going Home. By late October, the 71st and 72nd Brigades were transferred from the field and sent to the 16th Training Area around Tonnerre, France. The 72nd Brigade began its move back to the US on April 26, 1919, and the 71st Brigade on May 22. The steamship *Louisville* arrived in New York from Brest on June 1, with the first 1,897 troops of the 71st. On June 10 they left Hoboken, New Jersey, bound for Galveston on the steamship *Yale* where they boarded trains for Camp Travis. The 141st left Galveston first and as their trains reached Austin, they saw the tracks covered with a cheering crowd of well-wishers and stopped long enough for a parade. San Antonio planned an entire day of parades and "a big feast" when the 141st reached Camp Travis.[18]

The cruiser *Pueblo* followed in the wake of the *Louisville* carrying 1,799 soldiers of which most were part of the 142nd Regiment. They may have survived the war but not all survived the journey home – two men were killed and 60 injured when a large wave swept over the ship. Colonel A.W. Bloor and the 142nd arrived at Camp Bowie on June 13. During the three-day rail passage, crowds greeted them at every Texas train station, and Fort Worth was no different. A patriotic crowd waited all day before their expected arrival but were sent home by guards at about midnight. They returned the next day at 5:30 in the morning.[19]

A few of the Texas Eleven remained in France with the Regular Army and National Guard peace-keepers after most of their former teammates returned home. With no more machine gun or artillery fire to dodge, the soldiers who stayed behind organized a football league. The 36th Division team was represented by five former Second Texas Infantry players: Bill Birge, who was the offensive and defensive line coach, Phillip "Spitz" Clarke, "Big Jim" Kendrick, Eugene Dotson, and Grady "Rats" Watson. Major David R. Nelson was team coach.

Gone were the canvas tents and scrub scrimmage field of their past, the squad housed instead in "the chateau of a famous French Count and Countess," a palatial mansion surrounded by private hunting grounds. When the reformed 36th Division football won the First Army AEF championship at Bar-sur-Aube, near Paris, it was Spitz Clarke's field goal from the 28-yard line that decided the outcome. They had just one game left to win the AEF championship title in the All-Army Finals, but in a game witnessed by General Pershing and other top military brass, they lost the July contest by a score of 15 to 6. That summer, the footballers were shipped home.[20]

Recognition. For their battlefield valor, the Texans and Oklahomans of the 36th Division were awarded 30 Distinguished Service Crosses and two Congressional Medals of Honor. France conferred 129 Croix de Guerre medals for gallantry with the Fourth French Army. At least seven former footballers earned the Croix de Guerre. At a ceremony in France on March 20, 1919, Bloor was one of the first soldiers from the 36th Division to be pinned and by summer, Bill Birge, Bart Coan, Spitz Clarke, Whitey Davis, and David Nelson were honored. Bud Smith received his Croix de Guerre in 1920.[21]

AEF Commander-in-Chief John J. Pershing praised the 36th Division which, he wrote, was "thrown directly into the active battle" without the usual training, but "responded to every call made upon it." The French Minister of War wrote Major General W.R. Smith, Commanding General of the 36th Division, effusing that "your Division arrived in France at the time when the great battle was in progress which was to decide the fate of the War. It took a glorious part in it. The fighting which it did from the 8th of October, and which led to the Aisne, between Attigny and Givry, proved the valor and the spirit of discipline of your soldiers." He ended his recognition with: "France will not forget the generous help which they brought to her."[22]

Texas also recognized its 36th Division in ways large and small. October 10, 1919, was named 36th Division Day at the Dallas Fair. The same year a convention was being planned to form a permanent organization of the 36th Division Association, with Colonel Bloor as its first chairman. Members of the 36th Division were instructed to mail their names to Bloor for record-keeping and to register for the first convention.[23]

At the close of the Great War, just two years had passed since the names and athletic prowess of the Texas Brigade footballers were splashed across Lone Star newspapers. Some of those same names reappeared as war heroes. The highest praise went to Colonel Bloor. Major General W.R. Smith, commander of the 36th Division, recognized that Bloor's 142nd lost 70% of its officers and 57% of its enlisted men. Despite the losses, he told Bloor that "you are the only regimental commander of the division who brought the regiment to France, remained with it continuously while in France, and took it back to the United States." He continued with: "Your regiment participated in the hardest fighting of the division and was the best-handled regiment at that time."[24]

Bloor received two wartime military awards for his leadership during the Meuse-Argonne, the French Croix de Guerre, in 1919, and the US Army's Distinguished Service Medal in 1923. The Croix de Guerre was accompanied by the words: "During reconnaissance on the front line under a violent shell fire he displayed coolness and great contempt for danger. [Bloor] was a fine example for his men and contributed largely to the success of the operation." When Whitey Davis was presented his Croix de Guerre, he was acknowledged for his "great audacity, bravery, and technical knowledge," and touted as an inspiration to his fellow soldiers, unflinching "in spite of violent artillery and machine gun fire." Charlie Turner received a commendation from Brigadier General U.G. Alexander, the general congratulating him for "the splendid service that you rendered to [the 180th Infantry] Brigade" and adding you are "a credit to yourself and your organization."[25]

There is little doubt that similar high praise was bestowed on many of the other former footballers. Those words were likely part of the public record but, more than a hundred years later, are not easy to find. Perhaps they exist as yellowed pages in personal dairies and family papers. Should they resurface, they would likely tell of the individual heroism, great and small, of each of the famous footballers who served during the Great War.

From its Texas Independence roots to the Civil War, the Spanish-American War, and finally, the Mexican border, the Texas Brigade had been a Lone Star State military institution. When the Texas Brigade name was changed to the 36th Infantry Division in 1917, it wounded state pride and was only begrudgingly acknowledged in Texas and Oklahoma. It didn't take long, however, for the division to again become part of Texas lore. It quickly gathered nicknames, such as the Panther Division and the Arrowhead Division, the latter derived from the division insignia of an arrowhead representing Oklahoma and a 'T' for Texas that spawned a third nickname, the "T-Patchers." On the regimental crest of the 142nd Regiment is a damaged church steeple. It is the St. Étienne church tower that commemorates the first major battle of the reorganized 36th Division. Below are the words "I'll face you." They did.[26]

The Great War was over. Ocean-going ships brought the former footballers and warriors back to America's shores, and railroads took them to the cities nearest their homes. Their futures no longer belonged to the military, they belonged to them, and nearly all of them figured out what to do with it. The most common callings that the famous Second Texas Infantry followed were in sports, the military, and law. Not surprisingly, they were excelled at them.

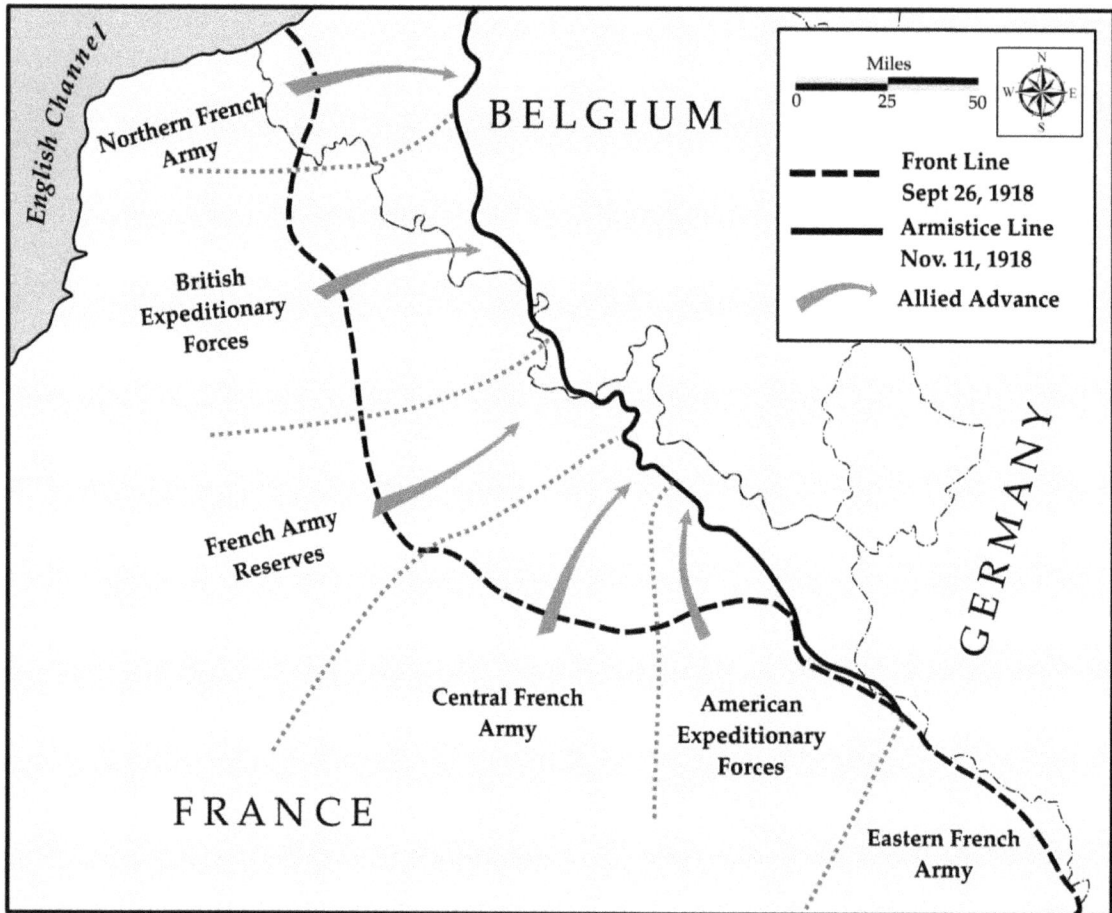

When America entered World War I, the Western Front of occupied France extended from near the Belgian-French border on the English Channel to the France-Germany boundary close to the Rhine River, a distance greater than 300 miles. Most of the former Second Texas Infantry footballers would serve in France as part of General Pershing's American Expeditionary Forces, or AEF, when the Allies initiated a series of joint attacks in late September called the "Grand Allied Offensive." The sector under American command was termed the Meuse-Argonne where, for 47 days between September 26 to November 11, 1918, over one million AEF soldiers participated in what was, up to that time, the largest and bloodiest battle in US military history. Drawing by R.K. Sawyer.

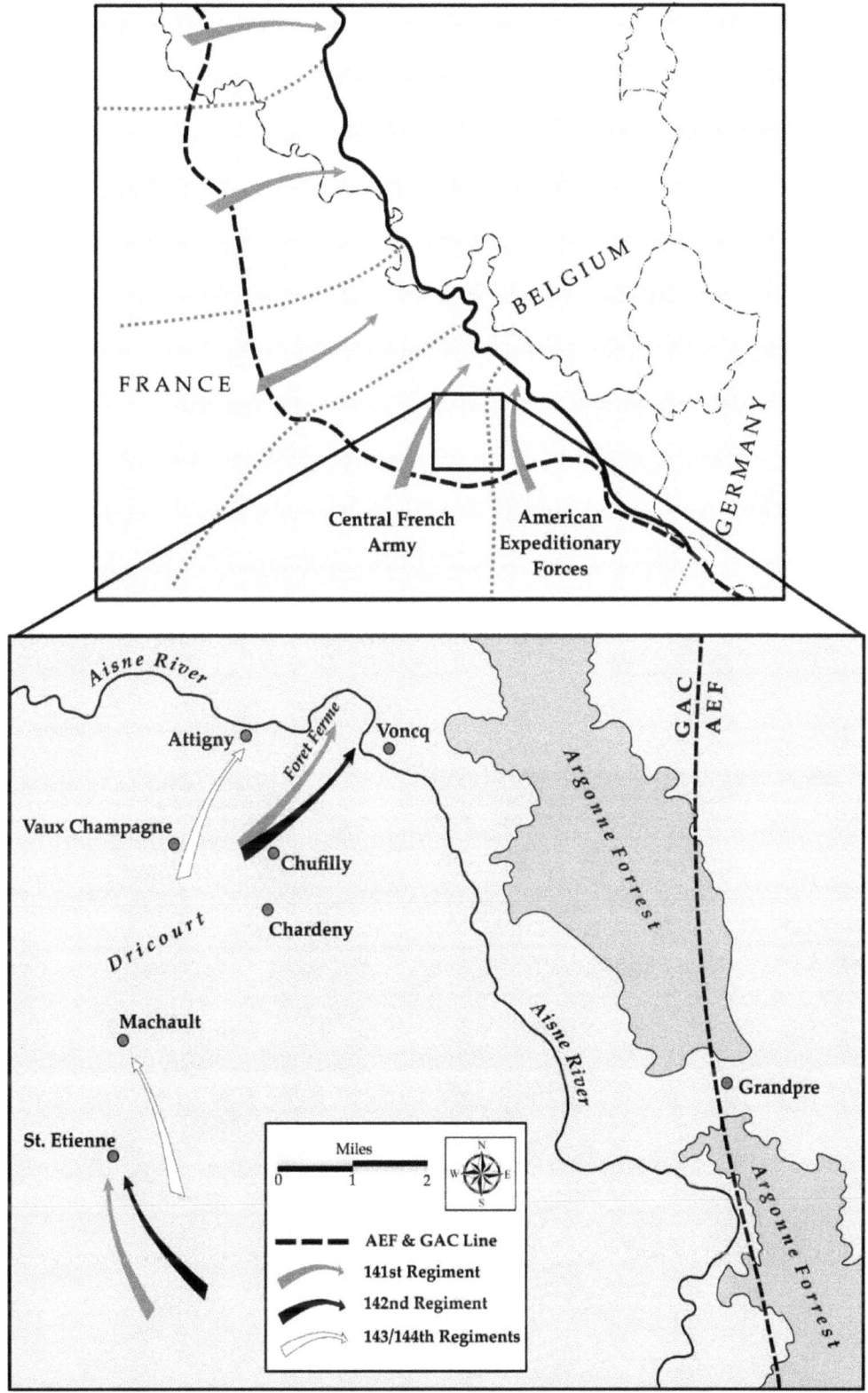

The 36th Division 71st and the 72nd Brigades were assigned to the French Army Group Centre (GAC). During October and November, the former footballers fought in the battles of St. Étienne and Forêt-Ferme. Drawing by R.K. Sawyer.

The incursion that started it all – the German Army crossing from Belgium to France in August 1914. *Library of Congress Prints and Photographs Division*, Washington, D.C., No. LC-USZ62-62437.

America's soldiers joined the Great War in 1918. *Library of Congress Prints and Photographs Division*, Washington, D.C., No. 9494.

Top: Germans building trenches that would eventually reach hundreds of miles across France and Belgium. *Library of Congress Prints and Photographs Division*, Washington, D.C., No. LC-USZ62-21422.

A bleak, worn torn landscape with German machine guns, one of the defining armaments of trench warfare during World War I. *Library of Congress Prints and Photographs Division*, Washington, D.C., No. LC-USZ62-136100.

Top: World War I is also remembered for the insidious use of chemical warfare. Delivered to the enemy by cylinders or artillery projectiles, the main gasses used were chlorine, phosgene, and mustard gas. Gas masks became the standard method for defense. Shown are US Marines with gas masks, France, 1918. *Library of Congress Prints and Photographs Division*, Washington, D.C., No. LC-USZ62-61594.

Left: Life in the French villages during World War I was one of gas masks and earthen fortifications to resist aerial and artillery bombardments. *Library of Congress Prints and Photographs Division*, Washington, D.C., No. LC-DIG-ppmsca-40805.

Allies digging in during an advance, Meuse-Argonne. Note the stretcher, center. *Library of Congress Prints and Photographs Division*, Washington, D.C., No. LC-DIG-ds-09803.

The 71st and the 72nd Brigades were assigned to the French Army Group Centre (GAC). Shown are GAC infantrymen in the Champagne region during the Forêt-Ferme offensive. *Library of Congress Prints and Photographs Division*, Washington, D.C., No. LC-DIG-ds-ls04024.

It was supposed to be the war to end all wars. Soldiers on both sides paid a heavy price for the geopolitical failings, as did citizens in French and Belgian towns. *Library of Congress Prints and Photographs Division*, Washington, D.C., No. LC-USZ62-62437.

CHAPTER 9

PART 1

Back to the Field

College football continued to dominate the national sports consciousness after the Great War, but pro ball, still bucking the headwinds of a rocky start, was gaining momentum. Salaried players in city athletic clubs made their appearance as early as the late 1800s, and in 1902, a regional pro football league was established in the Northeastern US that quickly moved west of the Appalachians to Ohio. Although team franchises and regional leagues came and went, between 1903 and 1919 the Buckeye State Massillon Tigers and the Canton AC, later the Bulldogs, dominated the nascent pro game. In 1920 the American Professional Football Association was founded, but it wobbled for two years before changing its name in 1922 to the National Football League.[1]

Sports brought them together as the Second Texas Infantry, and sports for many of the former Texas Brigade football players continued to provide them with opportunities after the war. Several who returned to college to finish their degrees played football again. Two former National Guard gridiron masters went on to play for pro ball clubs, and another chose professional baseball. At least six of the former footballers coached sports at the high school and college levels, and several were active in officiating Texas college and amateur football, baseball, basketball, and wrestling.

Spitz Clarke. Returning from overseas after the AEF football series in 1919, former Texas Eleven halfback Phillip Solomon Clarke III took a job as the Austin High School football coach, his Austin Eleven known as the "Spitz Clarke Gridders." Clarke's tenure lasted just a single season, the next year making a move to San Antonio as coach of the Main Avenue High School team. Clarke coached the Main Avenue "Red and White Football Machine" for three seasons. One anecdote from his winning 1922 season was published in 1937 after Vanderbilt beat LSU that year using a hidden ball stunt. An Austin sportswriter was quick to point out that the play wasn't the idea of the Nashville institution. The trickery had been developed 15 years earlier by Baylor's Frank Bridges and Spitz Clarke, the latter called the "crafty old San Antonio coach."[2]

Clarke immersed himself in Texas sports after he moved to San Antonio. Besides coaching, he officiated at high school, college, and Army games, and was a founder of the Texas Athletic Officials Association (TAOA), as both a charter member and its first vice president in 1923. San Antonio became the nucleus for Texas sports officials, its association chapter compiling the first official's rulebook, outlining the official's training, and developing and administering a qualifying test for officials. The program was adopted by other state chapters under the TAOA umbrella. Clarke was TAOA president in 1924 and 1925.[3]

Football coach and sports official Clarke also coached baseball for the Main Avenue team and various amateur league teams, and he added the title of promoter to his resume when he arranged local college baseball and golf tournaments. The industrious Clarke added a fourth job title in 1922 as Camp Mabry Athletic Officer, a job he kept until 1926. Demonstrating his interest in all things sports, he organized and coached Camp Mabry baseball and boxing.[4]

Not content with administration or coaching, Clarke played amateur baseball and competed in the local golf circuit. Mostly, he played football, and he was on the field often during the 1920s at San Antonio's celebrated Christmas Day contest between the Fort Sam Houston Army footballers and All-Star college players, whose roster included both students and alumni. Between 1921 and 1924, the series brought Clarke and several Second Infantry players together on the gridiron, both as teammates and opponents.

The 1921 Christmas Day contest pitted Clarke and Watson of the college All-Stars against K.L. Berry and the Army. Clarke, who made numerous running gains during the game, was as tough as ever. During one play, he was "laid out" after his "head struck [an opponent's] knees." With concussion protocols nearly a century away, the prostrate Clarke wobbled to his feet and continued the game. Two weeks later Clarke and Berry were selected to play with the college All-Stars in a benefit match against Centre College and this time they were in the same lineup. Their coach was former teammate Rats Watson. The 1923 Annual Christmas Day football matchup between the college All-Stars and the Army footballers at San Antonio's Schwab Field pitted K.L. Berry, the Army team captain, against former teammates player-coach Spitz Clarke and Eugene Dotson. John Diller, now at Yale, was scheduled to play but reached San Antonio too late to practice.[5]

1924 was the last year that any Second Infantry alumni played football in the popular college All-Star and Fort Sam Houston matches. Going into the game, the Army All-Stars had lost only one game during the regular season, the defeat to a San Antonio All-Star gridiron squad with Clarke and Dotson in the lineup. Christmas Day was a repeat performance when the Army lost 13-0 to a team with Clarke as coach and Dotson as fullback. Clarke coached and managed the collegiate All-Stars again the next year, its lineup devoid of any of the famous Second Texas Infantry footballers.[6]

Spitz Clarke left San Antonio for Laredo in 1927 and married Janet Gregory the next year. In 1929 he moved to Brownsville as the head of the Rio Grande Valley Texas Amateur Sports Federation. He also championed yet another sport, the Valley Amateur Basketball League, and served as its vice president. The next year, 1930, he was elected president of the Valley League and organized an amateur baseball team that he planned to develop into a semi-pro team.[7]

In 1932 Clarke left coaching to become a sporting goods salesman for W.A. Holt Sporting Goods Co. of Waco. Still following his wanderlust, he left Waco for San Antonio and Aransas Pass, where the avid saltwater fisherman bought two fishing boats. Clarke continued to appear throughout the state as an official for football, baseball, and basketball games at high schools and colleges until he moved to Brownwood in 1940, initially working for the Lowe and Campbell Sporting Goods Co., with headquarters in Dallas. He was the last of the Second Infantry players wounded in the Meuse-Argonne campaign to receive his Purple Heart, the recognition for an unknown reason delayed until 1943.[8]

In 1947 Clarke organized the Brownwood softball league and was named city softball commissioner, and he continued to officiate the softball league and local high school games. When he died in 1948, state newspapers carried only a brief obituary. None mentioned the cause of death, and he evidently had no children by "his wife here," who was nameless. Somehow, Phillip Spitz Clarke's 30 years of contribution to Lone Star State athletics managed to escape glowing tributes.[9]

Bart Coan. Second squad left end Bartlett E. Coan returned to West Texas and became a high school sports coach and teacher. In 1927 he moved to Fort Davis to take a job as Fort Davis School Superintendent and coached the Fort Davis Indians. Coan was known as a perfectionist as a coach and as an offensive strategist, he didn't believe in spending any practice time on defense. The Indians squad rarely had more than 13 to 14 players, but what they could do on the field was legendary, grinding out touchdowns "like a machine." One of the Houston native's nicknames was the "old wizard of football trickery," and he drilled his players in the mantra "deception-precision-deception-conditioning-deception." Opponents were often frustrated when Coan's runners were halfway down the field before they knew which player had the ball.

Coan left Fort Davis to serve as a captain in World War II and was stationed at Camp Bowie. He was discharged after five years, relocating to El Paso as a chemistry teacher at Austin High School. When he was asked to coach football again, newspapers heralded the return of the "old gray fox of the gridiron." Coan left Texas for Arizona in the 1970s to be near his daughter and died there in 1975.[10]

Rip Collins. Although most of the former Second Texas Infantry football team was serving in some capacity in the war effort during the spring of 1918, former first-string halfback Henry Warren Collins was pitching for the Cokes, a popular Austin amateur baseball team. Before he signed up in mid-summer to serve in the US Auto Mechanics School at Camp Mabry, locally called the SAM Brigade, he played baseball against their team. It was late June, and in a description that would portend his decade as a pro ballplayer, the writer said Collins "started on the firing line [as pitcher] for the Cokes, and although effective at times, was wild."[11]

Collins, whose kicking prowess was compared to such legends as Jim Thorpe, was to choose a pro baseball career over football. Although no statisticians tallied the figures during his college or Second Texas Infantry gridiron play, his career in pro baseball would be a judgment in numbers. Not just won-lost, which relied as much on a team's scoring ability as a pitcher's performance on the mound, but ERA (earned run average), which was the most important measure of a pitcher during the era. Representing the number of earned runs a pitcher allows per nine innings, a rule of thumb is that ERAs of 3.00 and below are exceptional and between 3.00 to 4.00 are good. Rip Collins' career ERA was all over the board, varying from exceptional to startling poor.

Collins' professional baseball debut was with the Dallas Marines minor league team, part of the Texas League, in the spring of 1919. His was a fair showing that season, with 11 wins and 12 losses, striking out 126 batters and allowing 166 hits in 25 games for a 2.36 ERA. But one writer noted of his minor league performance that "he was a bit wild, allowing 91 bases on balls." Another analyst thought his pitching "was weird and woozy" for most of the season, but during the last month of play, his record was the best in the league and included a no-hitter. That winter, the cash-strapped franchise had hurler Collins and the other Dallas ballplayers finish their contracts by rebuilding their ballpark. During spring, Collins was back in Austin as a high school basketball referee and a baseball coach at Austin High School. He was ready for an adventure when the New York Yankees signed him for the 1920 season.[12]

Collins pitched his first Yankees game in June 1920. In his third start, he hurled a one-hit shutout in front of a crowd of 38,000 in a 14-0 rout of the Boston Red Sox. By July he had six games under belt, with a record five wins and a single loss. Later that month, a cool Collins pitched relief against the Cleveland Indians, and with bases loaded, struck out the last batter for a win that pushed the Yankees, temporarily, into the American League lead. His hurling speed and untouchable curveball made him "the idol of New York fans," who began to call him "the Texas Wonder." In an interview in St. Louis, teammate Babe Ruth predicted he would be a leading American League pitcher. Collins played in 36 games during his rookie big league season and is credited with 14 wins, 8 losses, and a 3.22 ERA. Still "inclined to be a bit wild," he walked 79 hitters. That season the Yankees finished third in the American League.[13]

Collins' combination of Texas ethos and big-league baseball made him a popular profile in the nation's press, and at first, they couldn't get enough of him. Evidently, Collins had spent a few months with the Texas Rangers, and readers relished his purported Ranger border escapades, such as telling Austin reporter Norman E. Brown that he was "nicked by bullets four times." In another widely published interview, he conveyed more border tales and his quote: "Lissen, you gotta be some rider and a crack shot to ever climb into a Texas Ranger's saddle." The article was accompanied by photos of Collins in his Yankee summer "costume" and his winter Texas Ranger outfit, complete with cowboy hat, chaps, rifle, and holsters.[14]

Great things were expected from media prodigy and baseball hero Rip Collins in his second year. Instead, he delivered a lackluster performance. Although his win-loss record was a respectable 11-five, his ERA was 5.44. The Yankees won the AL pennant that year, but Collins, with his Yankees bidding for the 1921 World Series title against the cross-town rival Giants, struggled in his one inning of pitching.[15]

After the end of his second season, rookie adulation was replaced by reproach. He lacked discipline, according to the press, and was prone to rolling into his hotel room at dawn after nights in the New York clubs. His fondness for the good life included food, and he was gaining weight. An observer wrote that he was "eating himself out of big league baseball" and one of his nicknames, "Two-gun Collins" was changed to "Four Meal Collins." A Yankee manager later wrote that he knew of no other ballplayer who could "eat as long at a sitting" as Rip Collins.[16]

The *Boston Herald* charged that Collins "could not or would not keep the pace, and his work in the box has been generally disappointing." His 1921 bust year, wrote another journalist, was his own fault. "His temperament is not the best" and he is "erratic." An *Austin American-Statesman* sportswriter was unsparing. "His artistic temperament got the best of him," he wrote, and instead of attempting to play better, "began to discover stylish ailments and alibis." Most sportswriters posited that Collins simply wasn't trying, and they were probably closest to the truth.[17]

Others, however, blamed the much-maligned New York coach, Miller Huggins. Collins, wrote the *Austin American*, "is a glaring example of the poor discipline of Miller Huggins," continuing that "he is among those of the New York players who have no confidence in the Huggins' system and would welcome a change." But in a 1929 interview, Collins admitted the problem was his to own. "Don't blame Huggins," he said. There is "no one to blame but Old Rip Collins. You must stay in condition to pitch winning ball in the major leagues and Rip Collins failed to do that. Huggins gave me every chance and I was too young and thoughtless to take advantage of my opportunities. I wish I had that season to live over." He later added: "I didn't realize it at the time, but Miller Huggins gave me more consideration than I deserved."[18]

It didn't come out often in the press, but part of Collins' problem was alcohol. In a 1968 article, Collins confessed he started drinking when he was six years old – first beer, then corn whiskey. While the sanitized version of his nickname "Rip" was credited to his athletic prowess, Collins said of the name: "I don't particularly feel proud of the nickname Rip. There was a brand of whiskey fairly popular in my neck of the woods before Prohibition called Ripa Whiskey. Well, I could handle it pretty well, so you can draw your own conclusions."[19]

Rip Collins spent the fall of 1921 at his ranch in Blanco and that winter was traded to the Boston Red Sox. His was a mediocre showing through much of his first Boston season until late in the year when he delivered a startling winning streak of eight games in his last nine starts. One memorable win was against his former Yankee team. With the Yankees a game away from the 1922 pennant, the New York castoff pitched "masterly ball from start to finish" to give the Red Sox a 3-1 win. The Red Sox finished the season in eighth place in the AL.[20]

Collins was traded to the Detroit Tigers under player-manager Ty Cobb before the 1923 baseball season. A sports columnist doubted that "Rip Collins [will be] a star under Ty Cobb," and a Waco writer agreed, concluding that the Texas hurler suffered from two problems: lack of control and ambition. Of the latter, the writer offered a telling conversation that Collins supposedly had in the dugout. A teammate congratulated him on his play with: "Keep on pitching like that and they'll never send you back to the Texas League," to which Collins replied: "That is what is troubling me. If I pitched a [good game] down in the Texas League, the manager of the team would have let me go hunting or fishing until it was my turn to work again."[21]

In his debut Tiger season, Collins pitched for three wins and seven losses, the 1923 Detroit team placing second in the AL. Collins had a good year in 1924, ending the season with a 14-7 record and a 3.21 ERA. Holding out for a bonus clause, he returned his 1925 Detroit contract unsigned. When Detroit wouldn't budge, Collins relented. Then he lost his first six games of the season, limping through the year with six wins and 11 losses. In his fourth year as a Tiger, he pitched a career-best 2.73 ERA. But as sports writer Mark S. MacDonald Sr. puts it, "he must have pitched on the wrong days – when his teammates' bats were sleeping – as his exceptional ERA brought only a so-so W-L record if 8-8." Despite a 4.69 ERA in 1927, Collins had a good win-loss that year of 13-7. It was his last season under Ty Cobb.[22]

During the winter of 1927, the Tigers moved Collins to their Toronto Maple Leafs farm team. At first, he told Texas newspapermen that he didn't care where he played. Then he changed his mind, in March refusing to report to Toronto and insisting he be traded to a team in the Texas League. Toronto ignored him. The volatile Collins then went on to win his first five Toronto games. By July, he was at nine and two, averaging just seven hits per game. He pitched all 16 innings of a double-header in August, allowing only three hits and winning both. At season's end, his record was 17-8.[23]

At the end of the season, when Collins' contract was sold to the St. Louis Browns, a Waco sports columnist wrote: "It is not likely that he will star." He didn't, but he had a good 1929 season, finishing with 11-6. In 1930, the Browns were sixth in the AL, a year in which Collins went 9-7.[24]

Ball clubs were forced to cut salaries during the Depression, and Collins was no exception. When his $7,500 1930 salary was reduced the next year to $5,000, he responded by boycotting spring training camp. By early March 1931, he was one of only two St. Louis players who hadn't reported to West Palm Beach. All that anyone knew was that he was "apparently lost somewhere in Texas." By April, Collins was finally talking, but it wasn't about the Browns. Instead, he announced, he had offers to return to the Texas League. "If I can't come to terms with the Browns," he offered, "I expect I'll come back to Texas where I belong." The bluff worked, and week later he reported to spring training. He went 5-5 in 1931 with an ERA of 3.79, the first year he posted an ERA below 4.00 since 1926.[25]

When the Browns started spring training in 1932, "nothing had been heard from pitcher Rip Collins." Once again, the controversial pitcher was missing from the lineup, and yet again he returned his 1932 contract with the Browns unsigned. This time, he advised that due to health issues, his doctors told him "to drop baseball play for a season and live in the open to improve his health." His option for the open air was to join the Texas Rangers as a law enforcement agent. On his surprise exit from pro ball, he offered that it was a temporary assignment and that he was "just resting up so's to pitch better baseball."[26]

Warren "Rip" Collins spent 11 years in pro ball, accruing a career record of 108 wins, 82 losses, and an average ERA of 4.0. During those years, his off-season life was as colorful as his time in a baseball uniform. His passion was fishing and hunting, and each winter he traveled throughout Texas and Mexico to hunt turkey, quail, doves, waterfowl, deer, and rabbits. Before the 1929 World Series, he was asked by an Austin sports columnist which team he favored. Collins said he had no opinion; he was too busy dove hunting. Texas Game, Fish, and Oyster Commissioner William Tucker even named Collins a deputy in its game law enforcement agency, and his first order of business was putting a stop to illegal nighttime deer hunting near his ranch.[27]

Collins also remained active in local organized sports. He officiated various high school and amateur football games and even refereed boxing. Between 1925 and 1930, he alternated between UT and A&M as a pitching coach. One year he was kicking coach for the football team of the Texas State Deaf and Dumb Institute, which insensitively went by the name the "Silent Eleven" or the "Dummies."[28]

Although he didn't require assistance in making a name for himself off the field, he often got it anyway. One tale that surfaced in 1925 was particularly bizarre. A man named Charles Place posed as Rip Collins for three years, and he even married an unsuspecting woman who thought she was Mrs. Warren Collins, the wife of a pro ballplayer. The masquerade unraveled when the imposter Collins abandoned her and their infant, offering the excuse that he had been traveling the US looking for another ball club. While the plight of the unknowing Mrs. Collins circulated in newspapers, the real Mrs. Warren Collins – the former Leticia Ethel Pamele – was in Austin raising three young children.[29]

On January 17, 1933, Collins' Texas Ranger commission expired, and that spring, the Browns dropped him from their roster. He was negotiating with the Texas League for another season, but few in the league believed he was in "any kind of condition to pitch winning ball." He signed with the Austin City League in July and three weeks later was back in the Texas League with the Fort Worth Panthers. But it didn't last, and he threw his hat into the ring for Travis County Deputy Sheriff. He was appointed in September.[30]

Warren Rip Collins remained in law enforcement for the rest of his working career. After his exodus from the Texas Rangers and baseball in 1933, Collins worked as the deputy sheriff and sheriff of Travis County for the next four years, then returned to the Rangers from 1937 to 1940, and was elected Travis County Sheriff in 1940, a position he held for eight more years. He became Bryan Chief of Police in 1950 and retired from law enforcement in 1959. Collins was a highly regarded lawman, credited with apprehending a wide range of law-breakers, including bootleggers, ax murderers, robbers, and chicken thieves.[31]

The name Warren Collins was still carried often in the press. Texas front pages followed the arrests he made, and the sports pages announced his service as a referee or umpire. Just as newsworthy were his saltwater fishing trips and the size of the deer he killed during one of his many hunting trips. Nearly always, any mention of Collins recalled his 1915 A&M college football performance against UT, his 1916-17 football performance with the Second Texas Infantry, and his play in pro ball that was referenced in only glowing terms. Warren "Rip" Collins died in 1968 at 72.

Eugene Dotson. After his World War I service and the memorable 1918-19 AEF football season, the Baylor and Second Texas Infantry fullback returned to Baylor. Before he even took to the field that first autumn, sports pundits and fans alike predicted Dotson would end the season on the All-Texas team. They weren't counting on a nagging knee injury.[32]

Playing through knee pain, Dotson was unable to run his backfield magic or play more than a quarter or two at the quarterback slot. In the UT game that season, Dotson passed for both Baylor touchdowns in their 39-13 loss, but according to a Waco sports writer, the injured warrior was "seldom able to move more than ten yards from where he received the ball before the Longhorns were upon him. But if one of his ends got clear in that brief time, Dotson passed the ball to where he could get his hands on it." With "his big hand gripping the oval more than halfway around," Dotson still showed remarkable strength, in one play passed a 35-yard rocket waist high to the receiver. Baylor finished the 1919 season with a 5-3-1 record, losing games to Rice, UT, and A&M in three of its four Southwest Conference games. His Baylor Bear teammates elected him captain at the end of the season.[33]

Dotson's knee was better in 1920 but the Baylor Bears were not, producing a disappointing 4-4-1 record. Dotson's play at fullback was at times exceptional, but behind the center, he struggled. In the Baylor contest at Cotton Palace against Texas Christian University, he threw 14 passes without a single completion. In October, newspapers reassured sports fans that Dotson was not seriously injured in a game against Southwestern University. Taken to Baptist Hospital by ambulance, doctors reported no evidence of internal injuries, although "mild symptoms of cerebral concussion developed, but these are clearing rapidly."[34]

Dotson was on the Baylor Bear's track and field team for two seasons. Nicknamed the "Baylor Leviathan," he had near-perfect form in the shot put and discus throw. He lobbed the shot nearly 43 feet in a 1920 meet against Rice and the discus 126 feet at Southwestern, and both feats set new state records. Dotson won the shot put at every meet he entered except one. An admiring Waco sportswriter explained to readers that the only reason the gifted athlete lost was because "he traveled all night, coming from the baseball game at Austin." At the end of the 1920 season, Baylor awarded him three varsity letters.[35]

Dotson ended his Baylor athletic tenure with a track and field win in the Southwest Conference finals held in Houston in the spring of 1921. That June, he was playing amateur baseball with a Rockdale team and was at bat when a pitch hit him in the face. He was taken to the hospital unconscious with a broken jaw.[36]

When Rats Watson left his position as Port Arthur High School coach in the summer of 1921 to play professional football, Eugene Dotson took the job. His team started the football season strong, not losing a game until late October, then unraveled in November with a loss to Bryan 47-0. The next year he married Gladys Bush and moved back to San Antonio.[37]

Dotson during his short life remained a close friend of Spitz Clarke. The pair played various All-Star post-season football matches between 1921 and 1924, the most celebrated of which were the annual Christmas Day contests between the college All-Stars and the Fort Sam Houston footballers. Dotson and Clarke also officiated high school, college, and Army games together, and both were active in the Texas Athletic Officials Association (TAOA). Dotson was the TAOA vice president in 1924 when Clarke served as its president.[38]

Dotson played his last football game on New Year's Day in 1925 and that spring he was signed to a San Antonio semi-pro baseball team. His baseball tenure was short, however, because his health was failing. During the winter of 1926, he was confined to his bed for several months with "a serious throat malady."[39]

Between 1926 and 1932, Eugene Dotson left competitive sports, residing in San Antonio and Kerrville where he started a radio business. Thirty-eight-year-old Eugene Malcolm Dotson III entered the Legion VA Hospital near Kerrville in December 1931 and died there on March 18, 1932, from complications of the gangrene that ate away at his throat from the wound he suffered in the Meuse-Argonne.[40]

D.V. "Tubby" Graves. Second Texas Infantry coach Dorsett Vandeventer Graves returned to Texas A&M in the spring of 1917 as assistant coach to Dana Bible, and that year was responsible for founding and coaching A&M's wrestling program. He took the acting head coach position for the 1918 football season while Army pilot Bible served overseas in World War I. That year Graves had a 6-0 record going into the 1918 UT-Aggie Thanksgiving match, the Aggies losing the match 7-0. The Alabama native remained as the Aggie's assistant coach for another year before a two-year coaching stint at Montana State. Montana was followed by a long career at the University of Washington from 1923 to 1946. After he retired as coach he remained at Washington as assistant athletic director until his death in 1960.[41]

Big Jim Kendrick. The Second Texas Infantry's starting end James Marcellus Kendrick spent the Great War with the 141st Infantry and Fifth Artillery Observation School, 36th Division Headquarters, stationed at Camp Mills New York, and in France from

July 1918 to June 1919. Kendrick played the 1918-1919 AEF football season in France, returning to Texas in 1920. That fall, the legendary end was back in Waco as the Baylor Bears line coach and was reunited with his Second Texas Infantry teammate Eugene Dotson, the Baylor quarterback and fullback. Kendrick's sports career over the next 13 years was varied and demanding, ranging from pro football to minor league baseball, and he coached sports with at least ten different organizations.[42]

After Baylor, Kendrick joined the Canton Bulldogs, made famous by the incomparable Jim Thorpe. The Bulldogs, who were coming off a 5-2-3 season in the American Professional Football Association, were part of the new National Football League in 1922 and their 10-0-2 record took the championship that year. The rookie Kendrick played in four games as a defensive back and offensive end. According to author Jeffrey Miller, Kendrick also "snuck in" to play two games that year with the Toledo Maroons, joining the lineup with his former Second Texas Infantry colleague Rats Watson.[43]

The next year, Kendrick was at Centre College in Kentucky as assistant coach to his former A&M football coach, Charles Moran, and was head of the college's baseball and basketball teams. During his second year at Centre, he moonlighted in the Florida State Baseball League as player-manager for the Cleveland Indians minor league club in Bradenton. During the fall of 1924, Kendrick was back in pro football with the Chicago Bears. He appeared in nine games in a season in which the 6-1-4 Bears were second in the NFL. Following the rhythm of fall football and spring and summer baseball, he started 1925 as an outfielder for the Chicago Logan Squares in the Midwest Baseball League, then in the fall played football with the New York Buffalo Bisons, a team that managed only a 1-6-2 record that year.[44]

Likely inspired by the Second Texas Infantry's success in their final game against the First New York Cavalry, in which the team of all Texans trounced the best northern and eastern football players in the country, Kendrick offered the Buffalo Bison management his idea of building a team composed entirely of Texas and Oklahoma players. They agreed, and he became the experimental team's player, coach, and manager.

Fourteen newly signed footballers, who had never been east of the Mississippi River, made the trip from Waco to New York in five Fords during the summer of 1926 to join Kendrick's renamed Bison Rangers, the name a nod to the Lone Star State's famous law enforcement branch. The Rangers ended their first – and last – season with a 4-4-2 record. Kendrick was the team spark plug on the field, and in Jeffrey Miller's well-researched account of that season in "Jim Kendrick: The Man with the Plan" (2003), he follows Kendrick's every pass, run, punt, and extra point.[45]

The Buffalo franchise was renamed the Bisons for its 1927 season, but Jim Kendrick had already moved on. That fall he signed with the New York Giants, the team's 11-1-1 record taking the 1927 NFL championship title. True to his nature, he left at the end of the season, this time taking a position as head coach of the Rattlers football team at St. Mary's University in San Antonio. His training program was somewhat unorthodox, such as relocating his players to Corpus Christi in the late summer of 1928 for "an arduous conditioning course" that entailed mostly working manual labor. Theirs was not a winning season, however, and Kendrick resigned after his first season.[46]

In 1929, Kendrick was working in the Texas oil fields, and when he was home in Waco, officiated sports games. He was offered the opportunity to coach an Army Reserve football team for the Blanco Civilian Conservation Corps in 1932. In November of the next year, the team was traveling to a playoff game near Stephenville in an Army transport truck, with three men in the cab and 15 in the canvas-covered rear. The vehicle overturned. Two players were killed and the rest injured, some severely.

It was a truck with at least two heroes. Despite losing several teeth and ignoring a skull fracture, W.R. Lohse pulled several injured men from the carnage, and assisted in getting them to the hospital. Then he collapsed and died of a concussion. Jim Kendrick, with his right arm bone protruding through his skin at the wrist, was equally caring and refused treatment at the hospital until the last of his men were tended to. When he finally relented to the operating table, his arm had become infected and was amputated above the elbow. Kendrick was awarded the Soldier's Medal by the War Department for his peacetime acts of heroism. Interviewed by reporters as he recovered, he told them he would one day play football again, saying that the "brass nub on this stub I have left" will provide "the best stiff-arming machine you ever heard of."[47]

After 1934, Army Reserve Captain Kendrick divided his time between Waco and San Antonio. He died in his hometown of Waco, Texas, on November 17, 1941, after a stroke. Big Jim Kendrick was just 48 years old.[48]

Mullie Lenoir. Second-squad lineman Bertram Earl Lenoir spent the early spring of 1918 at the University of Alabama where he was vying for shortstop on the Crimson and White baseball team. He returned to Alabama after the war and played both baseball and football, winning All-Southern All-Star nominations in both sports. 1919 may have been his best baseball season, the centerfielder batting well over .350. As an Alabama running back, Lenoir was reported to be the nation's leading college scorer in 1919 and again in 1920. In 1919 the Crimson Tide won eight games out of nine and in 1920 won 11 straight games. Lenoir's 144 points on 24 touchdowns for the 1920 season remained the Crimson Tide's highest individual scoring record until as late as 1951. Lenoir left college in the spring of 1921 to try out for the American Association Columbus Senators baseball team but never made the roster.[49]

Lenoir went into coaching after baseball, his first job at Rosebud High School located between Waco and Austin and just south of his native Marlin. He left after four years to take a football coaching position at Georgetown University in Kentucky. In 1929, he relocated to Virginia as the Bluefield College Rambling Reds athletic director, coaching the school's football, basketball, and baseball teams until 1940. With a 79-18-2 gridiron record that included nine straight wins in 1933, the Virginia college inducted Lenoir into its Sports Hall of Fame in 1982. Lenoir remained in Virginia until 1972 then moved to Tennessee where the "high-class gentlemen of integrity and a top football coach" died in 1979.[50]

Charley Ogden. During the First World War, one-time Second Infantry starting lineman Charles Wesley Ogden served in the Regular Army's 57th Infantry and was stationed at Fort Sam Houston, Camp Pike in Arkansas, and Camp Benning, Georgia. Promoted to captain, he was at Camp Dix in New Jersey and Fort Sam Houston before retiring from the military in 1934. In both his military and civilian roles, the former first-string Second Texas lineman officiated sports games in Texas for over 40 years. Ogden worked as a referee, umpire, and timekeeper for high school and college football and basketball as a member of both the Southwest Football and Southwest Basketball

Associations. He remained in the Alamo City after his army service, working for an outdoor advertising firm and the Connecticut Mutual Life Insurance Company, then opened a branch office in Corpus Christi in 1936. He remained in Corpus Christi for the remainder of his life, his last job as personnel manager of Columbia Southern Chemical Corporation. Ogden died in 1968.[51]

Rats Watson. Stateside in 1919, Watson enrolled at the University of Texas. When the former Texas Eleven quarterback stepped onto the Longhorn practice field in the fall of 1919, Austin area newspapers trumpeted "the coming of Grady Watson, the greatest quarterback that ever stepped on a Southern gridiron." But he didn't play much under coach William Juneau, and that season UT went to the annual Longhorn-Aggie Thanksgiving match with a record of 6-2. The rival Aggies, however, dominated football in 1919 under returning head coach Dana X. Bible, outscoring its opposition 275-0 and winning ten games while not losing a single contest. The Aggies beat the Longhorns by 7-0 in the Thanksgiving game at Clark Field to earn the top spot in the Southwest Conference. UT was relegated to fourth, behind Rice and Oklahoma.[52]

1920 was an exciting year in Texas football. Both A&M and UT, the latter under new head coach Berry Whitaker, were undefeated. The 1920 Thanksgiving match at Clark Field would decide the Southwest Conference title, and it was, to that time, the best-attended game in Lone Star football history. Whitaker played Watson on punt returns and rotated him at the quarterback slot. The former Orange High School star made the longest run of the game, scrambling 45 yards on a kickoff return. Although he played in less than half of the contest, he gained more ground than any other UT player, and his game total of 61 yards matched the yardage of the entire Aggie team. The Longhorns won the contest 7-3 for the 1920 conference title. That year Watson was awarded his first varsity letter and was named an All-Southwest Conference quarterback.[53]

Watson's last year with the Longhorns was 1921. That year UT and A&M were again heading into the Thanksgiving game to decide the Southwest Conference crown. Fifteen thousand rooters packed Kyle Field and in a first for the Lone Star State, student radio operators from College Station and Austin joined to broadcast what was the first play-by-play radio transmission of a Lone Star football game. Watson, who had been out most of the season to injuries, was brought in at quarterback in the fourth quarter but only managed to complete a single pass. The defensive contest ended in a scoreless tie. The 1921 Southwest Conference title went to the Aggies who won more conference games.[54]

Nineteen Longhorns were awarded varsity letters for the 1921 season. The qualifying criteria for the varsity 'T' was for play in two or more quarters in "most" college games, or two quarters against rival A&M in their annual contest. Due to his injuries, Watson was not on the field enough to qualify, an inconvenience the University Athletic Council remedied by awarding him "an unqualified letter by special recommendation."[55]

At the close of the Longhorns 1921 season, Watson was selected to play on a national collegiate All-Star team with former Second Infantry teammate Spitz Clarke, their opponents an Army All-Start roster with K.L. Berry in the lineup. Ten thousand spectators were on hand at Camp Travis stadium for the Christmas Day game. In what was likely a first for the players, they wore numbers on their jerseys. Watson, number 11, alternated between quarterback and right halfback. Weighing in at a paltry 145 pounds during his

Second Texas Infantry days, he was now up to 178. Spitz Clarke played left halfback for the college All-Stars, and Berry was in the starting lineup at right tackle for the Army.[56]

The first half belonged to Rats Watson, who "could not be stopped by the soldiers." He "reeled off yard upon yard, and added first down after first down," contributing to the college boys' 19 first downs to the Army's one. In the first quarter, Watson made a sweeping 42-yard end run, then followed it by with a touchdown pass. He was also the team's punter, although he missed his only extra-point attempt. It must have seemed like old times when Berry intercepted a Watson toss, the only interception he threw during the half. At half-time, the Army was ahead 7-6. The college All-Star score should have been higher, but they were heavily penalized.

In the third quarter, Watson was charged with unnecessary roughness, a penalty that cost the team half of his punt return yardage. Arguing fiercely with the referee, the self-proclaimed "cocky" football player was ejected from the field. In the fourth quarter, the score unchanged, Watson invented a play from the sidelines and explained it to the offense. What happened next was talked about for years. The All-Star center held the ball on a fake snap and tossed a lateral to the right guard, who "held the ball on the back of his leg" while the left tackle came around the line and grabbed it, then crossed the goal while the Army defense "ganged up on a harmless player." Clarke kicked the goal. Watson's scheme led to the All-Stars winning touchdown, the final score 13-7.[57]

Watson returned to Orange in the spring of 1922, taking a position as the Port Arthur High School coach. He didn't make it through the summer. The Toledo Maroons, a formerly independent team that joined the new National Football League, signed him to play professional football and he was off to Ohio. He played in both seasons the Maroons were in Toledo, their record a fourth place finishing 5-2-2 in 1922 and 3-3-2 in 1923.[58]

Dallas had not yet become synonymous with pro football, and it was the Maroons that played the first professional football game staged in the city on Christmas Day, 1922. With the regular season ended, the Maroons brought in Jim Thorpe and other star players for a post-season tournament series. Dallas's first pro football game was a match between the Maroons and the Southern All-Stars, a collection of Texas and Southwestern US college players. Watson was one of the top ground gainers in a defensive contest that remained scoreless until the fourth period. Then Jim Thorpe did was he was famous for, winning the game with a drop-kicked 30-yard field goal for a final score of 3-0.[59]

Watson played against Thorpe for several seasons, and in a 1959 interview with Al Ward of the *Waco Tribune-Herald*, he spoke of the famously fierce and accomplished football player. Watson recalled the rivals were in a hotel room before a Cleveland game where Thorpe offered a warning: "Little man, I love you like a brother, but don't run [the ball] tomorrow. You do, I'm gonna hurt you." Watson, despite the threat, ran twice, and twice Thorpe "knocked me into the chairs." He added: "When Thorpe hit, he meant it. I wish you could see his shoulder pads. There was a heavy layer of felt, then a steel plate, then a leather covering. I couldn't lift them."[60]

After the Maroons, Watson briefly coached his former teammates K.L. Berry and Spitz Clarke in a January 1922 college All-Star match against the Army's Second Division. Then he answered the call of pro ball again, joining the Kansas City Blues, Hammond Pros, and Buffalo Bisons. He retired in 1925 after appearing in 20 NFL games. Watson next worked as a salesman, a stint as justice of the peace, then joined the Texas Liquor Control Board in 1936, where he remained for the next 24 years. He never lost his passion for the gridiron, and throughout his post-pro football career traveled the state as a college football referee and line umpire.[61]

When Watson retired from the liquor board in 1959, the Texas House of Representatives unanimously passed Resolution 256 recognizing Grady Watson for his service to the state and his distinguished football career, listing his Orange High School play, the Second Texas Infantry, his Longhorn years, and pro ball career. He was 62 years old when poor health, caused mostly by the German gassing in World War I, forced him to stop attending ball games. In what was perhaps his last interview, he spoke of the effect of the gassing the "scratched remorselessly at his lungs." He was no longer able to walk any distance, and climbing stairs and ramps was impossible. Watson died in Houston in 1965.[62]

GIANTS vs. YANKEES

NATIONAL LEAGUE — AMERICAN LEAGUE

World's Series

——BASEBALL——

Queen Theatre

Commencing Wednesday, Oct. 5, 1 p. m.

New Electric Scoreboard

8x10 Feet, Displaying 145 Lights in Four Colors, and all
Will Correctly Record Each and Every
Play the Instant Received On

DIRECT LEASER WIRE FROM THE BALL PARK

WHO SHALL IT BE?
RUTH VS. KELLY
MEUSEL VS. MEUSEL

Rip Collins, famous Second Texas football star, who was
located at Camp Scurry here is one of the Yankee
Pitchers.

Six-Game Ticket	$2.50
Single Tickets	50c
Children's Tickets	25c

TICKETS ON SALE AT THE AMUSU THEATRE

Left: Modern technology allowed Corpus Christi sports fans to watch the October World Series scoreboard live at the Amusu Theatre, the game featuring New York Yankee pitcher Rip Collins. Modified from *Corpus Christi Times*, Oct. 3, 1921.

Below: Warren "Rip" Collins as a Detroit Tiger pitcher, circa 1923. "Harry Warren (Rip) Collins, Texas A&M Legend," *Traces of Texas*, forum.tracesoftexas.com.

Left: Eugene Dotson. After his World War I service and the memorable 1918-19 AEF football season, the former Second Texas Infantry fullback returned to Baylor. Thirty-eight-year-old Eugene Malcolm Dotson III entered the Legion VA Hospital near Kerrville in December 1931 and died there on March 18, 1932. "1920 Round-Up Yearbook," *Baylor University Archives*, digitalcollections-baylor.quartexcollections.

Right: Bertram Earl "Mullie" Lenoir returned to Alabama after the war and played both baseball and football for the university, winning All-Southern and All-Star nominations in both sports. The Alabama running back was the nation's leading college scorer in 1919 and 1920. Lenoir's 144 points on 24 touchdowns for the 1920 season remained the Crimson Tide's highest individual scoring record until as late as 1951. "1920 Corolla," University of Alabama Libraries Special Collections, 27, 1920.

169

Grady "Rats" Watson enrolled at the UT in 1919 and played two seasons with the Longhorns. Both the top and bottom images are by Austin photographer Adkisson and are from the 1919 annual Longhorn-Aggie Thanksgiving Day match at Clark Field. The Aggies won the game 7-0. In the top image, the football is barely visible in the right center over the stands. Texas A&M University Libraries, Oak Trust, *Cushing Collection*, https://hdl.handle.net/1969.1/11 0559 and 110560.

Top: The 1920 University of Texas conference winning Longhorn team. Rats Watson is shown on bottom row, second player from right. "1921 Cactus Yearbook," *Texas Scholar Works*, University of Texas Libraries, http://hdl.hande.net/2152/61678.

Bottom: 1920 Thanksgiving Day game at Kyle Field. Both UT and A&M were undefeated, and the annual Thanksgiving match would decide the Southwest Conference title. Rats Watson played in a close contest that the Longhorns won 7-3. Texas A&M University Libraries, Oak Trust, *Cushing Collection*, https://hdl.handle.net/1969.1/110728.

Left: Rats Watson in 1921, his last season with the UT Longhorns. "1922 Cactus Yearbook," *Texas Scholar Works*, University of Texas Libraries, http://hdl.hande .net /2152/61677.

Below: Both Rats Watson and Jim Kendrick played football with the famous Jim Thorpe, shown carrying the ball in a 1915 game. Watson and Thorpe were rivals in the 1920s, although they played on the same team during the 1922 Maroon-All-Star game played in Dallas. After his Baylor years, Jim Kendrick joined Jim Thorpe's Canton Bulldogs. The Bulldogs were part of the new National Football League in 1922 and their 10-0-2 record took the championship that year. Rookie Kendrick played in four games as a back and end. "Jim Thorpe NFL File Photos," *NFL*, nfl.com.

CHAPTER 9

PART 2

Duty to Country

*D*uty to country was a strong common thread between most of the Second Texas Infantry's players, and it was apparent even after they parted ways. In 1918, most of them went to war, and many were the same heroes on the battlefield that they were on the gridiron. Seven former footballers were wounded during World War I. Many of the players remained in the Texas National Guard for decades after the Great War and several served in some capacity during America's next global conflict, World War II.

Of the players and management, ten either remained in or later joined the Regular Army. Three achieved the rank of brigadier general, a remarkably high number for the small sample size of a football team. The list of generals included Oscar Abbott, Kearie Lee Berry, and Pleas Rogers.

Ock Abbott. Former Second Texas Infantry quarterback Oscar Bergstrom Abbott married Elizabeth Stephens in 1918. Theirs was a military life full of transfers. Between 1920 and 1933 Abbott was stationed at Fort Benning in Georgia, Panama, San Francisco, and Fort Leavenworth, Kansas for two years in 1931. The newly promoted major went to Army War College in Washington D.C. in 1933, then enrolled in Washington College of Law and received his diploma in 1936. Abbott next returned to Texas as a Fort Sam Houston instructor but was back in Washington when World War II broke out.

Abbott's first assignment during the Second World War was as Military Personnel Director in the War Department. Then General Eisenhower personally requested his transfer to London as Chief of Staff, and the assignment came with a promotion from colonel to brigadier general. After the war he was placed in command of Camp Beale in California, then back to Washington before a transfer to Austin as commanding officer of the Texas Military District to administer the Army Reserves program. Abbott died in 1969 and was buried in Fort Sam Houston National Cemetery.[1]

K.L. Berry. First-squad offensive fullback and defensive lineman Kearie Lee Berry married Alice Fleming in 1917, the couple transferring to San Diego for the duration of the Great War where Berry was assigned to the 21st Infantry. Two years later, Lt. Berry spent nine months on the southeast Russian border with China as part of the 27th Infantry US expeditionary forces in Vladivostok during the Bolshevik Revolution. After a half-year stint in the Philippines, Berry returned as a captain and was posted as infantry commander at Fort Sam Houston in San Antonio, where he played football again.[2]

In 1921, Berry was on the Army All-Start roster during the annual Christmas Day Army-College All-Star game, playing against former Second Infantry teammates Spitz Clarke and Rats Watson. Since he was eligible for both the College All-Stars and the Army team, the next year he switched allegiances and played with Spitz Clarke under coach Rats Watson's All-Stars. For the 1923 Annual Christmas Day football matchup between the college All-Stars and the Camp Travis footballers, Berry was back with the Army and was the team captain, playing against player-coach Clarke and backfielder Eugene Dotson.[3]

The combination of National Guard duty and the threat of World War I had kept Berry from completing his UT degree, and in 1924 the Army captain was allowed to return to UT. He played Longhorn football, and at age 31, made the All-State Southwest Conference team. His nomination came with the accolades that he was not just an "outstanding guard," but he was probably also "the smartest football player in the conference" with "a great fighting heart" who "inspires his fellow [players]." At the end of the regular college season, Berry rejoined his Army team for the annual Christmas Day Army-College All-Star game. The Army lost 13-0 to a team with Spitz Clarke as its coach and Eugene Dotson as a fullback. It was Berry's last year as a player.[4]

After graduation, Captain Berry was assigned to Fort Benning, Georgia, and coached various Army athletic teams there and at North Carolina's Fort Bragg in 1926, where football coach Berry's assistant was his old coaching adversary from the 1917 Second Texas Infantry All-Star game, Dwight Eisenhower. In 1929 he was transferred to the University of Vermont as a military science and tactics instructor. After his stint in Vermont, he was posted in Tientsin China from 1934 to 1936 as a military advisor before returning stateside to San Francisco. By 1941 he was Lt. Colonel Berry, camp commander of Camp Bowie. In October, he was "directed to go to San Antonio where he will receive assignment to an unnamed post." It nearly killed him.[5]

In July 1941, President Franklin Roosevelt issued orders to fold the Philippine Army into the US Army Forces in the Far East (USAFFE) under commander General Douglas MacArthur, its goal to defend America's Pacific theatre military installations. That November, Berry was transferred to the Philippines as a senior instructor to the First Philippine Constabulary Regiment. The islands were assaulted by Japan just nine hours after the attack on Pearl Harbor. Berry was shifted to a field assignment as commander of the Third Infantry Regiment as part of the South Luzon Force before assuming command of the First Regular Division of the Philippine Army.[6]

With little support from America's crippled Far East Air Force or the Pacific Fleet, Japan made quick inroads into the main island of Luzon. Commanding from Fort Mills, situated on the island of Corregidor south of Bataan between Manilla Bay and the South China Sea, MacArthur ordered a withdrawal of the American and Filipino troops and consolidation in the mountainous jungle stronghold of the Bataan Peninsula.

The responsibility for the Bataan campaign fell to Lt. General Jonathan M. Wainwright, the highest-ranking officer on the ground during the Philippine defensive. Having fallen back from the north neck of the Bataan Peninsula after the first of January, the USAFFE prepared to form an east-west line of resistance, called the Bagac-Orion line, that stretched across the peninsula in a saddle between Mt. Natib and Mt. Mariveles. It was a hellish terrain dissected by rivers and streams converging from the concentric-shaped northern and southern volcanic highlands and joining in a confusing array beneath a canopy of thick jungle and bamboo.

Colonel Berry's role in the campaign was detailed in Louis Morton's 1953 *The Fall of the Philippines*. Morton wrote that General Wainwright gave command of the Philippine

Army's First Division to Colonel Berry in February 1942. By then, the Japanese had managed to penetrate a mile behind the main line of resistance in two strongholds, known as the Big and Little Pockets. Wainwright was as intent on reducing the Pockets as the Japanese were on reinforcing them. But after a week, every attempt by the USAFFE to dislodge them failed. Colonel Berry was directed to make his own plans to take the Little Pocket and began his offensive on February 7.

With the Little Pocket surrounded Berry was ready to make the final attack the next night. The enemy slipped away in the darkness and attempted to return to the Japanese lines. They were intercepted and offered the opportunity to surrender. When they responded with gunfire, they were killed to the last man. Colonel Berry next brought his force into the Big Pocket fight, supporting the USAFEE offensive that drove the last remaining defenders north through the jungle. Of the original 1,000 soldiers that made up the Big Pocket's invaders, just 377 returned to their division.[7]

The USAFEE had been under siege for over a month. Washington viewed Bataan as a lost cause and made little attempt to run the Japanese gauntlet to provide reinforcements or supplies, such as desperately needed medicine and food. Disease and an existence on half rations were taking a toll on the American and Philippine defenders. When the Japanese withdrew after the Pocket skirmishes to await reinforcements, one of the strategies they discussed was simply letting their enemy starve to death in the jungle. Japan was in a hurry, however, and chose a final assault.

MacArthur was ordered from his Corregidor Fort Mills command post to the safety of Australia, and after his departure on March 12, General Wainwright was given the unenviable task of directing the Philippine theatre as the Japanese offensive was renewed. The outgunned American and Filipino positions suffered aerial strafing and bombardment, as well as unrelenting artillery fire. On March 24, the Japanese attacked the defender's lines in wave after wave, day and night, their movement supported by field guns, bombing raids, and tanks and barges mounted with artillery.[8]

By the end of March, the situation was bleak. In their final fighting days, rations were cut from half to a third. Twenty thousand of the fighting force suffered from malaria, and thousands more fought dysentery, scurvy, hookworm, and beriberi. The remnants of the USAFEE were forced to abandon the Bagac-Orion position, withdrawing along the coast and to the south, making stand after stand during the retreat. There was no place left to go.

It was early April, and the defenders were beaten. When MacArthur communicated his orders for the fighting force to countermarch north across the entirety of the peninsula to attack Olongapo, on Subic Bay – a distance of 50 miles through occupied Japanese territory – it was clear he had either little compassion or an understanding of the situation in the field. Only a third of the 78,000 men were considered combat-effective, and most of these men were starving. They were simply too weak to fight. The USAFEE ignored his orders, sending emissaries forward with a white flag and surrendering the Bataan forces on April 9. History credits them with not being beaten militarily but by starvation and disease.[9]

The record is unclear whether Colonel Berry accompanied General Wainwright to Corregidor in March or was one of the approximately 2,000 fighting men and nurses who escaped Bataan in April and trickled across the Northern Channel the three miles to the rock fortress. Berry would spend the next month at the island command center, the next target of the Japanese offensive.[10]

Corregidor had an original 1941 reserve force of 6,000, the flow of refugees from Luzon after the fall of Bataan bringing the number to 10,000. Its occupants existed in two altered worlds. Non-combat personnel, doctors and nurses, command, and scores of the wounded subsisted in the Malinta system of tunnels carved beneath the verdant, jagged volcanic rocks of Malinta Hill, while the vestiges of the Marine, Navy, and Army manned its beaches and artillery posts.

From December 29 to January 6 the rock had been pounded daily, the raids intensifying after the Bataan surrender. Artillery from the heights of the Mariveles Mountains on Bataan and aerial bombing slowly reduced the rock fortress. On May 4, Corregidor shook with the thunder of 16,000 shells in just 24 hours. By then, its defensive infrastructure was obliterated, its barracks, hospital, airstrip, gun, and artillery batteries reduced to rubble, and the Navy's remaining minesweepers and launches sunk.

They came by barge at night on May 5. Despite stubborn resistance, the Japanese succeeded in establishing a beachhead on the island's northeast side. The fight along the narrow spine of the rock was intense, but effectively over when the Japanese landed tanks. Pushed west, the backs of the Marines and the Army were pressed to the foothills of Malinta Hill. On May 6, Wainwright issued order Pontiac, the code name for surrender. White flags flew over the Malinta tunnel.[11]

The Japanese command was not prepared for the nearly 80,000 prisoners that surrendered during April at Bataan and May at Corregidor. Most of the Bataan prisoners were force-marched in groups of a hundred from the southern tip of Bataan and up the peninsula's east coast to Camp O'Donnell in the Luzon central plain, a distance of about 65 to 85 miles. The Corregidor prisoners were divided between Cabanatuan in northcentral Luzon, the prison stockade in Manilla, and Camp O'Donnell. Colonel Kearie Lee Berry's fate as a POW was Camp O'Donnell, and he followed the trail of the 70,000 emaciated survivors of Bataan who, for the last month, had staggered up the coastal and inland route.[12]

In history, it's known as the Bataan Death March. By the time Berry and the Corregidor captives trudged along its track, the roadside was an image of startling carnage. Bodies of soldiers were everywhere. Some had fallen from disease, some from starvation, others from dehydration and exhaustion, but most at the hands of their captors. Any prisoner who collapsed along the way was killed immediately by bayonets, bullets, or beheadings.

Most of the Bataan POWs remained at Camp O'Donnell for two to three months. They received no medical supplies, subsisted on eight ounces of rice and a little soup a day, and were habitually beaten and tortured. About 400 men died each day, and most sources estimate that about 20,000 Filipinos and 1,500 Americans died as Camp O'Donnell POWs.[13]

Berry was transferred from Camp O'Donnell to the Formosa Karenko prison camp in 1942, and his time there overlapped with General J.M. Wainwright. Excerpts from Wainwright's writings, published in a series of newspaper columns across the United States in 1945, provide a stark image of what he, Berry, and the other POWs endured. Flies covered their ration of rice, the matrix of grains smattered with weevils and black-headed, inch-long worms. The more enterprising POWs searched for snails they plucked from the ground and boiled in water. On Christmas Day, 1942, their captors provided them with 30 ducks to share between 400 prisoners, and they each got an apple. A month later they were provided with their first protein, consisting of buckets of cattle stomachs, intestines, and lungs from a nearby slaughterhouse. Every day they suffered beatings and watched their friends die.[14]

For a year, K.L. Berry's family didn't know if he was dead or alive. In a letter he wrote in May 1942, Berry scribed that he was indeed alive, but he had lost 60 pounds. The letter didn't arrive until January 1943, the same month the family got a dispatch from the War Department advising that he had been captured and was being held prisoner on Formosa.[15]

Berry was moved from Formosa to an internment camp on Kyushu Island in southern Japan before he was shipped to Hoten-Mukden POW camp in Manchuria. Conditions there were better for those who had survived their months and years as POWs. The prisoners were housed in brick dormitories and given blankets and coal for heat during the bitter winters. They tended vegetable gardens in summer and most worked in a nearby factory. Some of the POWs remember that, to obtain meat, they baited camp dogs with their bread and corn meal rations, then beat them to death as they approached and ate the carcasses. According to another prisoner, whenever a captive escaped and was recaptured, the barracks were forced to assemble to witness them dig their graves before they were shot.[16]

K.L. Berry had been a prisoner for 40 months when, in September 1945, he was liberated from the Hoten-Mukden POW camp by Russian troops. By October, he was back in America and undergoing evaluation at Brooke Hospital in San Antonio. On special order of the War Department, Lt. Colonel Berry was promoted to brigadier general in February 1946. The same year he was awarded the Distinguished Service Cross for "extraordinary heroism" as First Infantry commander at the Battle of the Pocket's in Bataan. Other decorations he received for his wartime service included the Distinguished Service Medal, Silver Star, Bronze Star, the Philippine Legion of Honor, and the Purple Heart. His earning of the Purple Heart, according to a Texas newspaper, was because of a clubbing at the hands of his captors when he refused to give them his fountain pen.[17]

In 1946, Berry took a position in Austin as Executive Officer of the Texas Military District in Austin as head of the Reserve Officers Association. He retired from the Regular Army on May 2, 1947. Five days later, he was appointed as the Adjutant General of Texas in the Texas National Guard with oversight of the state's military department, which included the Texas State Guard, the Texas Army National Guard, and the Texas Air National Guard. Major General Berry was named to six additional terms by three governors before retiring after 14 years in 1961.[18]

In his official capacity, Berry was tireless in his battle to maintain funding for the National Guard as a budget-conscious Washington repeatedly sought to cut its funding. When the promised prisoners of war reparations were foundering, he joined his former commander J.M. Wainwright in 1950 to address the War Claims Commission. He fought for Texas armories and believed in the importance of state readiness for times of emergency. He was a force behind National Guard Muster Day which served to increase recruitment. As a participant in the annual National Guard conference, he was instrumental in collecting monies to erect the National Guard Memorial Building in Washington D.C. For a time, there was even a K.L. Berry Award for outstanding National Guard heroism and a K.L. Berry Humanitarian Award.

He probably didn't plan it that way, but from his return to Texas until 1961, General Berry was a Lone Star State celebrity. He traveled the state attending every National Guard review, ceremony, and officer promotion that his schedule allowed. He was a speaker at Armed Forces Week parades and celebrations and was requested as the master of ceremonies at town festivities and rodeo and stock shows. He volunteered his time with the VFW and as a speaker at civic groups.

In December 1952, the Texas governor designated Berry as the Lone Star State's official representative at President-elect Dwight Eisenhower's inauguration. That January, a 125-car special train left Dallas for the festivities. On board were six matched Palominos that would pull a golden carriage belonging to the Texas Cavaliers marching group from San Antonio, and Berry was to be its celebrated occupant. It must have been a singular moment as the two men reflected on their 1917 Second Texas Infantry-All-Star football clash and their time together coaching the Army's Fort Bragg gridiron team.[19]

In 1955, celebrity Berry was Texas Chairman of the March of Dimes. That year, a group of Austin citizens hosted a surprise tribute to Berry at the Driskill Hotel in Austin. Two of the hosts were former Texas governor Dan Moody and Col. Tom Mitchell, his former Second Texas Infantry football mate and now his Assistant Texas Adjutant General. Two years later, Berry was parade chairman at Governor-Elect Price Daniel's 1957 inauguration. Berry was a regular at Longhorn sports events and the three-letter man was honored in 1959 with induction to the UT Sports Hall of Fame.[20]

In July 1961, Berry was a pallbearer at the funeral of his old friend Tom Mitchell. Two months later, Berry was admitted to Brooke General Hospital in San Antonio. He remained bedridden for a month, much of that time in critical condition before he was released in early November. In January, he was admitted to Brackenridge Hospital in Austin. After over a month in its intensive care unit, he was transferred to Brooks Army Medical Center, and in March returned home. But he was hospitalized two more times in April.[21]

That August, he buried his son. Forty-three-year-old Colonel Kearie Lee Berry II, a 1943 West Point graduate, was commander of Paine Air Force Base in Washington when he was killed in a jet crash. Berry Jr. left behind an older son, K.L. Berry III, who was following in his father and grandfather's footsteps as a cadet in the Air Force Academy in Colorado Springs.[22]

The military bearing and smiling, chiseled face that had appeared so often in Texas newspapers between World War II and the onset of the Vietnam conflict was missing from the media between 1962 and 1965. Then, on April 25, 1965, K.L. Berry suffered a heart attack. Two days later he died at Brooke General Hospital in San Antonio. He was laid to rest with full military honors at Fort Sam Houston National Cemetery, next to his son.[23] That year, the Texas Senate unanimously passed a resolution recognizing Kearie Lee Berry for the "noble life of one of Texas' most distinguished public officials, gallant soldiers, and outstanding athletes and recognized with appreciation his many contributions to the state and nation."[24]

Mike Bloor. Alfred Wainwright Bloor was the Second Texas Infantry's athletic director. By the time he was made second in command of the Second Texas under Colonel B.F. Delameter, the 1895 A&M College graduate and 1904 UT law alumnus already had over 20 years of military service, including a tour of duty in Cuba during the Spanish-American War. After the decorated colonel returned from World War, I he settled in Austin to practice law.[25]

During his first months at home, Bloor wrote a three-part series on the history of the guard called *Texas National Guard in the World War*, published in the *Austin Stateman* in 1919. His narrative was unerring in its detail, and his description of the hardships of battle unflinching. In addition, his writings introduced his regiment's innovative strategy of recruiting Native American Choctaws to transmit coded messages during the war. In all, 14 Oklahoma soldiers of Bloor's 142nd Regiment participated in the "Code Talker" program that prevented the Germans from intercepting and decoding military communications. Bloor was invited to recite his war experiences before the Texas Legislature and gave talks at local civic clubs. Excerpts from Bloor's war memoirs continued to be published in US newspapers for the next 30 years.[26]

Bloor, who was a founder of the Texas National Guard Association, served as chairman of its executive committee in 1919. But the Austin lawyer was restless and didn't hesitate when the National Guard called him back into service the next year. In the summer of 1920, the Galveston docks were a war zone. A prolonged strike crippled its waterfront, its police department unable or unwilling to protect non-union longshoremen working the Mallory and Morgan Line docks from violence. Texas Governor W.P. Hobby responded by declaring martial law and dismissing the Galveston City Commissioners, city mayor, city attorney, and its police department for neglect of duty, replacing them with the National Guard and Texas Rangers.[27]

Colonel Bloor was given command of the military police and was responsible for stripping the Galveston peacekeepers of their badges and weapons. Over the next two months, he headed the campaign against illegal liquor operations, turning some 20 bootleggers over to federal custody. As he championed reforms in other areas of "vice in general," scores of "disreputable women" were said to have left the city. After the temporary lawmen restored order to the Galveston docks, the National Guard was decommissioned, and Texas Rangers remained in the city during early fall to monitor the police force.[28]

Bloor's recall to the National Guard precipitated his 1920 decision to return to the military. He enlisted in the Regular Army, leaving Austin for Fort Leavenworth, Kansas where the newly minted Army major graduated with distinction from the School of the Line in 1921, and was followed by General Staff School and Army War College in Washington D.C. He took a two-year assignment in the Philippines as assistant chief of staff in 1923 and was stateside at Fort Sam Houston for another two years.[29]

In 1927, Bloor was posted in Costa Rica and Nicaragua as US military attaché to the Central America Republics. US intervention in Nicaragua after 1912 led to a resistance and precipitated civil war from 1921 until 1927, and Bloor spent at least some time in the field during the struggle. No one should have been surprised that he documented at least one of his trips with the same detail as he did his WW I history series. Bloor's journal, complete with photographs, was only recently uncovered deep in the military archives of Nicaragua by Michael J. Schroeder, Professor Emeritus of History at Lebanon Valley College in Annville, Pennsylvania. Bloor was awarded the Nicaragua Medal by the US Marines in 1938.[30]

Bloor alternated between Washington and Fort Sam Houston until 1936 when he took an administrative role with the Army Reserves in Austin. He retired as a colonel in 1940.

Lawyer-soldier-citizen Mike Bloor died in 1952 at the age of 76 in Austin and was buried with full military honors.[31]

Whitey Davis. Captain Howard Herndon Davis enlisted in the US Army after World War I. The former Second Texas third squad player attended Army Infantry School at Camp Benning Georgia and in 1921 was ordered to Camp Travis for duty with the Citizen's Military Training Camp. He married Austin native Mildred Griffith in 1926 and was stationed that year at Schofield Military Base, near Honolulu. Other postings were in North Dakota and the Philippines. In 1937, he was back in Texas as a major in the Ninth Infantry and stationed in San Antonio at Fort Sam Houston. The next year he was ordered to the University of Arkansas to take charge of its Army ROTC program. In 1950, Colonel Davis was chief of the South Dakota Military District. He retired from the military in 1953 and moved to San Antonio. Davis died in 1969.[32]

John Diller. Former Second Texas Infantry first squad center and Illinois native John Cabot Diller enrolled at Yale after the war, playing center and tackle from 1921 until 1923. In the latter year, the Yale team went undefeated. He was inducted into the Skull and Bones Society during his senior year and graduated in 1924. He married Margaret Wells in 1927, settling in Connecticut where Diller worked as a personnel director at Yale and in 1932 was the Meriden Boys Club director.[33]

At the outbreak of World War II, Diller joined the Regular Army and was commissioned as a major in the Air Corps. He attended Officers Training Camp in Miami and Intelligence School in Virginia before a posting overseas in New Guinea and Queensland, Australia. He returned stateside in 1944 to Clearwater, Florida, but his stay was brief. Lt. Colonel Diller transferred to Japan between 1945 and May 1946 to serve on the Japanese War Commission. He remained for two more years as part of the legal and government board that restructured Japan's courts, police system, and public elections from Aug 1946 to March 1948. His wife died in Japan in 1946.[34]

Reassigned to the US in 1948, Diller had various military postings in California and Indiana before retiring in 1955. Colonel John C. Diller moved back to Illinois and died there in 1981.[35]

Tom Mitchell. Thomas D. Mitchell completed a law degree at UT after the War and returned to Waco where he owned an automobile dealership. The former second squad halfback moved to Los Angeles in 1927, then to Paris, Texas in 1935. He enlisted in the Army before World War II, and by 1943 was Major T.D. Mitchell, head of the Army Signal Corps' radio school in Kansas City. At war's end, he was commissioned as a colonel and served in China and Japan for three years. He retired from the Army in the late 1940s to take a position as assistant to the Texas Adjutant General – his old teammate from the Second Texas Infantry gridiron days, Kearie L. Berry. Mitchell died in 1961 after a heart attack.[36]

Pleas Rogers. Just days after their 1918 wedding, substitute player Pleasant Blair Rogers had to leave his new bride, El Paso native Clara Louise Fink, for the European theatre. After serving in France, he accepted the rank of Captain in the Regular Army and was assigned to the Ninth Infantry. Rogers in 1920 was at Fort Sam Houston and Camp Travis, then infantry school Fort Benning Georgia, cavalry school at Fort Riley, Kansas, and by 1930 was stationed in the Philippines. By 1937 he was Major Rogers and spent most of that year at Army War College in Washington D.C.[37]

In 1938, Rogers transferred from the Infantry to the Army Quartermaster Corps located in Front Royal, Virginia. At the onset of World War II, he was promoted to colonel and in 1942 was relocated to London, the next year the commanding officer of Army London Base Command and had charge of supply for much of the Allied European theatre. That year he was promoted to brigadier general. In 1945, he was transferred to France to command the Seine Base Section. The French awarded Rogers the Legion of Honor for his service in 1945, and back in America that Christmas, he was awarded the Distinguished Service Medal.[38]

Other than a few trips to visit family or attend funerals, Rogers rarely returned to Texas after 1946 and retired from the military in 1948. One of the retired general's passions was horses, and he relocated to the rolling hills and thoroughbred gentry of Front Royal and Warrenton, Virginia. He fine-tuned his knowledge of purebred cattle and thoroughbred horses as manager of the Walter P. Chrysler Estate in Warrenton for two years before purchasing a country estate called the "Llewellyn Farm." With his second wife, Rogers' new world was one of foxhunting, steeplechase, and other equestrian events. Each year, the couple held an annual Blue Ridge Hunt at their estate in Virginia that dovetailed with the famous Warrenton Hunt. They maintained a busy social schedule, entertaining at their home and traveling from New York to Florida.[39]

The retired general was learned in the horse and cattle breeding business. He maintained a network with other livestock raisers as an active member of the Clarke County Farm Bureau and was its president in 1953 and on the board of directors until 1955. He was known for his gifted eye at livestock auctions, making purchases as an owner and manager of a successful livestock company. By 1969, Rogers was living in Charles Town, West Virginia, where he bought two more country estates, called "Hawthorne Dale" and "Avon Bend." Rogers died in West Virginia at age 79 on Christmas Day, 1974.[40]

Sylvan Simpson. After his Leon Springs officer training, Sylvan B. Simpson joined the Regular Army and was promoted to captain in the 85th Infantry, 165th Depot Brigade. He served stateside during the war at Camp Travis, Camp Stanley, and Camp Gordon in Georgia. When he returned to Texas in the spring of 1919, Simpson scrambled to earn enough money to finish his degree at UT. The first-string lineman initially went to Waco, where he sold surplus army tents, then moved to North Texas and Oklahoma to work the oil fields. In 1921 he married, the couple living in Austin and Llano. Although he didn't have a law degree, Simpson announced for Llano County judge and was elected in 1932. The incumbent, J.W. Currie, lost by only 36 votes. Simpson ran again in 1934, but this time Judge Currie found the votes he needed to get his job back.[41]

Simpson moved his family back to Austin and in 1935 was given charge of the Texas Transient Bureau, a Depression-era relief program, before joining the Civilian Conservation Corps (CCC) as an Army Reserve officer. In 1936 he returned to active duty and had charge of the Brownwood CCC camp. He ran for Llano County Judge in 1938 and lost again. In 1940 he was CCC camp commander in Aragon, New Mexico and at the start of World War II was called to active duty at Lowrey Field in Denver as an infantry captain.[42]

In 1942 Simpson was given command of the Army Air Corps Training Detachment at Love Field, Dallas. That summer, he was posted in Louisiana and promoted to lieutenant colonel before shipping out to Europe. Simpson returned from Germany in 1950 and by

1954 was living in Pueblo, Colorado. He died at a VA hospital in 1970 and was buried in Llano County.[43]

Harry Stullken. Substitute lineman John Erwin "Harry" Stullken was commissioned as a lieutenant in the Regular Army's Sixth Division in 1917. When he returned from France in 1919 after serving with the 64th Infantry in the Meuse-Argonne Offensive, he was posted at Camp Grant, Illinois. Capt. Stullken next taught infantry school at Fort Benning, Georgia. Married and retired from the Army as a captain in 1925, he moved back to Austin. Stullken was prominent in Austin's Masons, Shriners, and the Travis County American Legion. He died in McClosky Veterans Hospital at 57 in 1953.[44]

Brigadier General Oscar Abbott. Abbott returned to Texas in the 1930s as a Fort Sam Houston instructor but was back in Washington when World War II broke out. General Dwight Eisenhower personally requested his transfer to London as Chief of Staff, and the assignment came with a promotion from colonel to brigadier general. "Charlotte L. Abbott Family Tree," *Ancestry.com.*

Brigadier General Kearie Lee Berry. On special order of the War Department, Lt. Colonel Berry was promoted to brigadier general in February 1946. The same year he was awarded the Distinguished Service Cross for "extraordinary heroism" as First Infantry commander at the Battle of the Pocket's in Bataan. After he retired from the Regular Army in 1947. Berry was appointed as the Adjutant General of Texas in the Texas National Guard. University of North Texas Libraries, *Portal to Texas History*, crediting Austin History Center, Austin Public Library, https://texas history.unt.edu.ark:/67531/metapth62660/.

US Military Attaché Major A. W. Bloor, far right, in Nicaragua in March 1927. Bloor was awarded the Nicaragua Medal by the US Marines in 1938. Michael J. Schroeder, "The Sandino Rebellion, Nicaragua, 1927-1934," No. USNA2-1.7, http://www.Sandino rebellion.com/PhotoPgs/1USNA2/PGS/pg1.html.

CHAPTER 9

PART 3

Lawyers and Laymen

*E*leven men on the Second Texas infantry team or its management completed law degrees. Some went into private practice, others used their degrees in the military, and several either ran for elected office or held political positions.

Bill Birge*.* First-string lineman William Samuel Birge Jr. was transferred to staff officer training at Langres, France after his battlefield tour. His military administrative duties weren't discussed as much, however, as his role as offensive and defensive line coach for the reformed 36th Division's football team of the AEF football program. After a brief tour in Italy, Birge sailed for New York and was back in Austin by August 1919.

Married to Josepha Pospeshenkse and with a young family to support, he immediately went to work as the founder of the oil and gas law partnership Smith & Birge. Smith in the partnership was former UT law student and third squad footballer Schuyler W. "Bud" Smith. The lawyers chose the town of Desdemona, located midway between Abilene and Dallas, to open their office in the First National Bank Building. With a string of nearby recent oil and gas discoveries, Desdemona was a wise choice. Birge relocated to Amarillo in the late 1920s and began to expand his business interests, owning and investing in a long list of companies by the 1930s.[1]

Birge devoted much of his time to the VFW. He was a founder of the John B. Golding Post No. 1475 in Amarillo in 1930, its post commander in 1933, then a state-wide departmental judge advocate. He was also active in the Amarillo and Texas State Bar Associations, heading the Bar's national defense legal committee at the beginning of World War II. An active Mason, Birge chartered the Palo Duro Lodge in 1938. Bill Birge died in 1973.[2]

Dan M. Cook*.* After the war, the Second Texas Infantry team manager returned to his native Titus County in northeast Texas to practice law, and he served as a two-term county judge. He moved in 1923 to the Texas Panhandle town of Plainview where he was a civil and criminal law attorney. Cook ran for District Attorney of the five-county 64th Judicial District in 1938 and lost. When Plainview formed a National Guard unit in 1940, the 67-man unit selected Dan Cook as its captain.[3]

Cook's law practice was interrupted in 1942 when he was returned to active duty and commissioned as an Army major. In a letter he wrote home in 1943, he was unable to disclose his war posting, but it was probably Northern Africa. He said of his war duty that it was "as hot as the hinges of hell," and described the sounds of "cannon and exploding bombs; the rattle of machine guns" and scenes of "the weird light of flares, star shells and tracer shells." Nightly German raids had the soldiers "diving for a slit trench" wearing only underwear and a tin helmet. After World War II service, Cook returned to Plainview and ran for District Judge of the 64th Judicial District. He lost. Dan Cook was active in the American Legion and was a member of the VFW, Elks Lodge, and a Mason. He was 78 when he died in the Amarillo Veterans Hospital in 1967.[4]

Baker Duncan. When 25-year-old Addison Baker Duncan filled out his WW I draft registration, he listed his occupation as a lawyer and farmer. With his father dead, he was managing the family farm for his mother. In 1919 he returned to Waco after his posting at Virginia's Fort Lee during the war. The former first-squad lineman practiced law for a few years before forming the Duncan-Smith automobile dealership. Duncan devoted much of his time to serving the city of Waco, and was named city commissioner in 1926, mayor in 1927, and in 1928 was chairman of the Waco City Charter Advisory Committee.[5]

When Baylor College was being lured from Waco to Dallas in 1928, Baker Duncan spearheaded the "Campaign Colonel's Divisions," a fund-raising organization that was structured like the military with a hierarchy of 240 volunteers reporting to captains who reported to its chairman, Colonel Duncan. In the end, Baylor remained in Waco. When the Baylor athletic program was struggling to compete against larger schools of the Southwestern Conference in the 1930s, it was Duncan with a team of Waco businessmen who formed the Baylor Big Brothers Inc. to provide financial assistance.[6]

Duncan married Francis Higginbottom, from Dallas, in 1926. Throughout the 20s and 30s, Francis Duncan spearheaded money-raising efforts for the McLennan Humane Society, Red Cross, area orphanages, and was chairperson of the Waco War Bond Committee "Women's Division." Unlike many of the women of that period, she was not confined to a social hostess role, her accomplishments far exceeding the expected life of floral arrangements and tea and cookies service. Mrs. Duncan was a learned historian who gave lectures on archeology, art, music, history figures, and even ancient Rome. She hosted study clubs, Bible studies, and was on the Waco Public Library Board of Directors.

Baker Duncan increased his business footprint during the 1930s and 1940s. He was a Director of the First National Bank of Waco and a Director of Texas Power & Light. When the Waco-based Southern Maid Bakery was heading for bankruptcy in 1948, Duncan was one of the many Wacoans who provided cash, and he served on the reorganized company board of directors as treasurer. His civic footprint was just as large. In 1938 he was on the board of directors of the Cotton Bowl Athletic Association, president of the Waco Chamber of Commerce, the YMCA Board of Directors, the Texas Episcopal Diocesan Council, chairman of the 1950 Waco-McLennan County Red Cross campaign, and he took pride in donating calves each year from his stock farm to the McLennan County 4-H Club. Addison Baker Duncan died in his sleep in 1952 at 60 years old.[7]

Thomas Gambrell. Capt. Thomas DeWitt Gambrell was in the Infantry Officer's Reserve Corps and was stationed during the war at Camp Greene in North Carolina, Camp Lee in Virginia, Washington D.C., and St Louis. One of the first things the former second-string halfback did after his 1919 discharge was volunteer his time and leadership skills to the American Legion. After attending the 1919 Texas American Legion convention in Dallas, he was elected an officer and remained active in the American Legion throughout his life. The Lockhart attorney married Josie Davis Francis in 1921, and that year penned a history of Caldwell County soldiers during World War I. He was elected county attorney the next year and county judge in 1925. In 1930 he ran for the Texas Senate and lost. The

UT Hall of Fame baseball star was a lifelong Mason and served on the Texas State Bar Association. He died in 1960 from a heart attack.[8]

Charlie Stewart. Former team manager Charles B. Stewart married Shreveport native Eunice Smith in 1917. The couple moved to Fort Worth in 1920 where Stewart opened the law firm of Clarence E. McGaw and Charles B. Stewart. When Eunice died in 1925, she left behind a four-year-old daughter, Virginia. Stewart remained in Fort Worth where he joined the legal staff of Shell Oil. He later moved to Tulsa to work for Continental Oil and Gas, and remarried. Stewart died of a heart attack at 51 in 1944.[9]

Bud Smith. In 1920, Schuyler William "Bud" Smith opened the law firm Smith & Birge, with Bill Birge in Desdemona, between Abilene and Dallas. He left the firm around 1927 and relocated to New Mexico where he practiced law and was active in the state's Republican party. During the 1930s, the Second Texas third squad player was elected Justice of the Peace for the New Mexico town of Dexter. He retired from law in 1950, then took a position as assistant superintendent of the state-run Juvenile Detention Home in Albuquerque. Bud Smith died in 1954 at age 63 when he was accidentally shot by his son, Schuyler Smith Jr., while they were deer hunting.[10]

Walter Woodul. Unofficial team manager Walter F. Woodul's political, civic, legal, and business resume was as rich as it was remarkable. Near the end of the Second Texas Infantry football season, Woodul left the National Guard, got married, and took his seat in the Texas House of Representatives for Laredo and Webb counties. He wasn't there long, resigning during World War I to serve his country. In his short time in the Texas Legislature, he had been chairman of the State Affairs Committee, vice-chairman of the Military Affairs Committee, and helped establish the Texas State Highway Commission.

Woodul joined the newly formed First Texas Cavalry as a first lieutenant, then quickly made major and was selected as the 36th Division Assistant Adjutant General, stationed at Camp Bowie. It was Woodul that Texas mothers called when their sons didn't make it home from the war, and as the soldiers began to filter back from overseas, it was Woodul that city politicians contacted to plan their welcoming parades and celebrations. At the war's end, he was instrumental in founding the Texas American Legion.[11]

After his 1919 military discharge, Woodul moved to Houston and established a law practice. He signed on as division attorney for the International and Great Northern Railroad Company, and in 1922, was named its company president. The civic-minded Woodul was a director in the Kiwanis Club, a member of the Harris County Bar Association, chairman of the precursor organization to the Harris County Drainage District, and in 1927 was named director of the Gulf Coast Good Roads Association.[12]

In 1928, Woodul decided to reenter politics. Early in the year, he worked to bring the Democratic presidential convention to Houston, although Chicago won out, and he was head of the Texas Democratic fundraising effort for presidential hopeful John Nance Garner. In a special election that November, the unfalteringly loyal Democrat won a bid as state senator representing Harris County's 16th District. Before he even took his seat, the man who so successfully negotiated the choppy waters of Army command to deliver the Second Texas Infantry its first football games, secured a 350-million-dollar bond for Texas highways. It was a profound achievement, the new legislator having "escaped the hatchets and knives of the factionists and emerged from the contest an easy winner."[13]

Woodul served three senate terms, not only excelling in the political arena, but relishing its processes of resolutions, amendments, and procedures. There was talk in 1932 of a Woodul run for governor at the end of Ross Sterling's tumultuous first term, but instead, Woodul ran for senate president pro tem. He was elected unanimously.[14]

In January 1934, Woodul announced he was running for the office of Texas Lieutenant Governor. It was a crowded field with six candidates on the July 28 ballot, but Woodul commented matter-of-factly that "I have no doubt of being elected." He won the popular vote by a wide margin, but not by enough to avoid a runoff which, as he predicted, he won handily.[15]

In 1938 Woodul announced his campaign for attorney general, and it was again a field crowded with five rivals. It was Texas politics at its best. His most vocal opponent, District Judge Ralph Yarborough, tried to convince crowds that Woodul's policies were responsible for the plight of blind children, impoverished families, and "kept thousands of elderly men and women off the pension rolls." He had even voted against the soldier's bonus. Little of it stuck, but what did hurt him was the perception of his alignment with big money interests. Woodul lost the contest to Southern Methodist University football star and Harvard Law School graduate Gerald Mann.[16]

Woodul left public office in 1939 and resisted its temptation for the rest of his career. He returned to his law practice in Houston and became a director of the Imperial Sugar Company. In the spring of 1945, Governor Coke Stevenson appointed him to the board of regents of the State Teachers Colleges, and in 1959, Governor Price Daniel appointed him to serve as a member of the Board for Texas State Hospitals and Special Schools. After retiring from his legal practice in 1958, the Woodul's moved to Austin, where he died on October 1, 1984, at the age of 92. He was buried in the Texas State Cemetery.[17]

Just A Regular Guy. Not every Second Texas Infantry football player made the newspapers for their exploits in sports, military, or legal careers. Some just got jobs and worked to support their families. They were simply everyday heroes.

Victor Bintliff. After the war, Sergeant Victor J. Bintliff moved back to Austin. The Purple Heart and Cross of Military Service recipient joined the US Immigration and Naturalization Service and was posted in El Paso, Del Rio, and Laredo, before relocating to Corpus Christi in 1931. He died of a heart attack at age 59 in 1954.[18]

Charlie Brown. Staff Sergeant Charles Wiley Brown did not return to college after the war, settling briefly in his Groesbeck hometown. He moved to Waco where he worked for the American Railway Express Agency for 34 years and died in 1960 of a heart attack.[19]

Tige Halphen. Louis Alcide Halphen, who was erroneously reported killed by a trench mortar during training at Camp Bowie, remained in Austin after the Great War as an iron worker. He was only 28 years old when he died from tuberculosis in 1923 at the American Legion Memorial Hospital in Kerrville.[20]

Dick Lane. In 1918, second-string utility player Richard G. Lane was stationed as Drillmaster at Simmons College Unit Students Army Training Corps in Abilene. That year his 20-year-old wife died. He remarried, raised two sons, and managed restaurants and motels in California, Oklahoma, and Colorado. He died in 1975.[21]

George Lane. First-squad end George H. Lane did not return to college after World War I, moving back to Waco where he worked as an electrician. He married Ethel Huse in 1920, the couple losing their five-year-old daughter Catherine to a ruptured appendix in

1928. Lane later owned a retail electric store and an electrical construction company, remaining in Waco until he died in 1972 of a heart attack.[22]

David Nelson. Second Texas Infantry second-string center and commander Bloor's right-hand man David R. Nelson moved to Taylor, east of Austin, after the war and returned to farming and ranching. With a widely respected reputation as a dairyman and stock farmer, he was just 31 years old when he was appointed as a director of the Williamson County Farm Bureau and agricultural agent for the First State Bank and Trust Company of Taylor. In the late 1920s, Nelson relocated to Orange when he was hired by W.H. Stark and his son Lutcher Stark, the UT football benefactor, to manage his cattle and agricultural interests.[23]

Nelson was nominated by Governor Dan Moody in 1930 to serve on the Texas Prison Board, and three years later was named by Governor Allred as Chairman of the Livestock Sanitary Commission. In 1935 he was solicited to head the Texas prison system. He held the job for just two weeks when, at only 46 years old, he died from complications of heart disease and pneumonia.[24]

Charles Schaedel. Third squad player Charles T. Schaedel and his wife Etta Lee traveled to Africa as Methodist missionaries from 1920 to 1928. Between trips to the African Congo, they lived in Bay City where they were deeply involved with the Methodist Church. Schaedel worked in Freeport as a civil engineer, and in the 1930s studied theology and added reverend to his resume. As late as 1960, he was still leading missionary study groups at churches across the state. For close to 50 years, his wife Etta served as an officer in the nationwide Woman's Division of Christian Service and the Women's Missionary Federation. She was involved in a long list of charity causes throughout their marriage, such as the Texas State Council of Methodist Women that served the needs of indigent Mexican children, and Texas prison reform. The Schaedel family remained in Bay City until at least the late 1960s before moving to Grapevine.[25]

Charles Turner. First Lt. Charles E. Turner served overseas for three months after the war with Seventh Army Corps before returning to Roswell, New Mexico. The former starting end worked as an electrical engineer in Detroit during the 1920s, then moved to Chicago. Turner died at age 53 in 1946 from a heart attack.[26]

189

VOTE FOR
Dan M. Cook

The Veteran's Candidate

for

DISTRICT JUDGE
64th JUDICIAL DISTRICT

Qualified to Handle the Office

A Veteran Himself, Who
Gave Up His Practice To
Serve His Country In
Both World Wars.

Your Vote Will Be Appreciated

After the war, the Second Texas Infantry team manager practiced law and served as a two-term county judge. Cook's law practice was interrupted in 1942 when he returned to active duty and commissioned as an Army major. After World War II, he returned to Plainview and ran for District Judge of the 64th Judicial District. He lost. Modified from *Tulia Herald,* July 18, 1946.

Vote Tuesday for the City Manager Candidates

A. Baker Duncan
S. R. Spencer
V. M. Cox

IT IS YOUR DUTY TO VOTE

Former first-squad lineman Baker Duncan practiced law for a few years before forming the Duncan-Smith automobile dealership. Duncan devoted much of his time to serving the city of Waco, and was named city commissioner in 1926, mayor in 1927, and in 1928 was chairman of the Waco City Charter Advisory Committee. Modified from *Waco Times Herald*, Feb. 14, 1926.

When Baylor College was being lured from Waco to Dallas in 1928, Baker Duncan spearheaded the "Campaign Colonel's Divisions," a fund-raising organization that was structured like the military with a hierarchy of 240 volunteers reporting to captains who reported to its chairman, Colonel Duncan. When the Baylor athletic program was struggling to compete against larger schools of the Southwestern Conference in the 1930s, it was Duncan with a team of Waco businessmen who formed the Baylor Big Brothers Inc. to provide financial assistance. Modified from *Waco Sunday Tribune*, Jan. 23, 1938.

Former team manager Charles B. Stewart moved to Fort Worth in 1920 where he opened the law firm of Clarence E. McGaw and Charles B. Stewart. Modified from *Fort Worth Star-Telegram*, March 9, 1921.

Walter Woodul, a lawyer, politician, statesman, and the man who organized the Second Texas Infantry's first games. "Woodul Family Tree," *Ancestry.com*, https://www.ancestry.com/mediauiviewer/collection/1030/tree/ 7949464/person/360001022841/media/97cc3269-a39f-4704-a744-4335a509 28ce?_phsrc= JuZ6&usePUBJs=true&galleryindex=2&albums=pg&showGalleryAlbums= true&tab=0&pid=360001022841&sort=-created.

EPILOGUE

Their Last Chapter

Although the Second Texas Infantry team never took to the field again after the frenzied 1916-1917 season, its players' paths sometimes crossed, and some even played together again. There were the 36th Division matches during "the lost year" between their Second Texas National Guard service and the Great War at McAllen and Camp Bowie that briefly brought together Victor Bintliff, Bill Birge, Spitz Clarke, Tige Halphen, George Lane, David Nelson, Pleas Rogers, and player-coach Jim Kendrick. The 90th Division Camp Travis football team collected John Diller, Eugene Dotson, Dick Lane, and Sylvan Simpson together on the field in the months before most of them sailed for Europe.

At the end of World War I, six former Second Texas Infantry footballers remained in France with the reformed 36th Division's football team and competed in the American Expeditionary Forces (AEF) gridiron league. David Nelson was team coach, Bill Birge the line coach, and the playing roster included Spitz Clarke, Jim Kendrick, Eugene Dotson, and Rats Watson. They won the First Army Championship but lost the AEF Championship title in the All-Army Finals.

Between 1921 and 1926, Kearie Berry, Spitz Clarke, Eugene Dotson, and Rats Watson met again as teammates or adversaries in a series of post-season All-Star games that pitted "the civilians," consisting of college and alumni players, against "the Army," comprised of mainly Fort Sam Houston Army players.

Probably the greatest gathering of players was in 1928, at a Texas National Guard-sponsored reunion of the 36th Division. Held at the American Legion Convention in San Antonio on the tenth anniversary of the battle of St. Étienne, Mike Bloor and Jim Kendrick were chairmen of the reunion committee. One of the scheduled events was a barbeque in honor of the Second Texas Infantry football team. Bill Birge, Spitz Clarke, John Diller, Eugene Dotson, Baker Duncan, Sylvan Simpson, and Rats Watson wired that they were coming, and "others of the team are being looked up to make the reunion complete." If any press covered the event, their words have yet to be discovered.[1]

A few former teammates were in the same room again reliving their storied football year with *Corpus Christi Caller-Times* writer Vic Cook in 1937. AP writer Harold Ratliff brought some of them together in 1956, and *Waco Tribune-Herald* sports editor Al Ward in 1959. But there were fewer players to interview as time went on.

Eugene Dotson, Tige Halphen, Jim Kendrick, and David Nelson did not live long enough to see the onset of World War II, and Charles B. Stewart died before he knew its outcome. Spitz Clarke and Charlie Turner passed away before the Korean War. Mike Bloor and Baker Duncan watched as Dwight Eisenhower, coach of the 12th Division All-Star team that opposed them in 1917, made his bid for the presidency in 1952. But they didn't live long enough to learn he was elected. Victor Bintliff, Harry Stullken, and Bud Smith died during Eisenhower's first term.

Charlie Brown, Tom Gambrell, Tubby Graves, and Tom Mitchell were alive when a former World War II PT boat commander named John F. Kennedy made a presidential run in 1960, but they died before Kennedy was assassinated in Texas in 1963. Rats Watson and K.L. Berry watched as Beatlemania came ashore in America and the first Green Berets landed in South Vietnam but died during former Texas senator Lyndon Johnson's first presidential term. Dan Cook did not live to see Johnson's speech declining to run again in 1968. The passing of Ock Abbott, Rip Collins, Whitey Davis, George Lane, Charley Ogden, and Sylva Simpson overlapped with student Vietnam War protests, racial riots, the shootings of Martin Luther King and Robert Kennedy, and the technological milestone of landing Neil Armstrong on the moon.

Bill Birge, Bart Coan, Dick Lane, Pleas Rogers, and Charles Schaedel lived to see the Watergate hearings dominate national television and President Nixon's fall from grace. Mullie Lenoir and John Diller lived through the Gerald Ford and Jimmy Carter presidencies, witnessing the Three Mile Island nuclear disaster and the Iran hostage crisis. Walter Woodul, who died in 1984, was the last of the Second Texas Infantry to leave the field.

APPENDIX

Souvenir Program
From the Final Game

SECOND TEXAS INFANTRY

VS

FIRST NEW YORK CAVALRY

JANUARY 20, 1917

The Souvenir Program for the final game of the Second Texas Infantry, collection Jim Moloney. The program was printed in advance of the game, and some of the names of the New York starting roster are not consistent with those who ultimately took to the field. Note that both Jim Kendrick's and Spitz Clarke's names were spelled wrong. Name misspellings were common in all forms of media of the day.

SOUVENIR PROGRAM

CAVALRY FROLICS

PRESENTED BY

FIRST NEW YORK CAVALRY
N. G. U. S.   ,

FOOTBALL

SECOND TEXAS INFANTRY

VS.

FIRST NEW YORK CAVALRY

SAN ANTONIO - - - - - - - TEXAS

SAN ANTONIO---

America's

Winter

Playground

AMUSEMENTS

San Antonio with its splendid modern hotels, its unsurpassed climate, has for many years established itself as one of the leading winter resorts of America. It is a city different from all other American cities and has many points of historic interest.

THE ALAMO AND MISSIONS

The great shrine of Texas liberty, the Alamo, is in San Antonio, and just outside of the city are four historic missions built by the Franciscan monks nearly two hundred years ago, and there are many other points of historic interest in the city.

AUTOMOBILING

San Antonio and Bexar County have 630 miles of paved streets and macadamized roads and 500 miles of graded roads. 115 miles of paved streets are in the city proper. 60 miles of the county roads are tarviated and 200 miles more will be tarviated during the next year. Automobiling is a pleasure enjoyed throughout the winter as the days are mild and sunny.

GOLF

In San Antonio Golf can be played the year round. At the Country Club links (18 holes), is a course as good as any in the East. There are two public courses, the Huisache Links (9 holes) and the Municipal Links (18 holes), in Brackenridge Park. This course is said by experts to be one of the best in the South. It is open at all times to visitors.

HUNTING

Near San Antonio is splendid quail, deer, turkey and wild duck hunting. There are many lakes near the city. The largest of these is the Medina lake, which is about 20 miles long by two or three miles wide.

SAN ANTONIO is yours for today and during every other day that shall come. We invite your attention to historic San Antonio, the Alamo and the four other Missions built here on account of the strategic location and the wonderful climatic conditions, more than 200 years ago by the Franciscan Fathers, who dreamed of controlling this great rich section through Monkish rule, under sovereignty of His Majesty the King of Spain.

San Antonio has been the center of every activity in this great Southwest since these first white men dared risk lives and limbs to explore and take charge.

We urge you to view San Antonio from the modern business standpoint. It is the gateway to Commercial Mexico.

San Antonio's trade territory covers an area containing 68,015 square miles, or 43,529,600 acres, an area larger by 3,850 square miles than the combined areas of Ohio, Massachusetts, New Jersey, Delaware, Rhode Island and Connecticut.

The population of this territory based on U. S. Census Bureau estimates is 884,130.

The Cotton raised in this section in 1916 is about 800,000 bales, with a total value of $80,000,000.00.

The total value of all agricultural products and live-stock produced, according to official figures of the State Comptroller for 1916, was $200,000,000.00.

The population is supported and the wealth produced according to official figures of the State Comptroller, on less than 15% development of the Agricultural lands. Therefore between 20,000,000 and 25,000,-000 acres of good agricultural land in this section is fit for cultivation, but is not now cultivated.

This section has 5,130 miles of improved wagon and automobile roads. It has 3,234.7 miles of standard gauged railroads constructed and in operation.

This is the last of the great partly developed areas of reasonably priced, high-grade agricultural lands.

In wealth of raw materials and undeveloped resources the San Antonio section offers great opportunities for new industries, branch manufacturing plants, distributing houses and colonization projects.

Facts About San Antonio

Population 1910, 96,614 U. S. Census
Population 1916, 124,225 U. S. Census Estimate
Population 1916, 126,000 City Directory
Soldiers included make population 142,000
Winter Tourists included make 182,000

TAXABLE VALUES

1910-11	$ 81,907,925
1911-12	88,674,375
1912-13	91,311,310
1913-14	96,233,005
1914-15	105,566,775

POST OFFICE RECEIPTS

1911	$324,134.22
1912	331,831.11
1913	354,340.60
1914	391,414.36
1915	404,559.30
1916 (April 1st to December 31st)	503,225.20

BUILDING PERMITS

1911-12, 3144 valued at	$2,813,992
1912-13, 2868 valued at	2,162,982
1913-14, 2815 valued at	2,913,390
1914-15, 2198 valued at	1,743,860
1915-16, permits will amount to more than	3,000,000

In behalf of every citizen of San Antonio, we welcome you of the First New York Cavalry, and ask that you return again and again to the "Land of Winter Sunshine, Palms and Good Cheer."

Any inquiry addressed to us will receive our best attention.

THE CHAMBER OF COMMERCE
San Antonio, Texas

THE FIRST CAVALRY FROLIC

PRESENTED BY THE MEMBERS OF THE

FIRST NEW YORK CAVALRY, N. G. U. S.

AT THE

EMPIRE THEATRE, SAN ANTONIO, TEXAS

FRIDAY AND SATURDAY NIGHTS, JANUARY 19th and 20th, 1917

FIRST PART---The Minstrels

Director............William A. Halloran, Jr.
Assistant Director................Herbert Kennedy
Orchestra Conductor................George Collins
Interlocutor....................Arthur McDermott

END MEN

James Kaye
Warren White
Hugh Riley
Keith Driscoll
John Mogge

Norman Duffield
Leroy S. Montgomery
Chester Shepard
Fred Schmidt
Phil Kearney

OLOISTS

Harold B. Jones
Harry Fries
Charles F. Taillie
Pascal Harrower
Clarence K. Boucher
Reginald H. Wood
Donald H. Wood

Frank Barry
Harold J. Nagell
Thomas H. McNalley
Josep A. Doyle
James Kaye
John Mogge
Fred Schmidt

Bayard T. Cummings

ORCHESTRA

Louis Drummond, Accompanist

Edward C. Christensen
T. Emerson Murphy
Sidney N. Riggs
Harold Shantz
Walton B. TenEyck
A. Calver King
George W. Cooper
John Bolton
Marmaduke R. Yawger

George A. Collins
Reginald V. Williams
Reginald B. Robinson
B. Potter Remington
Hamilton Downe
William G. Braid
Nicholas Mitrol
Carl W. Withse
Harry York

Frank E. Mendes
Valentine Seamen
Frank A. Barry
Frank J. Smith
Leroy S. Montgomery
Phil Kearney
Charles H. Johnson
Stanley Bosanko
Walter Kuhn

Henry C. Hackett
Philip W. Thorpe
Thomas H. McNally
Norman Duffield
Chester D. Shepard
Frederick Schmid
Herbert C. Ray
Philip J. Burns
George M. Johnson

Hugh S. Thompson

Otto F. Elbers
Jas. D. Ouchterloney
Bayard T. Cummings
Carl A. Hendershot
James H. Kaye
Thomas Barret
Harold R. Jones
Donald T. Jones
Reginald H. Wood
T. Harry Fries
Leo F. Forest
Edward Herendeen
David B. Hughes
Frank B. Henge
John C. Mogge
Marin C. Rutherford
Harold J. Boucher
Warren K. Lee
George Babcock
Herbert M. Wallace
Joseph A. Doyle
Lester V. Murphy
Donald Armstrong
Thomas F. Dolan
Howard Carpenter
Albert E. Latto
Warren P. White

Samuel Greason, Jr.
Courtney S. Bradley
Milton H. Bradley
Ralph W. Armstrong
James T. Lyons
Newton B. Sherwood
William Olson
Pascal R. Harrower
Donald H. Wood
George J. Dretmuller
Edgar L. Potter
George W. Peppard
Daniel E. Waugh
Ralph W. Shields
William F. Holmes
Charles F. Taille
Harold J. Nagell
Charles F. Aufderhar
Roosevelt W. Durkee
Robert Schuyler
William A. Tomes
John J. Burke
Henry F. Walker
Arthur C. Tileson
William J. Harding
Herbert Kennedy
James E. Fitzgibbon

Milton Van Benschoten

Musical Numbers

1. { a. The Cavalry
   { b. Here's to All Happin s } . . . . . . Company
2. End Song—The Good Ship Whippoorwill . . . James Kaye
3. A Long Time Since I've Been Home . . . . Frank Barry
4. New York Cavalry . . . . Harold J. Nagel
5. Mammy's Coal Black Rose . . . . Ralph W. Babcock
6. I Bury the Stiff . . . . Keith Driscoll
7. Come Back to Alabam' . . . . . John C. Mogge
8. Rose of Singapore . . . . . . T. Harry Fries
9. Father Wanted Me to Learn a Trade . . . Thomas McNally
10. Tenor Solo—My Laddie . . . . . Clarence Boucher
11. When I Get Back to the U. S. A . . . . Bayard T. Cummings
12. I May Look Foolish . . . . . . Fred Schmidt
13. When Uncle Sammy Leads the Band . . . Joseph A. Doyle

INTERMISSION 10 MINUTES

1. Selections by the B Troop Quartette . D. Wood, Harrower, R. Wood, Fries
2. Halloran . . THOSE TWO ENTERTAINERS . Drummond
3. THE COLORED CAVALRY BALL.

Written by Herbert Kennedy and William A. Halloran, Jr.

Staged by William A. Halloran, Jr.

CAST OF CHARACTERS

Rustus Nails, a tough . . . . Keith Driscoll
Lilly White, In love with Nails . . . . . Hugh Reilly
Prunella Snow, the Belle of the Ball . . William F. Holmes, Jr.
Artemus Johnson } In love with Prunella . . { John C. Mogge
Ephriam Jones } . . { James Kaye
Phil Kearney, a dead heat . . . . . Phil Kearney
Aby Cohn, a young chauffeur . . . . Fred Schmidt
George Washington Brown, master of Ceremonies . Leroy S. Montgomery
Alonzo, a lackey . . . . Norman Duffield

Musical Numbers

1. We've Come to You From Dear Old Broadway . . . Chorus
2. Pretty Baby . . . . Prunella
   Artemus, Ephriam and Chorus.
3. A Little Bit of Irish in Sadie Cohn . . . . Aby Cohn
4. Dancing Specialty . . . . Phil Thorpe
5. Dancing Specialty . . . . . Thompson and Burns
6. Ojo de Agua . . . . Kearney
7. Hello, I've Been Looking for You . . . Ephriam and Chorus
8. Specialty . . . . . Lilly White and Rastus Nails
9. The Ragtime Pipes of Pan . . . . Artemus and Chorus
10. Finale . . . . Company

During the course of The Colored Cavalry Ball

THROUGH AFRICA ON A BICYCLE

by Edward Streeter

Professor Finla Fogg, the Noted Explorer . . . Chester D. Shepard
His Boy Amonia . . . . By Himself

DANCING GIRLS

Messrs. Latto, Van Benschoten, Barrett, Sherwood, Aufderhar, Lee, Byrne, Ouchterlonie, Hackett, Harding, Olson, Murphy.

DANCING BOYS

Messrs. Hendershot, Hughs, Elbers, Greason, Cummings, White, Jones, Tomes, Herendean, Bosanko, Thorpe, Nagell.

EXECUTIVE STAFF

General Manager . . . . . . William A. Halloran, Jr.
Publicity Manager . . . . Stuart J. Saks
Stage Manager . . . . Howard Carpenter
Assistant Stage Manager . . . . . . James Noble
Electrician . . . . William Griffin
Wardrobe Mistress . . . . Frank Barry

FOOTBALL
2nd Texas Infantry *vs.* 1st New York Cavalry
LINE UP OF THE TEAMS

	TEXAS				NEW YORK	
PLAYER	WEIGHT	COLLEGE	POSITION	COLLEGE	WEIGHT	PLAYER
Kendricks	180	A & M	END	Princeton	170	Andrews
Duncan	185	Texas	TACKLE	Williams	189	Driscoll
Birge	180	Texas	GUARD	Syracuse	184	Shimer
Diller	197	Texas	CENTER	Syracuse	188	Forsyth
Berry	200	Texas	GUARD	N. Y. Semi Pro	186	Canlon
Simpson	195	Texas	TACKLE	Indiana	194	Jordan
Turner	155	Texas	END	Harvard	170	Little
Watson	150	South Western	QUARTERBACK	Cornell	178	Butler
Clark	155	Texas	HALFBACK	Syracuse	180	Wilkinson
Dotson	210	Baylor	HALFBACK	Syracuse	166	Glass
Collins	195	A & M	FULLBACK	Cornell	186	Miller
Ogden	200	Texas	SUBSTITUTE	Dartmouth	176	Potter
Nelson	190	Texas	SUBSTITUTE	Buffalo	155	Duffy
Abbott	150	A & M	SUBSTITUTE	Georgetown	185	Riley
Gambrell	150	Baylor	SUBSTITUTE	Pennsylvania	154	Cochensburger
Lane	155	Texas	SUBSTITUTE	Villa Nova	162	Hanlon

TEXAS

LIEUT. COLONEL BLOOR, Athletic Director
LIEUT. W. S BIRGE, Captain
"TUBBY" GRAVES, Coach

NEW YORK

CAPTAIN WILLIAM J. DONOVAN, Athletic Director
LIEUTENANT WILLIAM GILLESPIE, Financial Manager
SERGEANT MARCUS E. WILKINSON, Captain
CORPORAL HAMILTON ANDREWS, Coach
CORPORAL EVERETT E. WOOD, Manager

CAVALRY PRACTICE

CAVALRY BACKFIELD

FIRST NEW YORK CAVALRY ATHLETIC FIELD

COACH ANDREWS

CAPTAIN "RED" WILKINSON

FIRST NEW YORK CAVALRY
N. G. U. S.

LOCATED AT McALLEN, TEXAS   DATE OF ARRIVAL, JULY 7, 1916

FIELD AND STAFF
COLONEL CHAS. I. DeBEVOISE
LT. COLONEL CROOK McLEER

MAJOR EDWARD McLEER   ADJUTANT:
MAJOR MORTIMER BRYANT   CAPTAIN CHARLES CURRIE
MAJOR CHAS. I. TOBIN   SUPPLY OFFICER
                                         CAPTAIN JAMES C. MACLIN

MEDICAL OFFICERS
MAJOR JAMES PILCHER   CAPTAIN JAMES BROWN

Troop A.........Brooklyn.......... ...Captain Harold Donaldson   Troop G..........Utica...............Captain Henry Pickard
Troop B..........Albany.............Captain Livingston Miller   Troop H.........Rochester............Captain Charles Fiske
Troop C..........Brooklyn...........Captain George Backhouse   Troop I..........Buffalo..............Captain William J. Donovan
Troop D.........Syracuse...........Captain Chester H. King   Troop K.........Brooklyn............Captain Harry Spencer
Troop E.........Brooklyn...........Captain James Howlett   Troop L.........Brooklyn.... ......Captain A. F. Alpers
Troop F.........Staten Island.......Captain Hunter Platt   Troop M.........Avon...............Captain Dallas Newton
                              M. G. Troop...................Captain Anthony Fiala

References

INTRODUCTION

[1] *Austin American*, Jan. 2, 1917; *San Antonio Express*, Jan. 2, 1917.

[2] *San Antonio Express*, Jan. 2, 1917; *Austin American-Statesman*, Jan. 3, 1917; Ratliff, Harold V., *The Power and the Glory: The Story of Southwest Conference Football* (Lubbock: Texas Tech Press, 1957), 151.

[3] *Corpus Christi Caller-Daily Herald*, Nov. 21, 1916; *Austin American*, Jan. 14, 1917; *San Antonio Express*, Jan. 21, 1917; *San Antonio Express*, Jan. 28, 1917; *San Antonio Express*, Nov. 11, 1917; *Brenham Banner Press*, Jan. 10, 1928; *Corpus Christi Caller-Times*, Feb. 28, 1937; *Brady Standard*, Dec. 23, 1955; Ratliff, 141.

[4] *Austin American-Statesman*, Nov. 15, 1911.

[5] Prieto, Julie Irene, *The Mexican Expedition, 1916-1917*, CMH Pub. 77-1 (Washington, D.C., US Army Center of Military History), 18.

[6] Harris, Charles H., and Sadler, Louis R., *The Great Call-up* (Norman: Univ. OK Press, 2015), 19-20; *Report on Mobilization of the Organized Militia and National Guard of the United States, 1916* (Washington: Govt. Printing. Office, 1916), 153; Bruce A. Olson, "Texas National Guard," *Handbook of Texas Online*, https://www. tshaonline.org/handbook/entries/texas-national-guard; "36th Division in World War I," *Texas Military Forces Museum*, https://www.texasmilitaryforcesmuseum.org/36division/archives/wwi/white/chap 1.htm.

[7] *Austin American*, Sept. 19, 1916.

[8] *San Antonio Express*, Nov. 7, 1916.

[9] Patricia Benoit, "Automobiles Come to Texas in 1899 and Forever Change the Culture," In *Killeen Daily Herald*, Aug. 4, 2014.

CHAPTER 1

[1] *New Britain Herald*, March 14, 1925; "Camp and his Followers," *American Football: 1876-1889*, http://profootball researchers.org/Articles/Camp_And_Followers.pdf; *The History of the Walter Camp Foundation*, https://web.archive. org/web/20071218214118/; Spencer Parlier, *College Football History: Notable First Milestones*, June 30, 2022, https://www.ncaa.com.

[2] Richard Hershberger, "The Flying Wedge: The Greatest Play in Football," *Ordinary Times*, Sept. 15, 2015, https://ordinary-times.com/2015/09/14/the-flying-wedge-the-greatest-play-in-football/.

[3] *Houston Post*, Dec. 18, 1904; *Ibid.*, Dec. 31, 1906.

[4] *Ibid.*, Dec. 18, 1904.

[5] *Fort Worth Star-Telegram*, June 13, 1905.

[6] *Palestine Daily Herald*, Oct. 4, 1905; *Fort Worth Star-Telegram*, Oct. 6, 1905.

[7] *Ibid.; Ibid.*; *El Paso Times*, Oct. 10, 1905; *Ibid*, Oct. 12, 1905; *Fort Worth Star-Telegram*, Oct. 26, 1905.

[8] *Star Tribune*, April 5, 1903.

[9] *Saint Louis Post-Dispatch*, Oct. 16, 1905.

[10] *Houston Post*, Nov. 3, 1905; *Bryan Eagle*, Dec. 1, 1905.

[11] *Ibid.*, Nov. 24, 1905.

[12] *Boston Globe*, Nov. 26, 1905; *New York Tribune*, Nov. 26, 1905.

[13] *New York Tribune*, Nov. 26, 1905.

[14] *Austin American-Statesman*, Jan. 28, 1906.

[15] *Ibid.*, Dec. 29, 1905; *Ibid.*, Jan. 4, 1906; *Fort Worth Star-Telegram*, Jan. 12, 1906; *Ibid.*, Feb. 8, 1906.

[16] *Houston Post*, Feb. 25, 1906; *Fort Worth Star-Telegram*, April 1, 1906

[17] *Austin American-Statesman*, October 7, 1905; *Fort Worth Star-Telegram*, April 1, 1906; *Houston Post*, April 8, 1906; *Austin American-Statesman*, Aug. 20, 1906.

[18] *Houston Post*, Sept. 13, 1906; *Ibid.*, Feb. 6, 1906.

[19] *El Paso Herald*, Aug. 25, 1906; *Ibid.*, Oct. 6, 1906.

[20] *Fort Record and Register*, Sept. 23, 1906.

[21] *Houston Post*, Oct. 15, 1906; *Ibid.*, Dec. 31, 1906; *Austin American-Statesman*, Nov. 26, 1906.

[22] *Ibid.*, Oct. 15, 1906.

[23] *Ibid.*, Oct. 14, 1906; *Fort Worth Star-Telegram*, Nov. 18, 1906.

[24] *Austin American-Statesman*, Feb. 9, 1908; *Houston Post*, Sept. 25, 1910.

[25] *El Paso Herald*, Nov. 23, 1909; *NCAA History*, https://www.ncaa.org/sports/2021/5/4/history.aspx.

[26] *Washington Post*, Oct. 20, 1909; *Austin American*, Nov. 1, 1909; *El Paso Times*, Nov. 1, 1909; *Houston Post*, Nov. 8, 1909; *Wilkes-Barre Times Leader*, April 16, 1910.

[27] *Fort Worth Star-Telegram*, Dec. 1, 1909.

[28] *Houston Post*, Sept. 10, 1910; *El Paso Herald*, Sept. 24, 1910; *Houston Post*, Sept. 25, 1910; Mary Bellis, "History of Football," *ThoughtCo*, Aug. 26, 2020, thoughtco.com/history-of-football-1991800.

[29] *Austin American-Statesman*, Feb. 9, 1908; *Houston Post*, Sept. 11, 1910; *Houston Post*, Sept. 25, 1910.

[30] *Ibid.*

[31] *El Paso Times*, Feb. 4, 1912; *El Paso Herald*, Sept. 5, 1912; Spencer Parlier, *College Football History: Notable First Milestones*, June 30, 2022, https://www.ncaa.com.

[32] *Argus Leader*, Jan. 7, 1911; *Harrisburg Telegraph*, Nov. 24, 1914; *High Point Enterprise*, Nov. 29, 1915; *Houston Post*, Dec. 3, 1911.

CHAPTER 2

[1] *Austin Statesman*, April 4, 1917.

[2] *San Antonio Express*, Oct. 22, 1916,

[3] *Ibid.*; *Laredo Weekly Times*, Nov. 12, 1916; *San Antonio Express*, Jan. 17, 1917.

[4] *San Antonio Express*, Jan. 17, 1917; *Austin American*, March 9, 1917.

[5] Charles W. Ogden to Harold V. Ratliff, Letter dated April 23, 1956, Collection Jim Moloney.

[6] *San Antonio Express*, Oct. 22, 1916; *Ibid.*, Nov. 7, 1916; Ratliff, Harold V., *The Power and the Glory: The Story of Southwest Conference Football* (Lubbock: Texas Tech Press, 1957), 145.

[7] *Austin Statesman*, Jan. 15, 1917; *San Antonio Express*, Jan. 15, 1917; *Austin Statesman*, Jan. 17, 1917; *Denton Record-Chronicle*, Jan. 7, 1917; *Houston Post*, Jan. 7, 1917; *San Antonio Express*, Jan. 7, 1917. *San Antonio Express*, Jan. 29, 1917.

[8] *Galveston Daily News*, Oct. 12, 1910; *Galveston Daily News*, Oct. 16, 1910.

[9] *Fort Worth Star-Telegram*, Nov. 15, 1910; *Ibid.*, April 9, 1911; *Houston Post*, Feb. 10, 1913; *Austin American*, Nov 8, 1916; *San Antonio Express*, Dec. 16, 1916; *San Antonio Express*, Jan. 15, 1917; *Austin Sunday American-Statesman*, May 22, 1949.

[10] *Galveston Daily News*, Nov. 14, 1911; *Austin American-Statesman*, Nov. 24, 1911; *Houston Post*, Dec. 3, 1911; *Fort Worth Star-Telegram*, Dec. 1, 1911; *Fort Worth Star-Telegram*, Nov. 9, 1913; *Denton Record-Chronicle*, May 29, 1961; *Ibid.*, Dec. 31, 1969.

[11] *Fort Worth Star-Telegram*, Nov. 28, 1912; *Houston Post*, Nov. 29, 1912; *Ibid.*, Sept. 26, 1915; *Austin American-Statesman*, Nov. 26, 1915.

[12] *Austin American*, June 5, 1915; *Austin American-Statesman*, Nov. 27, 1915; *Fort Worth Star-Telegram*, Jan. 21, 1916; *Austin American*, April 22, 1916; *Houston Post*, April 28, 1916; *Austin American*, Nov. 8, 1916; *San Antonio Express*, Dec. 16, 1916; *Ibid.*, Jan. 15, 1917; *Houston Post*, Nov. 16, 1919; Ratliff, 143, "University of Texas Athletics," *UT Hall of Honor*, https://texassports.com/honors/hall-of-honor.

[13] *El Paso Herald*, Oct. 25, 1913; *Fort Worth Star-Telegram*, Nov. 9, 1913; *El Paso Herald*, Dec. 3, 1913; *Austin American-Statesman*, Nov. 27, 1915; *San Antonio Express*, Nov. 7, 1916; *Austin American*, Nov. 8, 1916; *San Antonio Express*, Dec. 1, 1916; *Ibid.*, Dec. 16, 1916; *Ibid.*, Jan. 15, 1917.

[14] *Austin American-Statesman*, Jan. 10, 1914; *Ibid.*, May 15, 1916.

[15] *Ibid.*, Dec. 21, 1913; *Ibid.*, Feb. 9, 1914.

[16] *Austin American*, Nov. 22, 1914; *Ibid.*, Dec. 4, 1914; *Fort Worth Star-Telegram*, Dec. 6, 1914.

[17] *Ibid.*, June 26, 1915; *Ibid.*, Aug. 10, 1915; *Fort Worth Star-Telegram*, Sept. 16, 1915; *El Paso Times*, Oct. 22, 1920.

[18] *Ibid.*, Nov. 14, 1914; *Ibid.*, Dec. 16, 1916; *Austin American-Statesman*, May 29, 1968; Bill Nowlin, "Rip Collins," *Society for Baseball Research*, https://sabr.org/bioproj/person/rip-collins/.

[19] *Bryan Daily Eagle and Pilot*, Nov. 20, 1915; *San Antonio Express*, Nov. 7, 1916; *Houston Post*, Dec. 10, 1916; *Ibid.*, Nov. 1, 1956.

[20] *Fort Worth Star-Telegram*, Dec. 7, 1915; *Waco News-Tribune*, Dec. 18, 1952.

[21] *San Antonio Express*, Nov. 19, 1916; *Waco News-Tribune*, Dec. 11, 1921; *Ibid.*, Dec. 18, 1952.

[22] *Waco Morning News*, Oct. 24, 1915.

[23] *Paris Morning News*, May 21, 1916.

[24] *Waco Times-Herald*, Sept. 16, 1914; *Waco Morning Sun*, Feb. 28, 1915; *Austin American-Statesman*, Nov. 26, 1915; *Houston Post*, Dec. 8, 1915; *News-Tribune*, Dec. 18, 1952.

[25] *Bryan-College Station Eagle*, May 23, 1916.

[26] *Houston Post*, Nov. 7, 1915; *Austin American*, Nov. 28, 1915; *Houston Post*, Nov. 28, 1915; *San Antonio Express*, Nov. 7, 1916.

[27] *Waco Times-Herald*, Dec. 20, 1914; *Ibid.*, Feb. 6, 1914; *Ibid.*, Sept. 12, 1915; *Waco News-Tribune*, Dec. 18, 1952; *Waco Times-Herald*, Oct. 19, 1972.

[28] *Ibid.*, Oct. 15, 1916.

[29] *Austin American*, Nov. 29, 1914; *Austin American-Statesman*, Nov. 27, 1915; Sawyer, R.K., and Moloney, Jim, *The Texas Tarpon Club* (Corpus Christi: Nueces Press, 2022).

[30] *Austin American-Statesman*, Nov. 27, 1915; *Ibid.*, Nov. 29, 1914; *US School Yearbooks, 1900-1926*, www.ancestry.com.

[31] *Austin American*, Oct. 10, 1915; *Austin American-Statesman*, Oct. 31, 1915; *Houston Post*, Nov. 7, 1915; *Fort Worth Star-Telegram*, Nov. 20, 1915; *San Antonio Express*, Dec. 10, 1916.

[32] *Houston Post*, Sept. 21, 1913; *Ibid.*, Oct. 19, 1913.

[33] *Austin American*, Oct. 25, 1914; "1915 Cactus Yearbook," *Texas Scholar Works*, University of Texas Libraries, http://hdl.hande.net/2152 /24283.

[34] *Fort Worth Star-Telegram*, Oct. 24, 1915; *Austin American-Statesman*, Oct. 31, 1915; *Houston Post*, Nov. 7, 1915; *Ibid.*, Nov. 28, 1915; *Fort Worth Record-Telegram*, Sept. 30, 1916; *Austin American*, Nov 8, 1916; *San Antonio Express*, Dec. 16, 1916; *Ibid.*, Jan. 15, 1917.

[35] *Austin American*, Oct. 18, 1915; *Ibid.*, Jan. 7, 1916. *Austin American-Statesman*, Feb. 12, 1937.

[36] *Waco Tribune-Herald*, March 1, 1959; Ratliff, 148.

[37] *Austin American*, Sept. 27, 1914; *Ibid.*, Sept. 25, 1915; *Ibid.*, Nov. 13, 1915; "Southwestern University Athletics History," *Southwestern Pirates*, https://www.southwesternpirates.com/information/history; "1915 Southwestern Pirates Schedule and Results," *Sports Reference College Football*, https://www.sports-reference.com/cfb/schools/southwestern-tx/1915-schedule.html.

[38] *Galveston Daily News*, Sept. 27, 1914.

[39] *Houston Post*, Sept. 20, 1914; *Ibid.*, Nov. 21, 1914; *Ibid.*, May 21, 1916; *San Angelo Morning Times*, May 21, 1947.

[40] *Houston Post*, Sept. 21, 1913; "University of Texas Athletics," *UT Hall of Honor*, https://texassports. com/honors/hall-of-honor.

[41] *Austin American-Statesman*, May 9, 1916; *Waco Times-Herald*, May 14, 1916.

[42] *Ibid.*, Oct. 3, 1915; *Ibid.*, Dec. 12, 1915.

[43] *Waco Morning News*, Dec. 10, 1913; *Waco Times-Herald*, May 12, 1916.

[44] *Waco Times-Herald*, Oct. 5, 1913; *Waco Morning News*, Nov. 23, 1913; *Fort Worth Star-Telegram*, Aug. 19, 1915.

[45] *Austin American*, Oct 11, 1914; *Waco Times-Herald*, Oct. 11, 1914.

[46] *Gainesville Daily Register and Messenger*, July 6, 1915; *Austin American-Statesman*, May 9, 1916; *Paris Morning News*, May 21, 1916.

[47] *San Antonio Express*, June 20, 1912; *Pearsall Leader and News*, June 13, 1913; *Pearsall Leader*, Oct. 15, 1915.

[48] Harris J. Weiss, Jr., "Rogers, John Harris," *Handbook of Texas Online*, https://www.tshaonline.org/handbook/entries/rogers-john-harris; "Capt. John H. Rogers," *Texas Ranger Hall of Fame*, https://www.texasranger.org/texas-ranger-museum/hall-of-fame/john-h-rogers/.

[49] *Fort Worth Star-Telegram*, Nov. 30, 1915; "Wentworth Annual Catalog 1914-1915," *Wentworth Military Academy Museum Yearbook Collection*, https://exportal.blob.core.windows.net/exportalresources/wma/Year bookWMA-1915.pdf.

[50] *Austin American-Statesman*, May 10, 1916; *Ibid.*, June 30, 1916.

[51] "1912 A&M Longhorn Yearbook," *Texas A&M University Libraries*, library.tamu.edu.

[52] *Houston Post*, Nov. 7, 1909; *Bryan Daily Eagle and Pilot*, Dec. 3, 1910; *Galveston Daily News*, Nov. 14, 1911.

[53] *Houston Post*, April 21, 1912; *Bryan Daily Eagle*, May 18; 1912; *Austin American-Statesman*, June 26, 1912.

[54] *Austin American*, Oct. 18, 1915; *Austin American-Statesman*, Oct. 20, 1915; *Austin American*, Jan. 7, 1916; *Austin American-Statesman*, Feb. 12, 1937.

[55] *Austin American-Statesman*, Nov. 27, 1915; *Austin Daily Texan*, March 12, 1948; *Austin American-Statesman*, Dec. 7, 1952.

[56] *Ibid.*, Jan. 2. 1910; *Ibid.*, Aug. 29, 1915.

[57] *Bryan-College Station Eagle*, Oct. 3, 1914; *Waco Times-Herald*, Feb. 6, 1914; *Fort Worth Star-Telegram*, Dec. 11, 1916; *Mexia Daily News*, Feb. 7, 1960; *Monitor*, Feb. 7, 1960.

[58] *Austin American*, March 14, 1915; *Fort Worth Star-Telegram*, Jan. 21, 1916.

[59] *Austin American-Statesman*, May 24, 1914; *Austin American*, June 28, 1915; *Austin American-Statesman*, July 9, 1915; *Austin American*, Oct. 17, 1915; *Ibid.*, April 3, 1916; *Ibid.*, April 24, 1916; *Austin American-Statesman*, May 29, 1916; *Austin American*, July 2, 1916.

[60] *Austin American*, Nov 8, 1916; *San Antonio Express*, Dec. 10, 1916; *Laredo Weekly Times*, Dec. 10, 1916; *Ibid.*, Dec. 17, 1916; *Austin American-Statesman*, Dec. 7, 1934.

[61] *Bryan Weekly Eagle*, July 29, 1897; *Shiner Gazette*, Feb. 22, 1899; *Rockdale Reporter and Messenger*, April 26, 1945; Gregory W. Ball, "Bloor, Alfred Wainwright," *Handbook of Texas Online*, https://www.tshaonline.org/handbook/entries/bloor-alfred-wainwright.

[62] *Austin American-Statesman*, July 20, 1901; *Austin Daily Statesman*, March 6, 1902; *Austin Statesman*, Dec. 9, 1905; *Houston Post*, Feb. 15, 1908; *Temple Daily Telegram*, Aug. 27, 1910.

[63] *El Paso Times*, April 5, 1905; *Austin American-Statesman*, Feb. 21, 1907.

[64] *Austin American*, Oct. 17, 1914; *Austin American-Statesman*, Feb. 28, 1915; *Austin American*, April 7, 1916; *Lubbock Avalanche-Journal*, June 16, 1967.

[65] *Austin American-Statesman*, April 4, 1919; *Ibid.*, Dec. 7, 1934.

[66] *The Times*, June 17, 1912; *The Times*, Sept. 28, 1912; *Austin American*, Oct. 28, 1915.

[67] *San Antonio Express*, July 21, 1916; *Austin American-Statesman*, Jan. 15, 1935; "Walter Woodul," *Ancestry*, https://www.ancestry.com/mediauiviewer/collection/1030/tree/7949464/person/360001022841/media/97cc3269-a39f-4704-a744-4335a50928ce?_phsrc=JuZ6&usePUBJs=true&galleryindex=2&albums=pg&showGalleryAlbums=true&tab=0&pid=360001022841&sort=-created.

[68] *Austin American-Statesman*, March 12, 1922; *Austin Statesman*, Nov. 30, 1924; *Corpus Christi Caller-Times*, Feb. 28, 1937; *Las Vegas Daily Optic*, Oct. 10, 1951.

CHAPTER 3

[1] *Austin American-Statesman*, Dec. 20, 1897; *Ibid.*, March 31, 1895; *Ibid.*, Dec. 4, 1904; *Ibid.*, April 25, 1910; *El Paso Herald*, Dec. 23, 1911; "American Football Database," *Southern Intercollegiate Athletic Assoc.*, https://americanfootballdatabase.fandom.com/wiki/Southern_Intercollegiate_Athletic_Association; *Texas A&M Football Database*, http://www.nationalchamps.net/NCAA/database/texasam_database.htm.

[2] *Fort Worth Record and Register*, Dec. 10, 1901; *Fort Worth Star-Telegram*, Dec. 12, 1901; *Houston Post*, Dec. 12, 1915.

[3] *Houston Post*, May 10, 1904; *San Antonio Express*, May 12, 1908; *Austin American-Statesman*, June 5, 1908; *Galveston Daily News*, Dec. 11, 1909; *Houston Post*, Nov. 14, 1909.

[4] *Austin American-Statesman* May 9, 1910; *Houston Post*, Nov. 30, 1913.

[5] *Waco Semi-Weekly Tribune*, Dec. 4, 1912; *Fort Worth Star-Telegram*, Dec. 5, 1912.

[6] *Fort Worth Star-Telegram*, Sept. 25, 1913.

[7] *Waco Times-Herald*, May 2, 1909; *Ibid.*, Jan. 2, 1910; *Austin American-Statesman*, May 9, 1910; *Fort Worth Record & Register*, May 14, 1910; *Ibid.*, Jan. 26, 1911; *Houston Post*, Nov. 30, 1913; "Texas Intercollegiate Athletic Association," *American Football Database*, https://americanfootballdatabase.fandom.com/wiki/Texas_Intercollegiate_Athletic_Association.

[8] *Fort Worth Star-Telegram*, Jan. 8, 1914; "Southwest Conference Annual Standings," *Football Record Book*, http://www.thompsonian.info/swc-historical-standings.pdf; "Southwest Athletic Conference: An Inventory of Its Records, 1914-1996", *Texas Tech University Southwest Collection/Special Collections Library*, http://resources.swco.ttu.edu/manuscripts/swac/swac-1.php; Eric M. Pfeifle, "Southwest Conference,"

Handbook of Texas Online, https://www.tshaonline.org/handbook/entries/southwest-conference; *NCAA History*, https://www.ncaa.org/sports/2021/5/4/history.aspx; Rick Waters, "The Original Conference Call," *TCU Magazine*, 1995, https://magazine.tcu.edu/winter-2011/original-conference-call/.

[9] *Austin American-Statesman*, Oct. 5, 1903; *New York Tribune*, Dec. 4, 1910; *Sioux City Journal*, Dec. 13, 1914.

[10] *Galveston Daily News*, Nov. 27, 1904; *Fort Worth Star-Telegram*, Oct. 16, 1909; *Austin American-Statesman*, Dec. 1, 1913.

[11] *Galveston Tribune*, Dec. 5, 1916.

[12] *Houston Post*, Nov. 27, 1910; *Ibid.*, Dec. 4, 1910; *Ibid.*, Dec. 11, 1911; *Austin American-Statesman*, Dec. 1, 1913; *Austin American*, Nov. 28, 1914.

[13] *Fort Worth Star-Telegram*, Nov. 30, 1916.

[14] *Houston Post*, Oct. 10, 1915; *Texas Longhorn Football History*, https://texassports.com/sports/2013/7/17/FB_07171 30240.aspx.

[15] *Houston Post*, Nov. 28, 1915; *Fort Worth Star-Telegram*, Jan. 26, 1916.

[16] *Ibid.*, Nov. 30, 1913; *Ibid.*, Nov. 28, 1915; "1914 Texas A&M Aggies Schedule and Results," *Sports Reference College Football*, https://www.sports-reference.com/cfb/schools/texas-am/1914-schedule.html.

[17] *Houston Post*, Nov. 14, 1909; *Ibid.*, Nov. 21, 1909.

[18] *Ibid.*

[19] *Ibid.*

[20] *Ibid.*

[21] *Ibid.*, July 17, 1910; *Austin American-Statesman*, Nov. 12, 1910.

[22] *Austin American-Statesman*, Jan. 22, 1911; *Ibid.*, Feb. 8, 1911.

[23] *Ibid.*, Nov. 15, 1911.

[24] *Ibid.*

[25] *Ibid.*; *El Paso Herald*, Dec. 23, 1911.

[26] *Bryan Eagle*, Dec. 4, 1911.

[27] *Houston Post*, Nov. 24, 1909.

[28] *El Paso Herald*, Dec. 23, 1911; *Houston Post*, March 12, 1912.

[29] *Houston Post*, Sept. 21, 1910.

[30] *Bryan Eagle*, Dec. 18, 1914; *Fort Worth Star-Telegram*, Jan. 8, 1914.

[31] *Bryan Daily Eagle*, Nov. 20, 1915.

[32] *Houston Post*, Oct. 10, 1915; *Ibid.*, Nov. 28, 1915; *Fort Worth Record-Telegram*, Dec. 11, 1915; "Southwest Conference Annual Standings," *Football Record Book*, http://www.thompsonian.info/swc-historical-standings.pdf.

[33] *Austin American*, Nov. 28, 1915; *Houston Post*, Nov. 28, 1915.

[34] *Bryan Daily Eagle*, Nov. 20, 1915; *Houston Post*, July 23, 1916.

[35] *Ibid.*; *Ibid.*; *Waco News-Tribune*, Sept. 3, 1922; "Harry Warren Collins," *The Association of Former Students, Texas A&M University*, https://www.aggienetwork.com/news/153413/harry-warren-collins/.

[36] *Bryan Daily Eagle*, Nov. 20, 1915; *Houston Post*, Dec. 5, 1915.

[37] *Ibid.*

[38] *Austin American*, Nov. 23, 1915; *Austin Statesman and Tribune*, Nov. 26, 1915.

[39] *Waco Times-Herald*, Dec. 2, 1906; *Austin American-Statesman*, June 1, 1906; *Houston Post*, June 1, 1906; *Ibid.*, Nov. 28, 1915; *Waco Times-Herald*, Dec. 7, 1915.

[40] *Waco Times-Herald* Oct. 9, 1915; *Houston Post*, Nov. 28, 1915.

[41] *Houston Post*, Nov. 28, 1915; *Waco Morning News*, Dec. 2, 1915; *Fort Worth Record-Telegram*, Dec. 11, 1915; "Southwest Conference Annual Standings," *Football Record Book*, http://www.thompsonian.info/swc-historical-standings.pdf.

[42] *Houston Post*, Sept. 20, 1914; *Fort Worth Record-Telegram*, Oct. 17, 1915; "Rice Owls Schedule and Results," *Sports Reference College Football*, https://www.sports-reference.com/cfb/schools/rice/1915-schedule.html.

[43] *Houston Post*, Nov. 21, 1914; *Fort Worth Record-Telegram*, Oct. 17, 1915; *Houston Post*, Nov. 9, 1915; *Ibid.*, May 21, 1916; *Ibid.*, Dec. 5, 1915; 1915 *Rice Owls Schedule and Results*, Sports Reference College Football.

[44] *Austin American*, Oct. 24, 1915.

CHAPTER 4

[1] Sawyer, R.K., *A History of Spread Oaks Ranch* (Corpus Christi: Nueces Press, 2023).

[2] Harris, Charles H., and Sadler, Louis R., *The Great Call-up* (Norman: Univ. OK Press, 2015), 14; Prieto, Julie Irene, *The Mexican Expedition, 1916-1917*, CMH Pub. 77-1 (Washington, D.C., US Army Center of Military History), 8-9.

[3] Harris and Sadler, 13-4.

[4] "The Mexican Revolution and the United States," *Collections of the Library of Congress*, https://www .loc.gov/exhibits/mexican-revolution-and-the-united-states/madero-presidency-to-assassination.html.

[5] Harris and Sadler, 15-6.

[6] *El Paso Herald*, Feb. 21, 1914; Prieto, 12.

[7] *Corsicana Semi-Weekly Light*, Dec. 17, 1915; Harris and Sadler, 52; Don M. Coerver, "Plan of San Diego," *Handbook of Texas Online*, https://www.tshaonline.org/handbook/entries/plan-of-san-diego.

[8] *San Antonio Light*, Oct. 19, 1915; *Brownsville Herald*, Oct. 21, 1915; *Texas City Times*, Oct. 21, 1915.

[9] *Brownsville Herald*, Aug. 9, 1915; *Ibid.*, Aug. 12, 1915; *Ibid.*, Sept. 20, 1915; *Ibid.*, Sept. 24, 1915; *Ibid.*, Oct. 27, 1915; *Ibid.*, Nov. 27, 1915; Moloney, Jim, "Camp Scurry: Corpus Christi and the Mexican Border Incidents," *Nueces County Historical Commission*, 3-1, Nov. 2006.

[10] *El Paso Times*, June 5, 1915; *Brownsville Herald*, Aug. 12, 1915; *Galveston Tribune*, Oct. 22, 1915; Harris and Sadler, 16-7, 53.

[11] *Brownsville Herald*, Dec. 1, 1915; Prieto, 16-9.

[12] Prieto, 18.

[13] Prieto, 45-8.

[14] Harris and Sadler, 19-20.

[15] Prieto, 42-4, 63-4.

[16] *Report on Mobilization of the Organized Militia and National Guard of the United States, 1916* (Washington: Govt. Printing. Office, 1916), 153; Bruce A. Olson, "Texas National Guard," *Handbook of Texas Online*, https://www. tshaonline.org/handbook/entries/texas-national-guard; "36th Division in World War I," *Texas Military Forces Museum*, https://www.texasmilitaryforcesmuseum.org/36division/archives /wwi/white/chap1.htm.

[17] *Austin American-Statesman*, April 1, 1913; *Ibid.*, May 24, 1914; *Austin American*, Aug. 18, 1914; *Ibid.*, Aug. 18, 1914; *Austin American-Statesman*, Aug. 29, 1915; *Ibid.*, Dec. 12, 1915; *Waco Times-Herald*, Dec. 13, 1915; *Austin American-Statesman*, May 6, 1916; *San Antonio Express*, May 13, 1916; *Matagorda County Tribune*, March 30, 1917; *Waco Times-Herald*, May 10, 1936.

[18] *Austin American*, Feb. 23, 1916; *Austin American-Statesman*, March 16, 1916; *El Paso Herald*, March 21, 1916; *Austin American-Statesman*, March 24, 1916; *Brownville Herald*, March 29, 1916; *Report on Mobilization of the Organized Militia and National Guard of the United States, 1916* (Washington: Govt. Printing. Office, 1916), 23, 138.

[19] *Fort Worth Star-Telegram*, April 11, 1916; *Austin American-Statesman*, May 6, 1916; *Ibid.*, May 6, 1916. *Corsicana Daily Sun*, May 9, 1916. *Austin American-Statesman*, May 10, 1916.

[20] *Austin American-Statesman*, May 10, 1916.

[21] Ratliff, Harold V., *The Power and the Glory: The Story of Southwest Conference Football* (Lubbock: Texas Tech Press, 1957), 143.

[22] *Austin American*, May 10, 1916.

[23] *Ibid.*, May 10, 1916; *Austin American-Statesman*, May 11. 1916; *Houston Post*, May 12, 1916; *Ibid.*, May 14, 1916; *Waco Times-Herald*, July 22, 1916; *Austin American*, March 27, 1917.

[24] *Austin American*, May 10, 1916; *Waco Times-Herald*, May 10, 1916; *Bryan-College Station Eagle*, May 12, 1916; *Bryan Weekly Eagle*, May 18, 1916; *Waco Times-Herald*, July 22, 1916; *Ibid.*, Aug. 6, 1916.

[25] *Corpus Christi Caller-Times*, Sept. 8, 1916; *San Angelo Morning Times*, May 21, 1947.

[26] *Waco Tribune-Herald*, May 10, 1936; Lonnie J. White, "Camp Travis," *Handbook of Texas Online*, https://www.tshaonline.org/handbook/entries/camp-travis.

[27] *Waco-Times Herald*, May 14, 1916.

[28] *Report on Mobilization of the Organized Militia and National Guard of the United States, 1916* (Washington: Govt. Printing. Office, 1916), 55.

[29] *Laredo Weekly Times*, April 8, 1916; *Austin American-Statesman*, May 14, 1916; *Laredo Weekly Times*, May 14, 1916; *Austin American-Statesman*, May 24, 1916; *San Antonio Express*, May 31, 1916; *Austin American*, Sept. 19, 1916.

[30] *Waco Semi-Weekly Tribune*, May 24, 1916; *Ibid.*, June 16, 1916.

[31] *Austin American*, May 25, 1916; *Ibid.*, May 26, 1916; *Ibid.*, June 6, 1916; *Ibid.*, June 16, 1916; *San Angelo Morning Times*, May 21, 1947.

[32] *Brownsville Daily Herald*, March 9, 1930; Bradshaw, Mike, *Texas Game Warden Chronicles* (Carrizo Springs: Mesquite Bean Press, 2009), 11.

[33] *Brownsville Herald*, July 12, 1932; Norman Rozeff, pers. comm. to Jim Moloney, Sept. 10, 2010; *Valley Star Monitor-Herald*, Oct. 10, 1937; *Brownsville Herald*, Sept. 19, 1922; *Ibid.*, Jan. 3, 1910; *Ibid.*, Nov. 18, 1938; *Ibid.*, Jan. 25, 1908.

[34] *Austin American*, June 6, 1916.

[35] *Waco Times-Herald*, Aug. 6, 1916.

[36] *Austin American*, June 6, 1916.

[37] *Corpus Christi Caller-Times*, Aug. 20, 1916; *Laredo Weekly Times*, Aug. 20, 1916; *Brownsville Herald*, Aug. 21, 1916; *Ibid.*, Aug. 22, 1916.

[38] *Austin American*, July 26, 1916; "Camp Scurry Post Return, September 1917," *Texas Adjutant General's Office, National Archives, Washington D.C.*; Harris and Sadler, 52.

[39] *Austin American*, June 16, 1916; *Ibid.*, July 26, 1916; *Ibid.*, Aug. 17, 1916.

[40] *Ibid.*, June 6, 1916; *Ibid.*, July 2, 1916; *Houston Post*, August 2, 1916; Moloney, 2006.

[41] *Ibid.*, July 2, 1916; *Ibid.*, Aug. 6, 1916.

[42] *Ibid.*, Aug. 6, 1916.

[43] *Ibid.*, June 30, 1916; *Waco Times-Herald*, Aug. 6, 1916; *Austin American*, August 9, 1916; *Ibid.*, Sept. 19, 1916.

[44] *Austin American-Statesman*, June 14, 1916; *Waco Times-Herald*, July 22, 1916; *Houston Post*, July 23, 1916; *Ibid.*, July 30. 1916.

[45] Moloney, 2006.

[46] *Brownville Herald*, Aug. 23, 1916; *Corpus Christi Caller-Times*, Sept. 8, 1916.

[47] *Corpus Christi Caller-Times*, Aug. 20, 1916.

[48] *Ibid.*, Sept. 7, 1916; *Ibid.*, Sept. 20, 1916.

[49] *Ibid.*; *Ibid.*, Sept. 8, 1916; Oklasodak, Sept. 27, 1916.

[50] *Ibid.*, Sept. 8, 1916; *Ibid.*, Sept. 14, 1916; *Los Angeles Times*, Oct. 3, 1916; *Corpus Christi Caller-Times*, Jan. 4, 1917; Allison Ehrlich, *Corpus Christi Caller-Times*, Oct. 7, 2020, https://www.caller.com /story/news/special-reports/building-our-future/throwback/2020/10/07/corpus-christis-camp-scurry-trained-wwi-soldiers-over-100-years-ago/5902451002/.

[51] *Austin Statesman*, June 9, 1903.

[52] *Corpus Christi Caller-Times*, Sept. 7, 1916; *Austin American*, Oct. 12, 1916.

[53] *Austin American*, Oct. 12, 1916. *Ibid.*, Oct. 13, 1916; *Corpus Christi Caller-Times*, Nov. 30, 1916; *Ibid.*, Jan. 4, 1917; Moloney, 2006.

[54] *San Antonio Express*, Nov. 1, 1956; *Austin American*, Nov. 2, 1916; *Corpus Christi Caller-Times*, Nov. 18, 1916; *Austin American*, Nov. 28, 1916.

[55] *Austin American*, Dec. 8, 1916; *Fort Cobb Record*, Dec. 21. 1916; *Brownsville Herald*, Dec. 22, 1916; *Corpus Christi Caller-Times*, Dec. 23, 1916.

CHAPTER 5

[1] *Austin American*, Sept. 19, 1916; *San Antonio Express*, Oct. 21, 1916; *Ibid.*, Oct. 22, 1916.

[2] *Ibid.*

[3] Ratliff, Harold V., *The Power and the Glory: The Story of Southwest Conference Football* (Lubbock: Texas Tech Press, 1957), 145.

[4] *Houston Post*, Oct. 22, 1916; *San Antonio Express*, Oct. 22, 1916; Ratliff, 145.

[5] *Laredo Weekly Times*, Oct. 29, 1916.

[6] *Ibid.*, Nov. 6, 1916.

[7] *Ibid.*, Oct. 29, 1916; *Ibid.*, Nov. 12, 1916.

[8] *Corpus Christi Caller-Times*, Sept. 21, 1916; *San Antonio Express*, Oct. 28, 1916; *Austin American*, Nov 8, 1916; *Corpus Christi Caller-Daily Herald*, Nov. 14, 1916; *Austin American*, Nov. 22, 1916.

[9] *Laredo Weekly Times*, Nov. 19, 1916; *Austin American*, Nov. 22, 1916; *Ibid.*, Nov. 25, 1916.

[10] *Corpus Christi Caller-Daily Herald*, Nov. 21, 1916; *Austin American*, Nov. 22, 1916.

[11] *Ibid.*, Nov. 21, 1916.

[12] *Ibid.*

[13] *San Antonio Express*, Nov. 7, 1916; *Ibid.*, Nov. 19, 1916; *Ibid.*, Nov. 21, 1916; *Ibid.*, Nov. 25, 1916.

[14] *Ibid.*, Nov. 15, 1916; *Ibid.*, Nov. 27, 1916.

[15] *Ibid.*, Nov. 26, 1916.

[16] *Ibid.*; *The Eagle*, Dec. 18, 1952.

[17] *San Antonio Express*, Jan. 28, 1917.

[18] Charles W. Ogden to Harold V. Ratliff, Letter dated April 23, 1956, Collection Jim Moloney.

[19] *Laredo Weekly Times*, Dec. 10, 1916.

[20] *Ibid.*

[21] *San Antonio Express*, Dec. 10, 1916; *Laredo Weekly Times*, Dec. 17, 1916.

[22] *Ibid.*

[23] *Ibid.*

[24] Ogden to Ratliff, 1956.

[25] *Laredo Weekly Times*, Dec. 17, 1916; Ogden to Ratliff, 1956.

[26] *Corpus Christi Caller-Times*, Feb. 28, 1937.

[27] *San Antonio Express*, Nov. 29, 1916

[28] *Ibid.*, Dec. 14, 1916.

[29] *Ibid.*, Dec. 10, 1916.

[30] *Ibid.*, Dec. 16, 1916.

[31] *Ibid.*

[32] *Austin Statesman*, Dec. 16, 1916; *Laredo Weekly Times*, Dec. 24, 1916; *San Antonio Express*, Dec. 16, 1916; *Ibid.*, Dec. 17, 1916; *Austin Statesman*, Dec. 17, 1916,

[33] *Austin Statesman*, Dec. 17, 1916.

[34] *Austin American*, Dec. 16, 1916; *San Antonio Express*, Dec. 16, 1916.

[35] *San Antonio Express*, Dec. 16, 1916; *Austin Statesman*, Dec. 17, 1916; *San Antonio Express*, Dec. 20, 1916; *Laredo Weekly Times*, Dec. 24, 1916.

[36] *Austin Statesman*, Dec. 17, 1916.

[37] *Corpus Christi Caller-Times*, Dec. 22, 1916; *San Antonio Express*, Jan. 28, 1917.

[38] *Ibid*, Dec. 22, 1916.

[39] *Ibid.*

[40] *San Antonio Express*, Dec. 13, 1916; *Ibid.*, Dec. 21, 1916. *Austin American*, Dec. 26, 1916; Ogden to Ratliff, 1956.

[41] *Austin American*, Jan. 2, 1917; *San Antonio Express*, Jan. 2, 1917.

[42] Ratliff, 151.

[43] *San Antonio Express*, Jan. 2, 1917; *Austin American-Statesman*, Jan. 3, 1917; Ratliff, 151.

[44] *Ibid.*, Dec. 24, 1916.

CHAPTER 6

[1] *San Antonio Express*, Dec. 24, 1916; *Corpus Christi Caller-Daily Herald*, Jan. 2, 1917; *San Antonio Light*, Jan. 2, 1917; *Houston Post*, Jan. 3, 1917; *San Antonio Express*, Jan. 7, 1917.

[2] *Houston Post*, Jan. 3, 1917; *San Antonio Light*, Jan. 5, 1917; *Houston Post*, Jan. 13, 1917.

[3] *Austin Statesman*, Dec. 29, 1916; *Austin American*, Dec. 30, 1916.; *Ibid.*, Jan. 3, 1917; *Ibid.*, Jan. 9, 1917; *Houston Post*, Jan. 13, 1917.

[4] *Ibid.*

[5] *San Antonio Light*, Jan. 7, 1917; *San Antonio Express*, Jan. 9. 191; *Ibid.*, Jan. 21, 1917.

[6] *San Antonio Express*, Jan. 5, 1917; *Ibid.*, Jan. 10, 1917. *Houston Post*, Jan. 13. 1916.

[7] *Austin American*, Dec. 31, 1916; *San Antonio Express*, Jan. 10, 1917; *Corpus Christi Caller-Daily Herald*, Jan. 24, 1917.

[8] *San Antonio Express*, Oct. 1, 1916; *San Antonio Light*, Jan. 11, 1917; *San Antonio Express*, Jan. 9. 1917; John S.D. Eisenhower, "Eisenhower, Dwight David," *Handbook of Texas Online*, https://www.tshaonline. org/handbook/entries/eisenhower-dwight-david.

[9] *Houston Post* Jan. 3, 1917; *Denton Record-Chronicle*, Jan. 7, 1917; *Houston Post*, Jan. 7, 1917.

[10] *Ibid.*, Jan. 10, 1917; "36th Division in World War I," *Texas Military Forces Museum*, https://www.texasmilitaryforcesmuseum.org/36division/archives/wwi/white/chap1.htm.

[11] *Ibid.*, Jan. 15, 1917; *Austin Statesman*, Jan. 17, 1917; *San Antonio Express*, Jan. 17, 1917.

[12] *Austin Statesman*, Jan. 17, 1917; *San Antonio Express*, Jan. 17, 1917.

[13] *San Antonio Express*. Jan. 17, 1917.

[14] *Austin American*, Jan. 16, 1917; *San Antonio Express*, Jan. 17, 1917.

[15] *San Antonio Express*, Jan. 17, 1917, *Corpus Christi Caller-Times*, Feb. 28, 1937.

[16] *Houston Post*, Jan. 13. 1916; *Austin Statesman*, Jan. 15. 1917; *San Antonio Express*, Jan. 17, 1917.

[17] *San Antonio Express*, Jan. 15, 1917; *Austin American*, Jan. 16, 1917.

[18] *Ibid.*, Jan. 7, 1917; *Ibid.*, Jan. 14, 1917.

[19] *Ibid.*, Jan. 20, 1917; *Corpus Christi Caller-Times*, Feb. 28, 1937; Ratliff, Harold V., *The Power and the Glory: The Story of Southwest Conference Football* (Lubbock: Texas Tech Press, 1957), 148, 151.

[20] *Detroit Free Press*, July 9, 1916.

[21] *Brooklyn Daily Eagle*, Jan. 6, 1917; *Democrat and Chronicle*, Jan. 15, 1917.

[22] *San Antonio Express*, Jan. 19, 1917; *Buffalo News*, Jan. 20, 1917.

[23] *San Antonio Express*, Jan. 14, 1917; Ratliff, 150-1.

[24] *Corpus Christi Caller-Daily Herald*, Jan. 2, 1917.

[25] *San Antonio Express*, Jan. 4, 1917; *San Antonio Light*, Jan. 8, 1917; *Austin American-Statesman*, Dec. 7, 1934.

[26] *Ibid.*, Jan. 4, 1917; *Ibid.*, Jan. 17, 1917; *Ibid.*, Jan. 20, 1917.

[27] *Ibid.*, Jan. 18, 1917; *Ibid.*, Jan. 19, 1917; *Ibid.*, Jan. 21, 1917; *Austin American-Statesman*, Dec. 7, 1934. p. 152.; Harris, Charles H., and Sadler, Louis R., *The Great Call-up* (Norman: Univ. OK Press, 2015), 133.

[28] *San Antonio Express*, Jan. 10, 1917. *San Antonio Express*, Jan. 14, 1917.

[29] *Ibid.*, Jan. 21, 1917.

[30] *Ibid.*; *Marshall Morning News*, Dec. 3, 1920.

[31] *Syracuse Herald*, Jan. 21, 1917; *San Antonio Express*. Jan. 28, 1917; *Corpus Christi Caller-Times*, Feb. 28, 1937.

[32] *San Antonio Express*, Jan. 21, 1917.

[33] *Laredo Weekly Times*, Jan. 21, 1917; *San Antonio Express*, Jan. 22, 1917; *Ibid.*, Jan. 25, 1917.

[34] *San Antonio Express*, Jan. 28, 1917; Harris and Sadler, 134; W.D. Cope, "Texas National Guard in World War I," *Texas Military Forces Museum*, https://www.texasmilitaryforcesmuseum.org/gallery/ww1/cope. htm.

[35] *San Antonio Express*, Jan. 25, 1917

[36] *Austin American*, March 9, 1917; *Waco Tribune-Herald*, March 1, 1959.

[37] Ratliff, 147; Ryan Christiansen, "T vs. Single-wing vs. Notre Dame Box," *Professional Football Researchers Association Forum*, https://www.profootballresearchers.org/forum/viewtopic.php?t=5995.

[38] *Waco Tribune-Herald*, March 1, 1959.

[39] *Corpus Christi Caller-Times*, Feb. 2, 1937.

[40] *Ibid.*

[41] *Brady Standard*, Dec. 23, 1955.

[42] Ratliff, 147.

[43] *Waco Tribune-Herald*, March 1, 1959.

[44] *Ibid.*, March 14, 1959.

[45] *Joseph E. Chance to Jim Moloney,* July 29, 2024.

[46] *Corpus Christi Caller-Daily Herald*, Nov. 21, 1916; *San Antonio Express*, Jan. 28, 1917; *Brenham Banner Press*, Jan. 10, 1928.

[47] *Austin American*, Jan. 14, 1917; *San Antonio Express*, Jan. 21, 1917; *Corpus Christi Caller-Times*, Feb. 28, 1937; *Brady Standard*, Dec. 23, 1955. Ratliff, 141.

[48] *San Angelo Standard-Times*, Jan. 28, 1943.

[49] *Brady Standard*, Dec. 23, 1955. Ratliff, 141.

CHAPTER 7

[1] *San Antonio Express*, Feb. 19, 1917.

[2] *Ibid.*, March 5, 1917; *Houston Post*, March 18, 1917.

[3] *Gainesville Daily Register and Messenger*, April 9, 1917.

[4] *Houston Post*, March 30, 1917; *Gainesville Daily Register and Messenger*, April 9, 1917; *Austin American*, April 2, 1917, *Austin Statesman*, April 1, 1919.

[5] *Austin American*, March 27, 1917; *Austin American-Statesman*, March 28, 1917; *Austin American*, April 18, 1917; *Austin Statesman*, Aug. 7, 1917.

[6] *Ibid.*; *Austin American*, April 2, 1917; "36th Division in World War I," *Texas Military Forces Museum*, https://www.texasmilitaryforcesmuseum.org/36division/archives/wwi/white/chap1.htm.

[7] W.D. Cope, "Texas National Guard in World War I," *Texas Military Forces Museum*, https://www.texas militaryforces museum.org/gallery/ww1/cope.htm; "2nd Battalion, 142nd Infantry Regiment," *Texas Military Department*, https://tmd.texas.gov/2nd-battalion-142nd-infantry-regiment; "143rd Infantry Regiment: A History Forged in Combat," *Southwest Foundation*, https://www.strongerwarriorfoundation.org/warrior-journal1/yme34zznukrpu9r46busye9x1se6xr-tfl77.

[8] *Houston Post*, March 30, 1917; *San Antonio Express*, Nov. 10, 1917; *Houston Daily Post*, Nov. 26, 1917; *Austin American-Statesman*, Nov. 30, 1922.

[9] *Fort Worth Star-Telegram*, Sept. 20, 1917; *Houston Daily Post*, Sept. 30, 1917.

[10] *Houston Post*, Dec. 16, 1917.

[11] *San Antonio Express*, Oct. 7, 1917.

[12] *Reconnaissance*, Oct. 6, 1917.

[13] *Fort Worth Star-Telegram*, Oct. 11, 1917; *Temple Daily Telegram*, Oct. 15, 1917; *Reconnaissance*, Oct. 20, 1917; *Pass in Review*, Nov. 17, 1917.

[14] *Fort Worth Star-Telegram*, Nov. 13, 1917; *Pass in Review*, Nov. 14, 1917; *Ibid.*, Dec. 1, 1917.

[15] *Tampa Bay Times*, Sept. 8, 1927; Lonnie J. White, "Camp Travis," *Handbook of Texas Online*, https://www.tshaonline.org/handbook/entries/camp-travis; John Manguso, "A short history of the 90th Division during its mobilization & training at Camp Travis," *Fort Sam Houston Museum*, http://90thdivisionassoc.org/90thDivisionFolders/WWONE/a_short_history_of_the_90th_divi.htm.

[16] *San Antonio Express*, Nov. 11, 1917; *Ibid.*, Nov. 30, 1917; *Denton Record-Chronicle*, Dec. 5, 1917.

[17] *San Antonio Light*, Nov. 12, 1917; *San Antonio Express*, Dec. 29, 1917.

[18] *Houston Post*, June 17, 1917; *Austin Daily Texan*, Sept. 30, 1917; *Houston Daily Post*, Oct. 9, 1917; *Pass in Review*, Dec. 1, 1917; *Houston Post*, Jan. 2, 1918; *Austin American*, March 24, 1918; *Austin Daily Texan*, April 25, 1918.

[19] *Galveston Daily News*, June 16, 1917; *Austin American*, Sept. 2, 1917; *Houston Post*, Sept. 2, 1917; *Houston Daily Post*, Oct. 9, 1917; *Austin American-Statesman*, Nov. 25, 1917; *Wichita Falls Times*, Nov. 27, 1917; *Houston Post*, Dec. 16, 1917; *San Antonio Evening News*, Dec. 25, 1917; *Austin American-Statesman*, Feb. 5, 1918; *Austin Statesman*, Sept. 10, 1918; *Houston Post*, Oct. 4, 1918; *San Antonio Evening News*, Feb. 5, 1919. *Houston Post*, Dec. 16, 1917.

[20] *Austin American-Statesman*, March 28, 1917; *Austin American*, April 2, 1917; *Austin American-Statesman*, Feb. 5, 1918; *Waco Times-Herald*, Feb. 10, 1918; "(Miscellaneous) World War I Draft Registration Cards, 1917-1918, No. 110;" *Ancestry.com*; *Waco Times-Herald*, July 22, 1952.

[21] *Bryan-College Station Eagle*, July 4, 1917; *San Antonio Light*, July 11, 1917; *Houston Daily Post*, Oct. 9, 1917; *Austin American-Statesman*, Nov. 25, 1917; *Austin American*, Dec. 6, 1917; *Houston Post*, Dec. 16, 1917; *Austin American*, Dec. 17, 1917; *Elgin Courier*, Dec. 10, 1953.

[22] *Houston Daily Post*, Oct. 9, 1917; *Fort Worth Star-Telegraph*, Dec. 12, 1917; Charley W. Brown, "US Army Transport Service Arriving and Departing Passenger Lists, 1910-1939," *Ancestry.com*; Howard Herndon Davis, *US College Student Lists for University of Texas, 1917*.

[23] *Austin American*, May 9, 1918; *Ibid.*, May 31, 1918; *Ibid.*, July 12, 1918.

[24] Moore, William E. and Crussell, James, *US Official Pictures of the World War* (Washington, D.C.: Pictorial Bureau, 1920), 108-9; Allen, B.H., *The Greatest Battle Never Told: The Meuse-Argonne Offensive, 1918*, Univ. of Mary Washington Senior Thesis, Nov. 9, 2015, 2; "36th Division in World War I," *Texas Military Forces Museum*.

CHAPTER 8

[1] Allen, B.H., *The Greatest Battle Never Told: The Meuse-Argonne Offensive, 1918*, Univ. of Mary Washington Senior Thesis, Nov. 9, 2015, 2-5.

[2] *Austin Statesman*, April 13, 1919, *Fort Worth Star-Telegram*, June 16, 1919; *Ibid.*, Oct. 1, 1933; W.D. Cope, "Texas National Guard in World War I," *Texas Military Forces Museum*, https://www.texasmilitary forces museum.org/gallery/ww1/cope.htm; "141st Infantry Regiment," *Texas Military Forces Museum*, https://texasmilitaryforcesmuseum.org/36division/archives/141/141lin.htm.

[3] *Austin American*, March 23, 1919.

[4] *Austin Statesman*, April 13, 1919; *Fort Worth Star-Telegram*, June 16, 1919; "143rd Infantry Regiment," *Texas Military Force Museum*, https://texasmilitaryforcesmuseum.org/36division/archives/143/ 14302.htm.

[5] *Austin Statesman*, April 13, 1919; *Blanc Mont: Meuse-Argonne-Champagne*, Monograph 9, June 1921 (Washington D.C.: Govt. Printing Office, 1922), 25; W.D. Cope, "Texas National Guard in World War I"; Peter Larsen, "Forêt-Ferme," *OK with the War, One Texan's Unlikely Journey Over There*, https://larsen link.com /2020/05/07/foret-ferme/.

[6] *Austin Statesman*, April 13, 1919; *Blanc Mont: Meuse-Argonne-Champagne*, 20-24; "141st Infantry Regiment," *Texas Military Forces Museum*, https://texasmilitaryforcesmuseum.org/36division/archives/141 /141lin.htm.

[7] *Austin Statesman*, April 13, 1919; "143rd Infantry Regiment," *Texas Military Force Museum*, https://texas militaryforcesmuseum.org/36division/archives/143/14302.htm.

[8] *San Angelo Morning Times*, May 21, 1937.

[9] Larsen, "Forêt-Ferme," *OK with the War, One Texan's Unlikely Journey Over There*.

[10] *Ibid.*

[11] *Austin Statesman*, April 13, 1919.

[12] *Fort Worth Star-Telegram*, Oct. 1, 1933.

[13] *Austin Statesman*, July 27, 1919; Alfred G Watson, "US Army Transport Service Arriving and Departing Passenger Lists, 1910-1939," *Ancestry.com*; W.D. Cope, "Texas National Guard in World War I."

[14] *Austin American-Statesman*, Jan. 20, 1918; *Austin Statesman*, May 8, 1918; *Austin American-Statesman*, Dec. 15, 1918; *Gainesville Daily Register*, Jan. 30, 1919; *Corsicana Daily Sun*, Feb. 20, 1919; *Gainesville Daily Register and Messenger*, June 19, 1919; *San Antonio Evening News*, July 1, 1919; *Corpus Christi Caller-Times*, Feb. 28, 1937; *Austin American-Statesman*, Oct. 24, 1943; "(Miscellaneous) Headstone Applications for Military Veterans, 1861-1985, DD Form 1330," *Ancestry.com*.

[15] *San Angelo Morning Times*, May 21, 1937; *Waco Tribune-Herald*, March 1, 1959"(Miscellaneous) Headstone Applications for Military Veterans, 1861-1985, DD Form 1330," *Ancestry.com*.

[16] Jim Marcellus Kendrick, "Military Service Record Form 84a-1," *Ancestry.com*.

[17] *Pass in Review*, Dec. 1, 1917; *Austin American*, March 24, 1918; *Ibid.*, May 9, 1918; *Ibid.*, May 31, 1918; *Ibid.*, July 12, 1918; *Austin American-Statesman*, April 11, 1920; Thomas DeWitt Gambrell, "Military Service Record Form 84a-1," *Ancestry.com*; *Austin Sunday American Statesman*, May 22, 1949; *Waco Times-Herald*, July 22, 1952; W.D. Cope, "Texas National Guard in World War I."

[18] *Gainesville Daily Register and Messenger*, June 2, 1919; *Galveston Daily News*, June 10, 1919; *San Antonio Evening News*, July 1, 1919; "141st Infantry Regiment," *Texas Military Forces Museum*, https://texasmilitaryforcesmuseum.org/36division/archives/141/141lin.htm; "143rd Infantry Regiment," *Texas Military Force Museum*; "144th Infantry Regiment," *Texas Military Force Museum*, https://texas militaryforcesmuseum.org/36division/archives/144/144lin.htm.

[19] *Gainesville Daily Register and Messenger*, June 2, 1919; *Ibid.*, June 14, 1919.

[20] *Fort Worth Star-Telegram*, March 9, 1919; *The Arrow Head*, March 13, 1919; *Austin American*, April 17, 1919; *Tulia Herald*, May 23, 1919; *Austin American*, July 5, 1919; *Austin Statesman*, July 27, 1919. *Austin American-Statesman*, Oct. 10, 1919.

[21] *Fort Worth Star-Telegram*, April 27, 1919; *Ibid.*, June 16, 1919; *San Antonio Evening News*, July 1, 1919; *Austin American*, Jan. 11, 1920; *Fort Worth Star-Telegram*, Oct. 1, 1933.

[22] W.D. Cope,"Texas National Guard in World War I."

[23] *Austin American*, Oct. 2, 1919.

[24] *Austin Statesman*, July 13, 1919; *Ibid.*, April 18, 1923.

[25] *Tulia Herald*, May 2, 1919; *San Antonio Evening News*, July 1, 1919; Alfred W. Bloor, "Military Service Record Form 84a-1," *Ancestry.com*.

[26] "2nd Battalion, 142nd Infantry Regiment," *Texas Military Department*, https://tmd.texas.gov/2nd-battalion-142nd-infantry-regiment.

CHAPTER 9-1

[1] "Chronology of Professional Football," *Pro Football Hall of Fame*, https://www.profootballhof.com/football-history/chronology-of-professional-football/.

[2] *Austin American-Statesman*, Sept. 10, 1920; *Ibid.*, Sept. 26, 1921; *Austin American*, Oct. 16, 1920; *San Antonio Light*, Sept. 11, 1923; *Austin American-Statesman*, Oct. 27, 1937.

[3] *Ibid.*, Oct. 7, 1922; *Ibid.*, Oct. 9, 1923; *Ibid.*, Sept. 16, 1924; *Fort Worth Record-Telegram*, Oct. 14, 1924.

[4] *Austin Statesman*, Aug. 2, 1922; *Austin American-Statesman*, Aug. 4, 1922.

[5] *Ibid.*, Dec. 26, 1921; *Austin American*, Jan. 6, 1922; *Austin American-Statesman*, Dec. 21, 1923; *San Antonio Light*, Dec. 24, 1923; *Ibid.*, Dec. 25, 1923.

[6] *San Antonio Light*, Dec. 26, 1924; *Ibid.*, Nov. 28, 1925; *Ibid.*, Dec. 9, 1925.

[7] *McAllen Daily Press*, Dec. 20, 1928; *Brownsville Herald*, Dec. 17, 1929; *Ibid.*, Feb. 18, 1930.

[8] *San Patricio County* News, Jan. 14, 1932; *Valley Morning Star*, Feb. 7, 1939; *Austin American-Statesman*, Oct. 24, 1943; Phillip S. Clarke, "1942 World War II Draft Registration," *Ancestry.com*.

[9] *McAllen Daily Press*, Dec. 20, 1928; *The Collegian*, Nov. 1, 1932; *Brownwood Bulletin*, Jan. 30, 1947; *Fort Worth Star-Telegram*, July 2, 1948.

[10] *San Angelo Morning Times*, May 21, 1937; *San Angelo Standard-Times*, July 20, 1950; *De Leon Free Press*, Oct. 30, 1975.

[11] *Austin American*, June 24, 1918.

[12] *Austin American-Statesman*, Feb. 20, 1919; *Ibid.*, April 7, 1919; *Waco Times-Herald*, Oct. 24, 1919; *Austin American-Statesman*, Nov. 10, 1919; *Ibid.*, Dec. 14, 1919; *Ibid.*, April 11, 1920.

[13] *Wichita Falls Times*, June 27, 1920; *Austin American-Statesman*, July 22, 1920; *Ibid.*, July 8, 1920; "Rip Collins," *Baseball Reference*, https://www.baseball-reference.com/players/c/colliri01.shtml.

[14] *Austin American-Statesman*, April 11, 1920; *Appleton Post Crescent*, May 19, 1921.

[15] *Austin American*, Sept. 20, 1921.

[16] *Ibid.*; *San Angelo Evening Standard*, Sept. 6, 1928.

[17] *Times Record*, Dec. 9, 1921; *Boston Herald*, Dec. 21, 1921. *Wichita Daily Times*, Dec. 21, 1921; *Austin American-Statesman*, Jan. 5, 1922.

[18] *Austin American*, Sept. 20, 1921; Bill Nowlin, "Rip Collins," *Society for Baseball Research*, https://sabr.org/bioproj/person/rip-collins/.

[19] *The Sporting News*, June 15, 1963; Nowlin, "Rip Collins."

[20] *Austin American-Statesman*, Feb. 12, 1922; *Waco News-Tribune*, Sept. 14, 1922; *Fort Worth Record-Telegram*, Sept. 29, 1922.

[21] *Waco News-Tribune*, Jan. 7, 1923; *Taylor Daily Press*, Aug. 22, 1923.

[22] *Fort Worth Star-Telegram*, Feb. 16, 1925; *Austin American*, May 24, 1925; Nowlin, "Rip Collins;" Mark S. MacDonald Sr., pers. com. July 22, 2024.

[23] *Austin American-Statesman*, Feb. 1, 1928; *El Paso Evening Post,* March 28, 1928; *Austin American-Statesman*, April 11, 1928; *Fort Worth Record-Telegram*, May 20, 1928; *Austin American*, July 12, 1928; *El Paso Times*, Aug. 30, 1928.

[24] *Fort Worth Star-Telegram*, Sept. 19, 1928; *Waco Tribune-Herald*, Jan. 7, 1923.

[25] *Brownsville Herald*, Feb. 26, 1931; *Abilene Daily Reporter*, March 4, 1931; *Austin American-Statesman*, April 8, 1931; *Austin American*, April 16, 1931; *Ibid.*, Feb. 27, 1932; *Fort Worth Star-Telegram*, March 7, 1932.

[26] *Amarillo Globe-Times*, March 29, 1932; *Fort Worth Star-Telegram*, June 15, 1932.

[27] *Waco News-Tribune*, Oct. 12, 1927; *Austin American-Statesman*. Jan 4, 1929; *Ibid.*, Oct. 11, 1929.

[28] *Austin American*, Oct. 10, 1924; *Wichita Falls Times*, Feb. 16, 1925; *Fort Worth Record-Telegram*, Feb. 26, 1926.

[29] *Boston Globe*, Aug. 4, 1925; *Daily Sun Times*, Aug. 6, 1925.

[30] *Valley Morning Star*, Jan. 8, 1933; *Fort Worth Star-Telegram*, April 28, 1933; *Austin American*, June 30, 1933; *Fort Worth Star-Telegram*, July 24, 1933; *Austin American*, Sept. 10, 1933.

[31] *Texas Ranger Museum*, https://www.texasranger.org/texas-ranger-museum/history/biographies-20th-century-texas-rangers/henry-warren-rip-collins/.

[32] *Waco Times-Herald*, Sept. 28, 1919; *Ibid.*, Oct. 25, 1919; *Corpus Christi Caller-Times*, Feb. 28, 1937.

[33] *Daily Herald*, Oct. 21, 1919; *Fort Worth Record-Telegram*, Oct. 28, 1919; *Waco Times-Herald*, Dec. 6, 1919.

[34] *Austin American-Statesman*, Sept. 26, 1920; *Waco Times-Herald*, Oct. 31, 1920; *Galveston Daily News*, Dec. 26, 1920.

[35] *Fort Worth Record-Telegram*, April 4, 1920; *Waco Times-Herald*, May 16, 1920; *Ibid.*, May 30, 1920.

[36] *Waco Times-Herald*, March 15, 1921; *Gilmer Mirror*, June 2, 1921.

[37] *Austin American*, Oct. 26, 1921; *Waco News Tribune*, Nov. 5, 1921.

[38] *San Antonio Light*, Sept. 16, 1924; *Fort Worth Record-Telegram*, Oct. 14, 1924.

[39] *Waco Times-Herald*, Jan. 2, 1925; *Ibid.*, April 8, 1925; *San Antonio Light*, March 20, 1926.

[40] *Tyler Morning Telegraph*, March 19, 1932.

[41] *Bryan Daily Eagle*, Jan. 20, 1917; *Austin American*, April 20, 1919; *Brownwood Bulletin*, Feb. 4, 1930; *Spokesman-Review*, Jan. 18, 1960; "My Aggie Nation, 1918," *Texas A&M Football History*, https://my aggienation.com/athletics_history/football/year_by_year/1918/article_bed1fbc0-f6f5-11e2-8dac-001a4bcf8 87a.html; "Dorsett Vandeventer Graves," *Remember the Rose Bowl*, Feb. 7, 2013, http://www.remember therosebowl.com/2013/02/dorsett-vandeventer-graves.html.

[42] *Austin American-Statesman*, Sept. 26, 1920; Jim Marcellus Kendrick, "Military Service Record Form 84a-1," *Ancestry.com*.

[43] *The Rattler*, April 16, 1928; Miller, Jeffrey, "Jim Kendrick: The Man with the Plan," *Coffin Corner*, 25, 6, (2003); "1922 Canton Bulldogs" *Pro Football Reference*, https://www.pro-football-reference.com/teams /cbd/1922_roster.htm.

[44] *Ibid.*; *Ibid.*

[45] Miller, 2003.

[46] *The Rattler*, April 16, 1928; Miller, 2003.

[47] *Stephensville Empire-Tribune*, Dec. 1, 1933; *Ibid.*, April 20, 1934.

[48] *Pampa Daily News*, Nov. 18, 1941.

[49] *Birmingham Post-Herald*, March 11, 1918; *Tuscaloosa News*, May 5, 1919; *Ibid.*, May 11, 1919; *Weekly Herald*, April 28, 1921; *Bluefield Daily Telegraph*, March 30, 1930; *Austin American*, Oct. 5, 1951; *Lubbock Evening Journal*, Nov. 8, 1957.

[50] *Houston Post*, Sept. 16, 1923; *Bryan Weekly Eagle*, Sept. 25, 1924; *Abilene Daily Reporter*, Dec. 30, 1926; *Bluefield Daily Telegraph*, May 16, 1979; *Ibid.*, Oct. 3, 1982; *Ibid.*, Sept. 25, 2011.

[51] Charles Wesley Ogden, "Military Service Record Form 84a-1," *Ancestry.com*; *St. Louis Times*, June 15, 1926; *Austin American-Statesman*, Dec. 7, 1934; *San Antonio Light*, March 26, 1940; *Corpus Christi Times*, Jan. 25, 1968.

[52] *Commerce Journal*, Oct. 10, 1919.

[53] *Houston Post*, Nov. 26, 1920; *Marshall Morning News*, Dec. 3, 1920; *Austin Statesman*, Nov. 24, 1921; "My Aggie Nation," *Texas A&M Football History*, https://myaggienation.com/athletics_history/football/ year_by_year/.

[54] Krista Smith, "A Look Back: Memorable Games And Historical Moments That Shaped The Texas A&M-University Of Texas Rivalry," *Texas A&M Today*, Nov. 21, 2011.

[55] *Waco Times-Herald*, Nov. 26, 1921.

[56] *Austin Statesman*, Dec. 23, 1921; *San Antonio Light*, Dec. 25, 1921; *Ibid.*, Dec. 24, 1921; *Ibid.*, Dec. 25, 1921.

[57] *Ibid.*, Dec. 26, 1921.

[58] *Orange Daily Leader*, Sept. 20, 1923.

[59] *Temple Daily Telegram*, Dec. 26, 1922.

[60] *Waco Tribune-Herald*, March 1, 1959.

[61] *Austin American*, Jan. 6, 1922; *Fort Worth Star-Telegram*, Oct. 5, 1935; *Waco Tribune-Herald*, March 1, 1959.

[62] "Journal of the House of Representatives of the State of Texas," *Regular Session of the Fifty-Sixth Legislature,* January 13, *1959* (Austin: Von Boeckmann-Jones Co., 1959), 556.

CHAPTER 9-2

[1] *Honey Grove Signal-Citizen*, March 22, 1946; *Austin Sunday American-Statesman*, May 22, 1949; *Express-News*, Oct. 29, 1960.

[2] *Denton Record-Chronicle*, Aug. 20, 1917; *Ibid.*, Jan. 29, 1920; Kearie Lee Berry Victory Medal Books from Rob SawyerBB Ap-plication, Aug. 9, 1920; Kearie Lee Berry, "US Army Transport Service Arriving and Departing Passenger Lists, 1910-1939," *Ancestry.com*.

[3] *Austin American-Statesman*, Dec. 21, 1923; *San Antonio Light*, Dec. 24, 1923; *Ibid*, Dec. 25, 1923.

[4] *Austin Statesman*, Nov. 30, 1924; *San Antonio Light*, Dec. 26, 1924; *Ibid.*, Nov. 28, 1925; *Ibid.*, Dec. 9, 1925; "University of Texas Athletics," *UT Hall of Honor*, https://texassports.com/honors/hall-of-honor.

[5] *San Antonio Express*, Aug. 23, 1936; *Fort Worth Star-Telegram*, Oct. 24, 1941; David Minor, "Kearie Lee Berry," *Handbook of Texas Online*, https://www.tshaonline.org/handbook/entries/berry-kearie-lee; "Memorial Day Weekend Tribute to Kearie Lee Berry," *Football Archeology*, https://www.football archaeology.com/p/todays-tidbit-memorial-day-weekend-3a3.

[6] Morton, Louis, "The Fall of the Philippines," *Center of Military History*, (Washington D.C.: US Army Govt Printing Office, 1953), 342.

[7] Morton, 338-345.

[8] *Wichita Falls Times*, April 9, 1942.

[9] Morton, 453.

[10] Morton, 461; Michael D. Hull, "Bataan and Corregidor: Valor Without Hope," *Warfare History Network*, June 2022, https://warfarehistorynetwork.com/article/bataan-and-corregidor-valor-without-hope/.

[11] *Sacramento Bee*, May 11, 1942; Hanson W. Baldwin, "The Fall of Corregidor," *American Heritage*, 17, 5, Aug. 1966, https://www.americanheritage.com/fall-corregidor; Hull, "Bataan and Corregidor: Valor Without Hope."

[12] "This Day in History May 6, 1942," *History*, https://www.history.com/this-day-in-history/all-american-forces-in-the-philippines-surrender-unconditionally.

[13] *Denton Record-Chronicle*, Dec. 7, 1945.

[14] *Fort Worth Star-Telegram*, Nov. 12, 1945.

[15] *San Angelo Standard-Times*, Jan. 23, 1943; *Fort Worth Star-Telegram*, June 25, 1944.

[16] "American POWs Remember Life in Japanese Prison Camp," *Reuters*, https://www.reuters.com/article/us-china-pows-idUSPEK37053320070525/; *Corpus Christi Caller-Times*, Sept. 25, 1945; *Denton Record-Chronicle*. Dec. 7, 1945; "Kearie Lee Berry," *Prabook*, https://prabook.com/web/kearie_lee.berry/1093844.

[17] *Denton Record-Chronicle*, Feb. 18, 1946; *Austin American*, Nov. 6, 1946; *Abilene Reporter*, Sept. 13, 1947; "K.L. Berry," *Texas Military Forces Hall of Honor*, Texas Military Forces Museum, https://texas militaryforcesmuseum.org/hallofhonor/berrykl.htm.

[18] *Austin American*, June 9, 1946. *Amarillo Daily News*, July 17, 1946; "K.L. Berry," *Texas Military Forces Hall of Honor*; "Journal of the Senate of the State of Texas," *Regular Session of the Fifty-Ninth Legislature, 1965* (Austin: Von Boeckmann-Jones Co., 1965).

[19] *Waco Tribune-Herald*, Dec. 21, 1952; "NBC 5/KXAS News Scripts (AR0787)," *Portal to Texas History*, University of North Texas Special Collections, ark:/67531/metadc.1836470/.

[20] *Austin American*, June 2, 1955; "Major General Kearie Lee Berry," *UT Hall of Honor*, https://texassports.com/honors/hall-of-honor/maj-gen-kearie-lee-berry/529.

[21] *Austin American-Statesman*, Oct. 23, 1961; *Corpus Christi Caller-Times*, Feb. 8, 1962; *Austin American*, Feb. 28, 1962; *Austin American-Statesman*, April 11, 1962; *Ibid.*, April 13, 1962.

[22] *Austin American*, July 30, 1962; *Brownwood Bulletin*, Aug. 1, 1962.

[23] *Austin American-Statesman*, April 28, 1965; Minor, *Kearie Lee Berry*.

[24] "Journal of the Senate of the State of Texas," *Regular Session of the Fifty-Ninth Legislature, 1965* (Austin: Von Boeckmann-Jones Co., 1965).

[25] *The Statesman*, June 20, 1919; *The Statesman*, Oct. 11, 1919; *Brenham Daily Banner-Press*, Oct. 12, 1915.

[26] "Letter from A.W. Bloor to Commanding General 36th Division dated Jan. 23, 1919," *War Department, 1918-1948*, Record Group 120; *The Statesman*, April 3, 1919.

[27] *West Texas Weekly News*, Sept. 5, 1919; *Marshall Morning News*, Sept. 19, 1919.

[28] *Marshall Morning News*, July 16, 1920; *Daily Herald*, Oct. 1, 1920; *Austin Statesman*, Oct. 11, 1920.

[29] *Austin Statesman*, April 28, 1923; *San Antonio Light*, July 8, 1923; *Austin Statesman*, Sept. 29, 1925; *Mobile New Item*, Feb. 25, 1927; *San Antonio Light*, March 1, 1927; *Wichita Falls Times*, Feb. 11, 1940; *Austin American*, July 5, 1952.

[30] *San Antonio Light*, Nov. 30, 1938; Craig Verniest, "The Sandino Manifesto and the Birth of the Nicaraguan Revolution," *Origins, Current Events in Historical Perspective*, https://origins.osu.edu/read/sandino-mani festo-nicaraguan-revolution?language_content_entity=en; Michael J. Schroeder, "The Sandino Rebellion, Nicaragua, 1927-1934," http://www.sandinorebellion.com/PhotoPgs/1USNA2/PGS/pg1.html.

[31] *San Antonio Light*, Jan. 29, 1928; *Ibid.*, Nov. 27, 1929; *Ibid.*, April 18, 1933; *Ibid.*, April 10, 1936; *Ibid.*, Nov. 2, 1938; *Wichita Falls* Times, Feb. 11, 1940; *Austin American*, July 5, 1952.

[32] *San Antonio Evening News*, May 24, 1921; *Austin American-Statesman*, Sept. 5, 1926; *Austin American*, June 11, 1933; *Weimer Mercury*, Jan. 28, 1938; *Northwest Arkansas Times*, Sept. 17, 1938; *El Paso Times*, Sept. 20, 1938; *Deadwood Pioneer-Times*, Aug. 4, 1950; *Austin American*, April 5, 1959; *San Antonio Light*, May 30, 1969.

[33] *Tampa Bay Times*, Sept. 8, 1927; *Austin American-Statesman*, Dec. 7, 1934.

[34] *Ibid.*; *The Journal*, Dec. 20, 1946; *Record-Journal*, June 12, 1981.

[35] *The Star*, June 4, 1981.

[36] *Waco News-Tribune* Jan. 23, 1925; *Ibid.*, Oct. 22, 1929; *Ibid.*, April 11, 1943; *Paris News*, Sept. 8, 1948; *The Monitor*, Dec. 5, 1950; *Austin American*, Nov. 2, 1951; *Paris News*, July 12, 1961.

[37] *El Paso Times*, July 21, 1918; *Austin American*, Nov. 12, 1930; *Wichita Falls Times*, Sept. 5, 1937; Pleas B. Rogers, "Selected US Military Records, 1862-1985," *Ancestry.com*.

[38] *Brownsville Herald*, Dec. 16, 1941; *Times Record News*, April 7, 1943; *El Paso Herald-Post*, April 29, 1943; *Austin American,* Feb. 13, 1944; *Austin American-Statesman*, Dec. 23, 1944; *Llano News*, April 14, 1945; *San Angelo Standard-Times*, July 12, 1945; *Austin American-Statesman*, Dec. 6, 1945.

[39] *El Paso Herald*, Jan. 7, 1946; *Austin American*, Aug. 22, 1947; *Cotulla Record*, July 9, 1948; *Winchester Evening Star*, Jan. 6, 1955.

[40] *Winchester Evening Star*, April 23, 1952; *Ibid.*, April 18, 1959; *Ibid.*, April 29, 1959; *Ibid.*, April 16, 1969; *Waco Times-Herald*, Oct. 22, 1970; *Winchester Evening Star*, Dec. 27, 1974.

[41] *Llano News*, April 24, 1919; *Ibid.*, Sept. 11, 1919; *Ibid.*, Dec. 25, 1919; Sylvan B. Simpson, "Military Service Record Form 84a-1," *Ancestry.com*; *San Antonio Express*, Jan. 1, 1932; *Llano News*, Sept. 15, 1932; *Ibid.*, June 25, 1936; *Austin American-Statesman*, May 5, 1954; *Llano News*, May 21, 1970.

[42] *Austin American-Statesman*, Feb. 24, 1935; *Brownwood Bulletin*, May 6, 1937; *Llano News*, June 2, 1938; *Ibid.*, June 25, 1936; *Austin American-Statesman*, May 5, 1954; *Llano News*, May 21, 1970.

[43] *Anderson Daily Bulletin*, June 26, 1942; *Llano News*, Nov. 12, 1942; *Austin American-Statesman*, May 5, 1954; *Llano News*, May 21, 1970; *Ibid.*, June 25, 1936; *Austin American-Statesman*, May 5, 1954; *Llano News*, May 21, 1970.

[44] *Austin American*, July 21, 1921; John Erwin Stullken, "Military Service Record Form 84a-1," *Ancestry.com*; *Austin American-Statesman*, Dec. 7, 1934; *Elgin Courier*, Dec. 10, 1953.

CHAPTER 9-3

[1] *San Patricio County News*, June 23, 1938; *Amarillo-Globe Times*, June 13, 1961.

[2] *Tri-Cities Sun*, June 22, 1933; *San Patricio County News*, June 23, 1938; *Amarillo Sunday News*, Aug. 14, 1938; *Shamrock Texan*, June 30, 1941.

[3] *Tulia Herald*, Jan. 27, 1938; *Amarillo Daily News*, Nov. 2, 1940.

[4] *Wichita Daily Times*, Aug. 26, 1942; *Tulia Herald*, July 1, 1943; *Amarillo Daily News*, July 29, 1946; *Lubbock Avalanche-Journal*, June 16, 1967.

[5] World War I Draft Registration Cards, 1917-1918; *Waco News-Tribune*, Oct. 26, 1924; *Ibid.*, Jan. 23, 1925; *Ibid.*, Feb.14, 1926; *Ibid.*, Dec. 11, 1925; *Ibid.*, April 18, 1928.

[6] *Ibid.*, May 27, 1928; *Ibid.*, Dec. 18, 1935.

[7] *Corsicana Semi-Weekly Light*, March 15, 1938; *Waco Times-Herald*, Oct. 28, 1938; *Ibid.*, Sept. 15, 1940; *Fort Worth Star-Telegram*, Feb. 14, 1945; *Waco Tribune-Herald*, July 7, 1946; *Ibid.*, Feb. 26, 1950; *Ibid.*, July 22, 1952.

[8] *San Antonio Express*, Oct. 16, 1919; *Austin American*, Oct. 16, 1920; *Liberty Vindicator*, June 10, 1921; Thomas DeWitt Gambrell, "Military Service Record Form 84a-1," *Ancestry.com*; *Galveston Daily News*, Nov. 25, 1922; *Austin American*, Dec. 21, 1927; *Austin American*, May 1, 1930.

[9] *Fort Worth Star-Telegram*, March 9, 1921; *Shreveport Journal*, Sept. 27, 1917; *Ibid.*, Jan. 16, 1925; *Fort Worth Star-Telegram*, Jan. 17, 1925.

[10] *Roswell Daily Record*, Sept. 20, 1930; *Ibid.*, Jan. 13, 1931; *Albuquerque Tribune*, Sept. 18, 1952; *Albuquerque Journal*, Nov. 19, 1954.

[11] *Houston Post*, April 5, 1919; *Ibid.*, May 3, 1919; "Walter F. Woodul," *The Texas Politics Project*, https://texaspolitics.utexas.edu/educational-resources/walter-woodul.

[12] *Galveston Daily News*, March 5, 1927; "Walter F. Woodul," *The Texas Politics Project*.

[13] *Austin American*, March 11, 1928; *Corpus Christi Caller-Times*, Feb. 1, 1928; *Wichita Falls Times*, Oct. 7, 1928; *Austin American*, Nov. 29, 1928; *Ibid.*, March 22, 1934; *Austin American-Statesman*, Oct. 2, 1984.

[14] *Austin American-Statesman*, Jan. 9. 1933; *Ibid.*, Jan. 10, 1933; *Austin American*, Jan. 13, 1933.

[15] *Austin American*, Jan. 7, 1934; *Ibid.*, June 12, 1934; *Austin American-Statesman*, July 31, 1934.

[16] *Ibid.*, Jan. 23, 1938; *Austin American-Statesman*, July 12, 1938; *Austin American*, July 23, 1938.

[17] "Walter F. Woodul," *The Texas Politics Project*.

[18] *Austin American-Statesman*, Feb. 20, 1927; *Corpus Christi Caller-Times*, Feb. 28, 1937; *Ibid.*, July 22, 1954.

[19] *Mexia Daily News*, Feb. 7, 1960; *The Monitor*, Feb. 7, 1960.

[20] *Austin American-Statesman*, Sept. 6, 1923; Louis A. Halphen, *US Death Certificates*, 1903-1982.

[21] *San Antonio Express*, Oct. 9, 1918; "Simmons College Unit Students Army Training Corps," *Catalog of Simmons College, 1918-1919*; Richard G. Lane, *1940 Federal Census*.

[22] *Waco Times-Herald*, Sept. 14, 1920; *Ibid.*, Oct. 19, 1972.

[23] *Austin American*, Dec. 29, 1919; *Austin American-Statesman*, March 4, 1921; *Cuero Record*, June 4, 1930; *Orange Leader*, Oct. 21, 1952.

[24] *Graham Daily Reporter*, Sept. 4, 1935; *Whitewright Sun*, Sept. 5, 1935; *Waco Tribune-Herald*, Nov. 17, 1935.

[25] *Daily Tribune*, Aug. 10, 1921; *Ibid.*, Aug. 12, 1922; *Ibid.*, Nov. 30, 1932; *Austin American*, July 11, 1936; Charles T. Schaedel, "1942 World War II Draft Registration," *Ancestry.com*; *Palacios Beacon*, April 18, 1946; *Fort Worth Star-Telegram*, Jan. 9, 1960; *Tyler Morning Telegraph*, March 30, 1946; *Ibid.*, March 26, 1953.

[26] *Roswell Daily Record*, April 29, 1919; *Ibid.*, July 10, 1926; *Southern Economist*, June 16, 1946.

EPILOGUE

[1] *Amarillo Daily News*, Jan. 26, 1928; *Crosbyton Review*, May 11, 1928; *Sealy News*, May 25, 1928.

INDEX

Photographs, maps and charts are shown in parentheses.

Cisco (town of): 27.

Civilian Conservation Corps: 181.

Clark Field: 26, 51, 107-9, 128, *170*.

Clarke County (WV): 181.

Clarke, Phillip: 1, 19, 20, 22, 23, *36*, 68, 72, 95, 96, 99-102, 109, 112-6, 127, 128, 131, 144, 145, 155-7, 162, 165, 166, 173, 174, 193.

Cleveland Indians: 32, 158, 163.

Coan, Bart: 19, 27, 50, 52, 68, 70, 99, 101, 114, 131, 142-5, 157.

Coastal Sand Sheet: 70, 71.

Cobb, Ty: 159.

Code Talkers: 179.

Cokes (baseball team): 157.

College Station (town of): 51, 68, 93, 165.

Collins, Warren: 1, 19, 20, 22-5, 32, 50-2, *62*, 68, 72, 95, 96, 99-102, *106*, 109-17, *121*, *122*, 127, 128, 131, 157-161, *168*, 194.

Columbia Southern Chemical Corporation: 165.

Columbus Senators: 164.

Columbus, New Mexico: 2, 65, 66, *82*, *83*.

Company E (Austin National Guard): 19, 20, 27, 29, 30, *41*, 67-9, 72, *90*, *91*, 128, 131.

Company F (Austin National Guard): 19, 20, 22-4, 27, 28, 31, 32, 67-72, 128.

Company G (Third Texas Infantry Regiment): 68.

Company G (Waco National Guard): 67, 69, 72, *91*.

Company I (Laredo): 32, 69, 70.

Company K (Third Infantry): 68, 70.

Congressional Medal(s) of Honor: 145.

Connecticut Mutual Life Insurance Company: 165.

Cook, Dan: 21, 30, 31, 33, *42*, 67, 114, 128, 130, 185, 186, *190*, 194.

Cook, Vic: 115, 193.

Cookville (town of): 31.

Corpus Christi: 1, 2, 32, 50, 63, 65, 69, 73-5, *76*, *87*, *88*, 93-9, 101, *103*, *104*, 107-10, 112, 114, *120*, 127, 165, *168*.

Corregidor: 174-6.

Cotton Palace: 161.

Coy, Ted: *16*, 116.

Coyote(s): 72, 99.

Cragin, C.C.: 7.

Criollos: 63.

Croix de Guerre(s): 145, 146.

Culberson, William: 107.

Farmers (A&M): 46.

Ferdinand, Franz: 132.

Ferguson (Texas governor): 67, 109.

Fifth Artillery Observation School: 162.

Fink, Clara Louise: 180.

First American Army: 141, 144.

First Florida Infantry: 101.

First Missouri Artillery All-Stars: 96-8, *122.*

First Missouri Artillery: 94-7, *103-5, 122.*

First New York Cavalry: 63, 98, 101, 107, 108, 110-2, *119, 120, 122.*

First New York Infantry: 112.

First Oklahoma Infantry: 128.

First Regular Division of Philippine Army: 174, 177.

First Texas Volunteer Infantry: 31, 74.

First Virginia Artillery: 27, 98, 99, 102, *105, 122.*

First Wisconsin Infantry: 96, 102, *122.*

Fleming, Alice: 173.

Flying wedge: 5, 7, *13.*

Flyting tackle(s): 5, 8, 9.

Football (American): 5, *17.*

Football (college): 1, 3, 5, 6, 43, 50, 155.

Football (helmets): *13, 15, 74,* 93.

Football (injuries): 5, 6, 7, 9, 10, 21, 22, 23, 25, 28, 49, 93, 99, 108, 111, 113, 145, 161, 164, 165.

Football (professional): 155.

Football (rubgy): 5, *17.*

Football, AEF: 145, 155, 161, 163, 185, 193.

Football, All-American (All-Star): 1, 45, 108, 110, 112.

Football, All-Southwestern: 22, 24, 26, 32, 45, 165.

Football, All-State (Texas): 21-4, 26, 29, 45, 50, 174.

Football, All-State Southwest Conference: 174.

Football, Army All-Star team: 156, 162, 165, 166, 173, 174.

Football, college All-Star team: 156, 162, 165, 166, 173, 174.

Ford, Gerald: 194.

Forêt-Ferme: 142, 143, *149, 153.*

Formosa (POW camp): 177.

Forsythe, Ben: 112.

Fort Bliss: 131.

Fort Bragg, 174, 178.

Fort Davis Indians: 157.

Fort Leavenworth: 179.

Fort Lee, 131, 144, 186.

Fort Mills: 174, 175.

Fort Riley: 180.

Fort Sam Houston: 68, 69, 98, 102, 107-9, 112 131, 144, 156, 162, 164, 173, 178-80, 193.

Fort Worth (city of): 44, 128, 129, 132, *135*, 145, 187.

Fort Worth Panthers: 161.

Fort Worth Polytechnic: 44.

Fort Worth University: 44.

Fort Worth Warriors: 23.

Forward pass: 6, 8, 9, 10, 21, 26, 95, 97, 113.

Fourth French Army: 145.

Fourth Minnesota Infantry: 101, 110.

Fourth Nebraska Infantry: 22, 27, 101.

Fourth Texas Infantry: 69, 70.

France, 132, 141, 143-6, *148, 150, 152*, 162, 193.

Francis, Josie: 186.

French (military): 141-3.

French Army Group Centre: 141, *149, 153*.

Funston, Frederick: 64, 66, 67, 73, 107-9, 112, 114, 127.

Gainesville (town of): 8.

Galveston, martial law: 179.

Gambrell, Tom: 19, 27, 33, *38*, 68, 71, 72, 127, 128, 131, 144, 186, 194.

Garrison (town of): 24.

Gas (hydrocarbon): 3, 185.

Gas (in war): 129, 141, 143, 144, *152*, 167.

General (Military Rank): 21, 29, 33, 173, 177, 181.

German (military): 141-3.

Germany: 3, 63, 66, 73, 127, 132, 141, 143, *148*, 181.

Glass, Walter, 112.

Glaze, Ralph: 44.

Glenn Springs: 66, 73.

Goat(s): 72, 99, 130.

Goodman, Howard: 100, 107, 109.

Gorman (town of): 22.

Grand Allied Offensive: 141, 143, *148*.

Grapevine (town of): 189.

Graves, D.V.: 20, 21, 31, 46, 100, 108, 110, 116, *121*, 162, 194.

Great War, 4, 33, 141, 146, 147, 155, 162, 173, 188, 193.

Greble, General: 129.

Greene, General: 109.

Gridiron (def): 5.

Griffith, Mildred: 180.

Groesbeck (town of): 30, 188.

Gulf Coast Exposition: 94-6, 103, *104*.

Gulf of Mexico: 69, 73, *88*.

Gumm, C.C.: 44, *54*.

Gunter Hotel: 99.

Halphen, Louis: 19, 20, 30, 67, 128, 131, *138*, 145, 188, 193.

Hanson, Runt: 50.

Harlan, Edwin H.: 46, 50.

Harlingen (town of): 69-71, 74, *76*.

Harold, Marion: 49.

Harrell's (of Austin): *119*.

Harvard (football): 6, 7, 9, *14*, 109, 111.

Harvard (University): 1, 6, 7, 8, 110.

Higginbottom, Frances: 186.

Hill, Lon C., 70.

Hillside (town of): 24.

Hobby, W.P.: 179.

Hoten-Mukden (POW camp): 177.

Houston (city of): 6, 27, 52, 107, 187, 188.

Houston Lights Company A: 17, 27, 68.

Huerta, Victoriano: 64.

Huggins, Miller: 158, 159.

Hulen, John: 69, 74, 75, 107, 112, 114, 127.

Hurricane: 71, 73, *85, 87*.

Huse, Ethel: 188.

Hutchings, Edwin: 141.

Hutchings, Henry: 131.

International and Great Northern Railroad Company: 187.

Interscholastic Athletic Association: 8, 10.

Ironmonger, J.W.: 109.

Israel, R. Scott Israel: 108.

Japan (in war): 132, 174-7.

Japan (POW): 33.

Japan: 180.

Javelina(s): 72, 99.

John B. Golding VFW Post: 185.

Johnson, Lyndon: 194.

Johnson, Walt: 98, 100, 102, 107-9, 114.

Jones, Casey: 50.

Jones, Tad: 10.

Jordan, Louis: 45.

Juneau, William: 165.

K.L. Berry Award: 177.

K.L. Berry Humanitarian Award: 177.

Karenko (POW camp): 176.

Kelly Field Aviators: 130.

Kelly Smiths: 23.

Kendrick, Jim: 1, 19, 20, 21, 24, 25, 32, *37*, 49, 49-52, *62*, 67-9, 72, 95, 96, 99, 100, 102, *106*, 107, 109, 111-3, 116, *122*, 127-9, 131, 144, 145, 162-4, 193.

Kennedy, John F.: 194.

Kennedy, Robert F.: 194.

Kerrville: 162, 188.

Kick breakaway: 115.

Kick formation: 100, 115.

King, Martin Luther: 194.

Korea (War): 193.

Kyle Field: 50, 165, *171*.

Kyle, E.J.: 47.

Kyusha Island (POW camp): 177.

Lane, George: 1, 19, 20, 25, 67, 68, 96, 99, 102, *122*, 127, 128, 131, 188, 193, 194.

Lane, Richard: 19, 21, 27, 28, 67, 69, 72, 96, *122*, 130, 131, 144, 188, 193, 194.

Langres: 185.

Lawyer(s): 33, 71, 179, 185, 186, *192*.

Lenoir, Bertrand: 19, 20, 27, 28, 32, 68, 127, 164, *169*, 194.

Llano (city of): 181.

Llano (County): 25, 181, 182.

Long, O.W.: 44.

MacArthur, Douglas: 174, 175.

MacDonald, Mark S.: 159.

Machault: 142.

Machine gun (Company/Battalion): 69, 72, 128, 131, *135*, 144.

Machine gun(s): *80*, 129, 141-6, *151*, 185.

Madero, (city of): 69, 70, 72, *76*.

Madero, Francisco: 64.

Madero, Raul: *79*.

Madisonville (town of): 31.

Main Avenue High School: 155, 156.

Malinta: 176.

Manilla (Bay): 174.

Manilla (city of): 176.

Mann, Gerald: 188.

Manor (town of): 31.

Marine(s) (military): *152*, 176, 179.

Marines (Dallas baseball team): 157.

Marlin (town of): 28, 164.

Mascot: 72, 97, 99, 112, 130.

Mass play(s): 5, 6, 10.

Massillon (Ohio) Tigers: 155.

Mather, W.T.: 48.

McAllen (town of): 64, 69-71, *76*, 111, 112, 128, 129, 193.

McBee, Albert: 65.

McCain, E.S.: 65.

McClosky Veterans Hospital: 182.

McLennan (County): 186.

Menger Hotel: 112, *118*.

Mercedes (town of): 69, *76*.

Mery (town of): 143.

Mestizos: 63.

Meuse-Argonne: 141, 144, *148*, 156, 162,

Mexican Revolution: 2, 63, 70.

Mexico: 2, 3, 21, 63-6, 70, 96, 132, 144, 160.

90th Division: 128-131, 134, 144, 193.

Nixon, Richard M.: 194.

Norias (King Ranch): 65: 76, 77.

North Carolina: 3, 178, 190.

North Dakota: 180.

North Fort Worth Warriors: 23.

Notre Dame: 22, 51, 115, 116.

Nueces Bay: 73.

Nueces Hotel: 74, 95, 96.

Ogden, Charles Wesley, Sr.: 25.

Ogden, Charles Wesley, Jr. "June": 19, 20, 25, 51, 67, 69, 96-8, 114, 115, *122*, 131, *135*, 144, 164, 165, 194.

Oklahoma A&M (University): 45.

Oklahoma (University): 26, 45.

Oklahoma National Guard: 76, 128, 144.

Oklahoma (state): 28, 32.

Olongapo, Philippines: 175.

Olson, Homer: 117.

Orange (city of): 26, 32, 68, 70, 110, 112, 114, *125*, 165-7, 189.

Orange High School: 113.

Paine Air Force Base: 178.

Panther Division: 146.

Paris, Texas: 180.

Parker, Brigadier General James: 1, 93.

Parks, Pvt. William Joe: 72.

Paris (France): 64, 141, 145, 180.

Parral (Mexico): 66, 70.

Parrott(s): 99.

Peacock Military Academy: 28, 108.

Pearl Harbor: 174.

Peavy, John R.: 78.

Penn State (football team): 98.

Pennsylvania (University of): 1, 7, 111.

Pennsylvania (state): 31, 98, 102, 116, 179.

Pershing, Brigadier General John "Black Jack": 2, 66, 68, *81, 82*, 141, 145, 148.

Petersburg Virginia: 144.

Pharr, Texas: 74, *85*, 111.

Philippine Islands: 173, 174, 179, 180.

Philippine Legion of Honor: 175.

Pinckney, Stephen F.: 48.

Plainview, Texas: 185, 186, *190*.

Plan of San Diego; 64, 65.

Polytech College: 44.

Port Arthur High School: 166.

Pospeshenkse, Josepha: 185.

Potter, Russell: 112.

Princeton University: 1, 6, 9, *16*, 48, 111, 112, 116.

Pueblo, Colorado: 182.

Pueblo (ship): 145.

Punitive Expedition: 2, 68, 70, *83-85*, 136, 145.

Purple Heart: 156, 177.

Queensland, Australia: 180.

Racoon(s): 72.

Randall Macon College: 99.

Ratliff, Harold; 97, 117, 193.

Rattlers (football team): 163.

Red River: 28.

Reid, W.T.: 7, 8.

Republic of Mexico: 63.

Rhine River: 141, *148*.

Rio Grande River: 2, 21, 66, 69, 71, 72, *78,* 100.

Rio Grande Valley: 73, 75, 105, 117, 160.

Ripon College: 109.

Rix Burton: 50, 53.

Robertson, Doak: 107.

Rockne, Knute, *17,* 117,

Rodgers, C.P.: 3.

Rogers, John Harris: 28.

Rogers, Pleasant "Pleas": 19, 20, 27, 28, 29, 33, *39*, 51, 68, 69, 72, 86, *90, 91*, 114, 127, 128, 131, 173, 180, 181, 193, 194.

Rogers, T.: 20.

Rosebud High School: 164.

Roosevelt, Ethel, *14.*

Roosevelt, Franklin: 174.

Roosevelt Theodore: 6, 7.

Roosevelt, Theodore, Jr. 6, 7.

Roswell, New Mexico: 26, 189.

Rotary Club (of Corpus Christi): 73, 75.

Ruggles, William B.: 52.

Sabine River: 24.

St. Étienne: 141-143, 147, *149.*

St. Louis Browns: 32, 127, 160.

St. Louis, Brownsville & Mexican Railway: 65, *76, 78.*

St. Louis College: 108.

St. Louis Post-Dispatch: 6.

St. Louis Star: 45.

Saks, Stuart J.: 108.

San Angelo, Texas: 23, 142.

San Antonio & Aransas Pass Railroad: 75, 99.

San Antonio Express: 20, *105*, 108, 114, *118-121*, *125*, 130.

San Antonio, Texas: 21, 23, 25, 27, 28, 67-69, 75, 99, 102, 107, 108, 112-4, 129, 130, 145, 155, 156, 162, 174, 180, 193.

San Diego, California: 144, 173.

San Francisco, California: 174.

San Marcos, Texas: 30.

Schaedel, Charles T.: 19, 29, 45, 49, *55, 56,* 68, *137,* 189, 194.

Schaendel; See Schaedel.

Sehaedel: See Schaedel.

Schraedel: See Schaedel.

Schofield Military Base: 180.

Scott; Army Chief of Staff Hugh: 66, 67.

Seay, James: 31, *42.*

Second Florida Infantry:114.

Second Texas Infantry National Guard (football team): 1, 2, 3, 4, 10, 11, 19, 20, 25, 28, 29, 30, 32, 43, 49, 50, 51, 53, 63, 94-102, 107, 110, 113-118, 128-130, 141, 144, 145, 147, 148, 155-157, 164-7, 169, 173, 174, 178, 180, 185, 187-190, 192-4.

Second Texas Infantry National Guard (regiment): 21, 93, 127, 128, 131, 132, 178.

Seine Base Section: 181.

Seton Hospital: 67:

71st Brigade: 128, 131, 141-5, 149.

72nd Brigade: 128, 141-5, 149.

74th New York Infantry: 1, 25, 28, 29, 101, 102, 107

Sewanee University: 22, 25, 26, 45, 48.

Shell Oil: 187.

Shreveport, Louisiana: 24, 31, 32, 87.

Simmons College Unit Students Army Training Corps: 188.

Simpson, Sylvan: 19, 25, 26, *42*, 51, *58, 60*, 67, 72, 109, 111, 112, *121, 122*, 128, 130, 131, 144, 181, 193, 194.

Sims, Bob: 110, 117.

Skull and Bones Society: 180

Smith & Birge: 185, 187.

Smith, Buhl: 21.

Smith, Eunice: 187.

Smith, Schuyler Jr.: 185.

Smith, Schuyler William "Bud": 19-21, 23, 27, 29, 30, 33, *40*, 47, 67, 72, *122*, 128, 131, 141, 144-146, 185-187, *190*, 194.

Smith, Virginia: 187.

Smith, Major General W.R.: 146.

Snake(s): 72.

South China Sea: 174.

South Dakota Military District: 180.

South Luzon Force: 174.

Southern All-Stars: 166.

Southern Conference: 43.

Southern Intercollegiate Athletic Association (SIAA): 43-7, 49.

Southern Maid Bakery: 186.

Southern Methodist University: 188.

Southwest Conference (SWC): 43, 44, 50. 52, 53.

Southwest Basketball Association: 164.

Southwest Football Officials Association: 97, 164.

Southwestern Intercollegiate Athletic Association (SWIAA): 43, 44, 46, 47.

Southwestern University:1, 25-7, 44, 46, 50.

Spanish-American War: 31, *41*, 68, 74, 146,178.

Spitz Clarke Gridders: 155.

Spring (town of): 30.

Stagg, Amos Alonso: *13*.

Stark, W.H.: 189.

Stark, Lutcher: 189.

Stark, H.J. Lutcher: 110.

Vanderbilt University: 45, 155.

Vaux Champagne: 142.

Veracruz, Mexico: 63.

Verdun, France: 141.

Vietnam: 194.

Villa, Pancho: 2, 66-8, *81-4*.

Virginia (state): 131, 144, 164, 180, 181, 186, 187.

Virginia (University of): 1, 24, 110, 130.

Waco Chamber of Commerce: 186.

Waco City Charter Advisory Committee: 186, *190*.

Waco-McLennan County Red Cross: 186.

Waco Public Library: 186.

Waco, Texas: 24, 25, 27, 28, 30, 33, 53, 67-9, 156, 159-164, 166, 180, 186, 188-191, 193.

Waco Tribune-Herald: 166.

Waco War Bond Committee "Women's Division: 186.

Wainwright, General Jonathan M.: 174-8.

War Claims Commission: 177.

Ward, Al: 166, 193.

Warden (12th Division All-Star): 110.

Warner, Glenn Scobey "Pop": 10.

Warrenton, Virginia: 181.

Washington and Lee University: 1, 114.

Washington College of Law: 173.

Washington, DC: 65, 73, 173, 175, 177, 179, 180, *183*, 186.

Washington (state): 178.

Watson, Grady: 1, 2, 21, 26, 27, 32, 52, 53, 68, 70, 93, 96, 99-102, 111-6, 122, 125, 170-172.

Water Street: *87*.

Weatherford (Texas): 12, 23.

Webb County (Texas): 32, 94, 187.

Weidman (12th Division All Star): 109.

Wells Fargo Express Company: 75.

Wentworth Military Academy: 28, 29, *39*.

West End Park: 107.

West Point: 1, 9, *15*, 45, 108-10, 178.

West Virginia (state): 181.

West Virginia University: 1, 109.

Books from R.K. Sawyer

A Hundred Years of Texas Waterfowl Hunting:
The Decoys, Guides, Clubs, and Places, 1870s to 1970s

Texas Market Hunting:
Stories of Waterfowl, Game Laws, and Outlaws

Images of the Hunt
A Photographic History of Texas

The Tarpon Club of Texas
And the Genius of E.H.R. Green

Copies are available from https://robertksawyer.com

BOOKS AVAILABLE
FROM
NUECES PRESS

1919 – The Storm
Corpus Christi – A History
A Soldier's Life
Great Tales from the History of South Texas
Recollections of Other Days
Perilous Trails of Texas
Columns   2009 – 2011
Columns 2 2012 – 2013
Columns 3 2014 – 2015
Columns 4 2016 – 2018
Streets of Corpus Christi Texas
Thomas Noakes Diary of War & Drought
100 Tales of Old Texas
Water Woes
Corpus Christi Handbook and Murphy Givens Index
At a Bend in the River – A History of Spread Oaks Ranch
Zachary Taylor's Army in Texas
The Tarpon Club of Texas

Copies and more information
are available at
www.nuecespress.com

www.ingramcontent.com/pod-product-compliance
Lightning Source LLC
Chambersburg PA
CBHW061231150426

42812CB00054BA/2563